LATEST

WORD

ON THE

LAST

DAYS

ABOUT THE AUTHOR. . .DR. C. S. LOVETT

Dr. Lovett is the president of **Personal Christianity,** a fundamental, evangelical interdenominational ministry. For the past 29 years he has had but one objective—**preparing Christians for the second coming of Christ!** This book is one of over 40 of his works designed to help believers be **prepared for His appearing.**

Dr. Lovett's decision to serve the Lord resulted in the loss of a sizable personal fortune. He is well equipped for the job the Lord has given him. A graduate of American Baptist Seminary of the West, he holds the M.A. and B.D. degrees conferred *Magna Cum Laude.* He has also completed graduate work in psychology at Los Angeles State College and holds an honorary doctorate from the Protestant Episcopal University in London.

A retired Air Force Chaplain (Lt. Colonel), he has been married to Marjorie for over 38 years and has two grown daughters dedicated to the Lord.

LATEST WORD ON THE LAST DAYS

C. S. LOVETT
M.A., B.D., D.D.

president of Personal Christianity Chapel

author of fourteen best selling books including:
Dealing With The Devil
Soul-Winning Made Easy
"Help Lord — The Devil Wants Me Fat!"
Jesus Wants You Well

editorial assistance and
illustrated by Linda Lovett

published by:
PERSONAL CHRISTIANITY CHAPEL
Box 549
Baldwin Park, California 91706

© C. S. LOVETT 1980

No part of this book may be used or reproduced in any manner whatsoever without written permission of the copyright owner except in the case of brief quotations in articles and reviews.

ALL RIGHTS RESERVED

This book is dedicated to all the MARANATHA MEN and WOMEN who are preparing themselves for the appearing of the Lord and are dedicating themselves to helping others get ready as well.

Nothing in this book is intended to discredit or malign any living person (or organization) regardless of his religious affiliation or theological position.

PRINTED IN THE UNITED STATES OF AMERICA

ISBN No. 0-938148-00-1

Contents

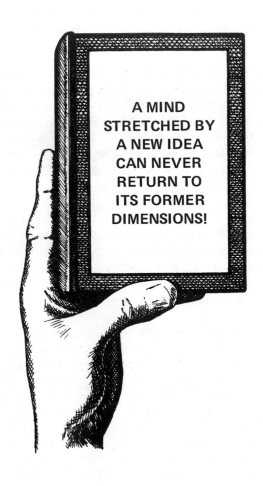

A MIND
STRETCHED BY
A NEW IDEA
CAN NEVER
RETURN TO
ITS FORMER
DIMENSIONS!

Your thinking should not be the same after you read this book, for you are going to encounter startling ideas that may run counter to some things you've learned previously. If you are able to hang your previous conditioning "on a peg," you'll meet some astonishing insights guaranteed to stretch your mind.

I am **not claiming** NEW REVELATION in the writing of this book. I have simply put God's Word and circumstances together, interpreting them with the LIGHT He's given me. Should the scenario prove to be accurate, it won't be because I possess special knowledge. I do not. It will simply be God's working through me to meet the needs of His people, — as He has in the past. If I am "on target," the doing is His, not mine.

This book is NOT a commentary on the book of Revelation. Rather it is a scenario of end time events. You will not find me setting any dates, but instead giving you a sequence to observe. That way, you will be able to watch the news headlines and judge for yourself the timing of the Lord's return.

This book was written in response to God's call upon my life . . . "PREPARE MY PEOPLE FOR MY APPEARING!" Why would I expect to do that with a book on prophecy? Ah — prophecy is a great motivator. It captures the Christian's imagination and is able to shift his interest from this world to the Lord's return. So while this book will definitely satisfy your curiosity concerning future events, it will also MOTIVATE you to get ready for Jesus' return. As you behold this age drawing to a close, it will change your life and fill you with anticipation of appearing with the Lord in the sky! (1 Thess. 4:16, 17).

"Come Up Hither!"

Years before I had ever heard of the "RAPTURE" there was a longing within me to fly through the air. I mean, go as high as I could and see if it brought me any closer to God. And you know what? The day came when I tried to satisfy that longing.

In 1943, I was a flight instructor stationed at the Pecos Army Air Base. Instructors were allowed to use the planes during their free time to improve their flying skills.

On this particular day, I chose a BT-14, a 450 horse-power, single engine trainer and determined to fly as high as I could go. I was excited over the possibility of being "closer to God." I wasn't saved then, so I didn't know any better. I thought God was "up there."

I sat in takeoff position waiting for the tower to clear me, my heart pounding in anticipation. Then it came — "235 cleared for takeoff." Suddenly I was thrust against the back of the seat as the engine roared to life, hurling me down the runway. "Here we go," I thought to myself as I pulled back on the stick. In that same second I was free — airborne — with the earth which held me captive left behind.

For the better part of an hour the nose of that plane pointed upward. Something seemed to be saying, "Come up hither." I wanted to do that — very much. Finally the plane could go no higher. I leveled off and trimmed the ship to fly by itself. Then I closed my eyes to see if the inner ache felt better now that I was "closer to God." It didn't. Another 50,000 feet or 50,000 miles wouldn't have made any difference. But I didn't know that then.

Four years later I accepted Jesus' offer to come into my heart and give me eternal life. That ended the ache, But the "come up hither" never left.

WHAT'S THAT GOT TO DO WITH PROPHECY?

There's a connection.

9

Shortly after I was saved, a friend gave me a Scofield Bible and a copy of "Rightly Dividing the Word of Truth." I started through the New Testament. It wasn't long before I came upon the rapture of the saints. Wow — something clicked in my spirit! As you might guess, my soul seized the idea of meeting the Lord in the air. Now I had an explanation for the feelings I had when I flew that plane to its limit.

You may smile at this, but the truth of the rapture kindled such a fire in my soul I couldn't leave the Word of God alone. From then on, I was hooked on prophecy. I had to know more. I devoured the Bible to see what God had in store for me, now that I was His child.

The more I studied, the more the plan of God unfolded before me. The more I learned, the more excited I became. I found myself spellbound. Obviously this is why God gives us glimpses into things to come. He knows we're fascinated by the future. He counts on that fascination to shift our interest from the things of the world to the things of God.

Did you know that prophecy can get a man involved in the Word quicker than anything else? That's why more than ONE-THIRD of the Bible is devoted to prophecy. Then, after that Word lays hold of us, we're motivated to live for Christ rather than ourselves. I'm sure I'm not the only one who has found this to be so.

PROPHECY MADE THE DIFFERENCE FOR ME

When I was saved, I was doing well in business, speculating in real estate, building hotels and motels. I loved it. It was fun making big money and enjoying the "good life" that went with it. When I came to Christ, I saw no reason to be anything but a successful Christian businessman. And while I was happy to have everything the Lord cared to give me, my commitment to Him was only half-hearted.

It was prophecy that changed my attitude.

When God's overall plan began to surface from the Word, I was enamored. It thrilled me to see a sequence of events emerge from the pages of the Bible. With news headlines heralding the last days, I realized I could no longer fool with fortune or fame, I had to be involved in what God was doing.

So I quit my business, which cost me a sizeable fortune, and went on a **spiritual** treasure hunt. I purchased some Bible tools, like *Halley's Bible Handbook* and began reading various authors such as John Walvoord, De Haan, Ladd, Larkin, Mauro, English, Ironside, Reese, Leon Morris and Leon Wood. Before very much time had passed, God had me in a new business — HIS!

My point is this: **had it not been for prophecy, I would never have thrown myself into studying God's Word with such vigor.** It was the power of the Word that changed me. Just think — if the headlines of 30 years ago were heralding the end of the age, what must they be screaming today!

THAT'S WHY I WANT TO
SHARE PROPHECY WITH YOU

I won't be interpreting the news headlines for you. You can see why. If I did that, this book would be out-dated before it went to press. Things are happening too fast now. Instead, I want to lay out for you the SEQUENCE OF EVENTS as the Holy Spirit has revealed them to me and set forth what they mean to you personally. The next big event could explode at any moment. And when it does, I'm hoping this grasp of prophecy will do for you what it did for me.

The purpose of prophecy is to MOTIVATE us to let go of the world and invest ourselves in Christ. I mean it

11

should get us so excited about Jesus that we'll put Him ahead of family, career or financial security. Now you know the reason for this book.

This is what I want for you — I would like to see you so turned on to Christ, that all that matters to you is living for His pleasure. To my mind, nothing will do this quicker than a clear grasp of what lies ahead. And I mean JUST AHEAD.

I DON'T HAVE ALL THE TRUTH

Go to a good-sized Christian bookstore. Stand in front of the prophecy section. Look at all those books! Should you start reading through them, you'll find each has its own peculiar twist or thrust. Each interprets the Scriptures concerning end time events a bit differently. Ah, but this is not a bad thing. It appears the Lord has DELIBERATELY left gaps in prophecy so that there would be differing opinions. Why? It gives us a chance to love each other in spite of our different views.

I see the genius of God in leaving things so vague, that we might differ and still be led of the Spirit. O, what wisdom. **It's the Lord's desire, of course, that we will "agree to differ, but resolve to love." You've got to admit it is a unique test to see if we'll put "unity of the Spirit" ahead of doctrinal exactitude (Eph. 4:3).** But it is a hard test when you consider most would "rather fight than switch!"

● Having said that, I want to make it clear I am sharing MY OPINION. I could easily be wrong and hasten to admit it. I do not have all the truth. I am setting forth matters as the Spirit has revealed them to me, but I am still an "earthen vessel" handling God's truth amidst my weaknesses. Therefore I do not want anyone who has a SETTLED VIEW of prophecy to change his views because of what I write here.

If your doctrinal position already motivates you to put your heart and soul into making Christ NUMBER ONE, you'll gain nothing by shifting to my views. I seek to change NO ONE'S prophetic outlook, except as it would help him get ready for that glorious day when we meet Jesus in the air. That day is coming and we'll be discussing it in one of the chapters.

So let's have fellowship in this book, not on the basis of how much light you or I have, but on the basis of our mutual love in Christ. If we differ on some points, why not let it add spice to our fellowship, rather than hinder. How much fun would it be if we all thought alike? Not much. I want you to know I love you. . .and proof of my love is that I seek **your** profit, rather than getting you to think as I do.

Naturally, my hope is that those who already have FIRM CONVICTIONS concerning future events, would profit from this book. The Holy Spirit will surely give me things that will add to what He has given you. Some lingering questions are bound to be answered; some parts of the puzzle should get a lot clearer. Even if your views differ from mine, if this work is of God, it will bring blessing to every reader. In any event, I'm going to assume you are too wise to throw out the baby with the bathwater.

While I do not have all the truth, neither will I be so far off that you'll get into trouble embracing my views. My work lies solidly within the historic, fundamental, premillennial position, adopted by most scholars.

We all need a place to start. So if you have no prophetic convictions or you're hazy on the subject, accept mine — at least until the Spirit leads you to some that motivate you even more. I write because I love my brethren and the Lord's appearing. It is my longing to help every reader get ready for the days ahead. Here's how I'm praying this moment:

13

"Precious Lord, I feel a great need just now. I am beginning a work in which I could differ with men who serve you night and day, and whose love and zeal put my poor efforts to shame. Give me the right words, O Lord, lest I offend those who love you with all their hearts. Spirit of the gentle Christ, make me gentle. Spirit of Truth, make my teaching inoffensive."

C. S. Lovett

Baldwin Park, California

PART ONE

PROPHECY
WITH A
PURPOSE

Chapter One

The Next Big Event In Prophecy!

"Brrrrrrrnnnnnnnnng!"

The red phone startles everyone in the Oval Office. It is the Moscow/Washington hotline. An aide seizes the instrument.

"President Nixon's office."

The voice at the other end is hard and cold. "Please hold for Mr. Brezhnev. He wishes to speak to the President."

It is October 23rd, 1973. As Mr. Nixon walks to the phone, he is aware of its purpose — to prevent war.

And we were at the brink of World War III.

REMEMBER THE SITUATION?

The Jews were celebrating Yom Kippur — the Day of Atonement — the holiest day of the Jewish calendar. Most Israelis, including members of the armed forces, were with their families or in synagogues in prayer. Armed with Soviet equipment, the Arabs launched a sneak attack that caught the tiny nation off guard. For the first time since 1948, the Jewish people were involved in a surprise war without having their equipment and troops on **standby alert.**

No one believed the Egyptians and Syrians would dare move in such a concerted attack without the knowledge of the Soviets, if not without their direct encouragement. But as God would have it, the battle slowly turned. A daring thrust by Israeli armor crossed the Suez and encircled the Egyptian Third Army.

The Russians were startled by this unexpected turn of events, but a crafty notion entered their minds. By way of the hotline, they suggested that Russia and the U. S. jointly send troops into the area to stabilize the situation. However, before the U. S. had time to react to the idea, Brezhnev sent word that Russia would move on her own if the U. S. refused to join the effort.

What would the United States do?

The decision fell on President Nixon, already burdened by vicious attacks in the press and waning popularity in the polls. Watergate was crashing down on him. After conferring with Haig and Kissinger, it was agreed that the threat of Soviet intervention was real. The President knew the U. S. must act, or Israel would be helpless. Besides, we had vital interests in that part of the world which holds 53% of all known oil reserves.

On the night of October 24, Secretary Kissinger

17

brought word to the President that 85 Soviet ships, including landing craft and those with troop helicopters, were in the Mediterranean. It was also reported that huge air transports had been recalled from Egypt to move seven Soviet Airborne divisions, numbering 50,000 men. The final jar came when an American Intelligence officer intercepted a "troop alert" order.

DECISION TIME FOR THE PRESIDENT

At 11 o'clock that same night, the President met with his closest advisers in the White House Situation Room. He then pressed the button that put ALL American forces, including nuclear forces, on worldwide alert.

Mr. Brezhnev picked up the first signs of the American alert and read the situation correctly. The U. S. was not ready to be intimidated by Soviet military might. And the Soviets were not quite ready for an East-West confrontation.

Today it would be a different story, but then — **the Russians backed away.** It was not time for a Russian takeover of the Middle East.

But that was a few years back. Since then, the Soviets have been pouring a huge chunk of their gross national income into armaments, desperately racing for military superiority. **They no longer have to back down.** What's more, they know the Mideast is ripe for plucking. The weakness of Israel, the confusion of the Arabs, as well as the political unrest throughout the region all make the prospect of a takeover very inviting.

In spite of Russia's eagerness, God is holding her back from an all out attack against Israel, limiting her actions to secondary thrusts and probing actions. Yet, any day now, God will give the signal and then the "Bear" will come out of the North!

18

RUSSIA IS THINKING ABOUT IT

"Next time it will be Russia!"

Those words came from Moshe Dyan, former Minister of Israeli Defense. Undoubtedly he was thinking of the communist encirclement of the Mideast, rather than biblical prophecy. All Israeli defense leaders, reported the Los Angeles Times in a recent article, feel the Soviets hold all the advantage over the next few years and will move to exploit that advantage.*

As MASTERS OF CHAOS, the Communists know how to fan the fires of unrest. By means of two combustible products — nationalism and religious fervor, they can easily set a troubled country on fire (as in the case of Iran). The tactic of supplying arms (via underground) to dissidents within a country easily creates a violence that can topple any shaky government.

The lack of strong leadership in the nations surrounding the Mideast oil deposits makes it tempting for the Russians to go after them one by one (as in the case of Afghanistan). The cover of TIME MAGAZINE (January 15th, 1979), pictures the "Bear" gobbling up what commentators call the "Crescent of Crisis."

Zibigniew Brezenski, President Carter's national security adviser, refers to this region as the "arc of insecurity." **He notes how skilled Soviet agents have become in toppling rulers and governments by instigating religious and political violence. With the entire Mideast so unstable and Arab countries controlled by a few ruling families, he sees the area an irresistible plum.

---

*Los Angeles Times, December 17, 1978, Part V, Page 1
* *U. S. News and World Report, January 15, 1979

19

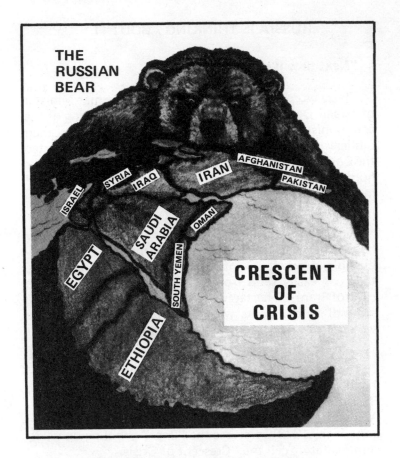

THE
RUSSIAN
BEAR

ISRAEL

SYRIA

IRAQ

IRAN

AFGHANISTAN

PAKISTAN

EGYPT

SAUDI
ARABIA

SOUTH YEMEN

OMAN

ETHIOPIA

**CRESCENT
OF
CRISIS**

RUSSIA'S EVIL MOTIVATION

While God controls the timing of the Soviet invasion of Israel, the Russians will be motivated by evil intentions. The prophet Ezekiel makes that clear (Ezekiel 38:1—39:16). Keep in mind what they stand to gain by seizing that part of the Mideast:

- **The richest oil fields in the world,**

- **The chemical deposits of the Dead Sea, estimated to be worth trillions of dollars,**

20

- **The only land bridge between Europe, Asia and Africa.**

Inasmuch as Russia has clearly admitted her intentions to rule the world, the land of Palestine is probably the most strategic piece of real estate on this globe — as far as she is concerned. She's determined to have it, though presently playing a waiting game. In the meantime . . .

RUSSIA WANTS THAT OIL

Imagine — all that oil just for the taking. Don't think it doesn't tantalize the Kremlin. They'd love to have control of it. Why they could choke off the lifeline to the West, cripple Japan and put Europe in its pocket. What a tempting morsel that is, how inviting. As long as the U. S. doesn't put up any real challenge, the Soviets can pull it off . . . **until they come to Israel.**

OIL SUPPLY. Russia is keenly aware the world's supply of oil is limited. The production of petroleum energy, according to M. King Hubbert, of the U. S. Geological Survey, will peak in roughly 15 years. By the year 2015, it will be only 50% of what it was at its peak. Mexican reserves, said to equal those of the Persian Gulf States, could be flowing by 1983-1985. This could take some pressure off the U. S. while we develop alternate energy sources. Therefore the ideal time for the Soviets to seize control of Mideast oil is while most of the world is still dependent on it. That advantage will fade when Mexican oil begins to flow and alternate energy sources are developed.

RUSSIA MUST MOVE SOON

"I see no evidence that the Soviet Union is exercising one iota of restraint in its ongoing nuclear and conventional weapons buildup."

Those were the words of General Alexander Haig,

21

former U. S. and NATO commander in Europe. In a recent address, he sought to show how Russia was arming herself as fast as she could . . . and this in the face of her SALT I pact with the U. S. (Treaties apparently mean nothing to the Soviets, except as they give them the advantage.) The general's sentiments were echoed in an article in the *U. S. NEWS & WORLD REPORT* that carried the bold headline . . .

New Alarm Over Russian Threat!

"What will the Soviet Union do with the immense military power it is amassing? Fear of American strategists: Kremlin leaders will be tempted to cash in on their advantage before it is lost."

The article continued:

"By 1983, most analysts predict, Russia will achieve an unprecedented . . . strategic advantage over the U. S. . . . and will be able to hold it for an optimal period of five years or so. The overwhelming question, therefore, is whether the Soviet Union will try to take advantage of this optimal period before problems beset them in the later 1980s." *

The same article went on to show how the Soviets spend roughly 13% of their gross national product on weapons, whereas the U. S. spends but 5.2% of its GNP. I'm certain you've seen plenty of tables and charts in the news magazines comparing our military strength with that of Russia. We are clearly getting weaker, warn many of our generals, while the Soviets are getting stronger.

The Russians Think Differently Than We Do

The United States is interested in having enough wea-

U. S. News and World Report, October 30, 1978

pons to deter aggression or to be able to retaliate, should we be attacked. **But the Russian philosophy is geared to a FIRST STRIKE.** The Soviet is desperately striving to build a supply of weapons that can ruin ours BEFORE we can fire them. They want to catch our B-52 fleet on the ground, our atomic subs in port and destroy our missile sites. And after that, have plenty of warheads left to threaten our cities, should we dare use any weapons that survive their initial strike.

• *The Kiplinger-Washington Newsletter*, which does a superb job in ferreting facts, states the overall nuclear capacity of the U.S. is about even at the moment. But in the 1980s, the Russians will easily move ahead of us. Right now, the Russians could dramatically reduce our response capability with a FIRST STRIKE. It is clear the U.S. **won't** strike first. So — how likely is it that we would use any of our remaining weapons if the Soviets still had plenty of missiles aimed at our cities?*

CIVIL DEFENSE. The civil defense system of the U.S. is in shambles. For the last decade it has been all but forgotten. It would take months (perhaps years) to gear up and condition our cities for a full blown civil defense program. The Soviets, on the other hand, have worked furiously to develop theirs. Many of their factories are underground. Miles of tunnels connect important centers, with those same tunnels providing bomb shelters for much of the population. A nuclear strike against Russian cities would be far less crippling than one against ours. So while Soviet armed forces will suffer annihilation against the mountains of Israel, the U. S. could be wiped out at home.

It is estimated that Moscow cannot continue pouring its income into arms for more than FIVE YEARS. By then, the country will have become so drained, she could face a revolt from within. At the very least, say the ex-

---

*U. S. News and World Report, February 2, 1979

23

perts, her production would come to a standstill through decay. **Therefore SHE MUST MOVE SOON.** If she doesn't, her huge arms buildup and military superiority will be meaningless.

RUSSIA WILL MOVE ON GOD'S TIMETABLE

Moshe Dyan looks at the practical situation, **"War with Russia is likely by 1983."** He may be right. But the timing remains in God's hands. How do we know? The Bible says so. The moment of the Russian invasion of Israel awaits God's signal.

● Down in Babylon, around 587 B. C., the prophet Ezekiel had a vision concerning a mighty nation to the North. Bible students universally agree that the prophecies of Ezekiel 38 and 39 pertain to Russia and her invasion of Israel. The Bible foresees her huge army rising up and coming against the tiny state, newly returned to the land after being scattered among the nations of the world. The prophet explains in detail how God manages the timing:

"I will . . . put hooks into thy jaws, and I will bring thee forth, and all thine army . . . thou shalt ascend and come like a storm, thou shalt be like a cloud to cover the land, thou, and all thy bands, and many people with thee" (Ezekiel 38:4, 9).

And here's how God sets the hook . . .

"Thus saith the Lord God; it shall also come to pass, that at the same time SHALL THINGS COME INTO THY MIND, and thou shalt think an evil thought" (vs. 10).

And here's the idea God uses in the minds of the Russian leaders . . .

"... thou shalt say, I will go up to the land of unwalled villages; I will go to them that are at rest, that dwell safely . . . to take a spoil, and to take a prey; to turn thine hand upon the desolate places that are now inhabited, and upon the people that are gathered out of the nations..." (Ezek. 38:11,12 KJV).

Then God announces the outcome of the Russian invasion . . .

" . . . I am against you, Gog, prince of Rosh, Meshech, and Tubal. I will turn you about and drive you, I will fetch you from the far recesses of the North and bring you to the mountains of Israel. . . There on the mountains of Israel YOU SHALL FALL, you and all your squadrons, and your allies..." (39:1,2, 4 NEB).

Ezekiel goes on to explain how it will take SEVEN MONTHS to bury the dead bodies of the slain intruders. It is this little detail that JARS the reader, suddenly making him realize TWO BIG BATTLES are being described in these chapters and not just one. At first reading, a person easily supposes he is faced with an account of the battle of Armageddon only. But when he thinks about the dead bodies and disposal of weapons, it strikes him the LAW OF DOUBLE REFERENCE must be applied.

THE LAW OF DOUBLE REFERENCE

A word about the Law of Double Reference. The prophets often saw only the MOUNTAIN TOPS of future events. Sometimes a smaller mountain will blend in with a larger one in the distance. To the casual observer they look like one mountain. In prophecy, a seer can behold what looks like ONE EVENT, when actually there are two. That's what we have here. There are **two battles** described in these chapters of Ezekiel. The first one, the invasion of Israel, is the smaller one (38:1 — 39:16). But to the prophet's eyes it blends in with the bigger one (Armageddon), the great day of God's wrath (39:17-20).

MARK YOUR BIBLE. Are you one who marks his Bible? Good. You will want to draw a line between verses 16 and 17 of Ezekiel Chapter 39. That's where the change occurs. Everything before that line pertains to the Russian invasion of Israel. That which follows refers to Armageddon. The language of the latter part is almost identical to the prophecy of Christ's dealing with antichrist at HIS return. The second great battle ushers in the Millennium. The whole earth is changed at that time, with seas disappearing and the land mass levelled (Rev. 6:14). With the earth in convulsion and perhaps billions dying, there won't be any people running around trying to bury bodies for seven months. There won't be any need for it. This observation alerts us to the fact that two battles are being referred to here.

THE TWO GREAT
BATTLES IN EZEKIEL

Second Battle
Armageddon
Ezek. 39:17-22

First Battle
War with Russia
Ezek. 38:1 to 39:16

SEVEN YEAR TRIBULATION PERIOD

Once it is discovered that Ezekiel's prophecy refers to **two battles,** the Scriptures are much easier to handle. For very clearly the Russian attack is directed against the tiny nation after she has been newly regathered out of the world and stands helpless before this mighty adversary from the North (Ezekiel 38:8, 11, 12).

In my opinion, dear reader, the **destruction of the armies of Russia against the mountains of Israel is the NEXT BIG EVENT IN PROPHECY.** And from what we've already seen, it will probably occur within the next few years. When it does, it will be right on schedule according to God's timetable.

A SUMMARY OF THE SITUATION

Circumstances indicate Russia must move before long:

1. OIL — there is only so much oil in the world. Russia wants it and it is all but within her grasp right now. Control of Mideast oil would put her hand at the throat of the industrialized nations. Who could resist her socialistic doctrine then? She could squeeze any nation to death.

2. INSTABILITY of the Arab nations — skilled in exploiting national unrest (as well as generating it), Russia is grabbing off Mideast nations with relative ease. She merely topples the existing regime and helps obedient puppets come to power.

3. ECONOMIC DRAIN — She cannot continue draining her resources to achieve military superiority. She has five years, say the experts, after which chaos will follow. So she must make use of it or it will be wasted.

4. MILITARY SUPERIORITY — Russia is close to nuclear equality with the West. With her FIRST STRIKE philosophy, she could perhaps neutralize the

U. S. right now. In another few years, she will have unquestioned superiority and the U. S. will pose far less threat to her.

5. AMERICAN WEAKNESS — as a West German columnist put it . . .

> *"The Americans are no longer the unquestioned leaders they once were. Their dollar is weak. Their president is weak. Their will is weak."*

Who can argue? It is clear that Americans no longer have the will to arm themselves and fight.

When we consider these facts, common sense tells us it won't be long before Russia moves. Move she will, but her "troop alert" will come only **when God puts the "hook" in her jaws and brings her forth.**

What's God waiting for? That's next.

Chapter Two

What Is
God Up To?

"Israel annihilated!"

No, that's not a future headline. It's an old one —
a very old one.

Should you visit the Cairo museum, there's one object you won't want to miss. It is a stone about 12 feet
high and 6 feet wide, polished on both sides. It carries
an inscription dating back to the days of Ramses II,
about 1400 B.C. After describing the blazing victories
of the Pharaoh, the inscription ends with this announcement . . .

"Israel Annihilated: Israel Will Have No Posterity!"

You chuckle as you read those words. "How little
that fellow knew of our God and the power of His promises!" The words sound even funnier when your mind
travels across the Sinai to consider the nation that has

risen out of the ashes of the past. The state of Israel stands as a monument to the unfailing power of God's promises.

GREATEST SIGN TODAY

For hundreds of years, Bible scholars predicted the return of the Jews and the rebuilding of the nation. Standing on God's Word alone, they insisted He would bring His people back. Sceptics laughed when Bible believers said the nation would be resurrected. Such a thing had never happened before. What nation ever vanished from history to return again?

Around the turn of the century, there were less than 10,000 Jews in all of Palestine. Then the miracle began to take place and the scoffers weren't laughing any more.

But why would God want the Jews back in Palestine? What is He up to?

The answer takes us back 4,000 years. To see it, we have to flashback to the beginning of the Jewish story.

THE STORY BEGINS WITH ONE MAN — ABRAHAM
2000 B. C.

In God's eyes, this is likely the greatest man of the Old Testament. God appeared to **Abraham** in his hometown of Ur, in Mesopotamia. He ordered him to uproot his family and journey to a land He would show him. After some years passed, He finally brought him to the region we know as Palestine. Abraham was 75 when he arrived in this land, then occupied by the Canaanite nations.

This man thrilled God with his unquestioning obedience. The Lord was so delighted with him, He made a number of personal appearances to him. Each time He would affirm His pleasure in him and reveal His plans for him. So intense was God's pleasure, that He entered into a covenant with Abraham, a covenant that included three things:

1. NATION — God never had a nation on earth which He could call His own, but He wanted one. He chose to build it through this man. Even though Abraham never had any children, and his body was now too old, God promised his descendants would outnumber the stars of heaven (Gen. 15:5).

2. TERRITORY — A nation must have a land. So God laid out a territory bordering on the Mediterranean, from the river of Egypt in the South and Hamath in the North and extending to the Euphrates (Gen. 15:18). By some interpretations, this includes oil-rich Arabia. God affirmed this land would one day belong to Abraham's descendants.

3. KING — A nation must also have a ruler. So God promised that through Abraham's seed (descendants) would come an individual Who would not only be the Ruler, but also the Savior of the world.

These three elements make up what is known as the Abrahamic Covenant. It is because of this covenant that the nation of Israel exists today. Because God keeps His Word, it has been impossible to wipe out the Jew. And there have been those who tried.

● As the story unfolds, a twist occurs, revealing Abraham to be as human as the rest of us. As we often do, he tried to help God fulfill His promise concerning a son. So at the suggestion of Sarah, his wife, he took her maid, Hagar, and had a son by her. He named him Ishmael. As Abraham's FIRST BORN, he could normally expect to be the patriarch's heir. But God overruled common practice, saying in effect, "No, Ishmael

31

is NOT YOUR HEIR. You will yet have a son by your wife Sarah, and he shall be your heir. All of the promises I made to you are to be fulfilled through him" (Gen. 17:15-21).

> **ISHMAEL.** This goof on Abraham's part is the basis of the Arab/Israeli conflict today. Modern Arabs descend from Ishmael. If Abraham had continued to wait on the Lord, rather than taking matters into his own hands, there'd be no Arabs today. Even though Ishmael was Abraham's first born, the Arabs DO NOT lay claim to Palestine on that basis. They know the Bible clearly DISAVOWS Ishmael and CONFIRMS Isaac as the only heir to the promises. Modern Arabs contend the land is theirs by virtue of having lived in it for nearly 2,000 years, while the Jews claim it as a divine promise.

In due time **Isaac** was born as promised. Apart from digging a few wells in the Negev, he didn't do much. But then he didn't have to. All that was to happen to him was based on God's promise to his father. However, God also appeared to Isaac, and reaffirmed the covenant He had made with Abraham:

> "Sojourn in this land and I will be with you and bless you, for to you and to your descendants I will give all these lands and I will establish the oath which I swore to your father Abraham. And I will multiply your descendants as the stars of heaven . . . because Abraham obeyed me and kept my charge . . . " (Gen. 26:3-5 NAS).

● With that confirmation to Isaac, the nation of Israel was on its way. Isaac married Rebecca and had two sons . . . JACOB and ESAU. Though **Esau** was older (first born), God chose **Jacob** as the one who would inherit the promises. **Jacob,** whose name God later changed to **Israel,** had twelve sons. These were the founders and heads of the twelve tribes of Israel. **Thus three men, Abraham, Isaac and Jacob, are the patriarchs of the nation God was raising up to be His personal nation in the world** (Gen. 35:9-29).

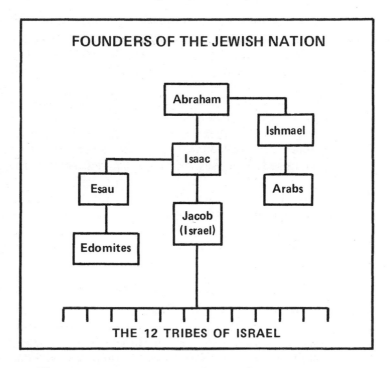

FOUNDERS OF THE JEWISH NATION

THE 12 TRIBES OF ISRAEL

The story gets more complicated from here on.

THE INFANT NATION GOES TO EGYPT

Jacob's favorite son, **Joseph,** was sold by his jealous brothers as a slave to a caravan headed for Egypt. But God's hand was on Joseph to the place where he ultimately became the governor of Egypt. Then famine struck the Mideast and the rest of Jacob's family was affected. Because of his exalted position in Egypt, Joseph was able to arrange for the whole clan, 70 persons by now, to move bag and baggage into Egypt where

33

he could care for them. As God had promised, the people multiplied until they were indeed a nation, numbering about 3½ million (Gen. 37:1 — 50:26). They remained there 300 years.

• When it was time for God to bring His nation out of Egypt and back to the land promised to the patriarchs, He raised up a fierce Pharaoh who severely afflicted the Israelites, as they came to be called. God used these afflictions to wean their hearts from Egypt. After living there for 300 years, you can imagine how "Egyptian" they had become. The U. S. isn't that old.

To effect their deliverance from the stubborn Pharaoh, God raised up **Moses.** Empowering His servant to perform mighty miracles, God brought the people out of Egypt, taking them through the Red Sea and gathering them before Himself at Mt. Sinai (Ex. 1:1 — 19:4).

OFFICIALLY DECLARED GOD'S NATION
(1300 B.C.)

While God had personally appeared to Abraham, Isaac and Jacob, He had yet to appear to the mass of people and confirm them as His own nation. This He did when they were assembled before Him at Sinai. Speaking through Moses, He offered them a deal, a covenant actually:

 "If you will obey Me and keep the Law which I am about to give you, you will be a unique treasure to Me. I will take you to Myself as My own personal nation and bless you and protect you. And through you, fulfill the promises I made to Abraham."

I have not quoted the passage verbatim, but this is the essence of God's offer as set forth in Exodus 19:5, 6. The Israelites happily accepted the deal and the whole thing was sealed with blood sacrifices (Ex. 24:7, 8). It wasn't long, though, before they forgot their bargain with God and embraced false gods. As chastisement, God kept that unbelieving generation in the wilderness of the Sinai deserts for 40 years, until all the adult males had died off (Num. 14:26-38). Under **Joshua,** the next generation was allowed to enter the promised land (Palestine).

ISRAEL DEMANDS A KING

God blessed the new generation by raising up Joshua and going before him to drive out the Canaanite nations from the land (Josh. 1:1-9). But wouldn't you know, before long, the people tired of being ruled by God's leaders. They liked being God's nation, but they hated being DIFFERENT from the surrounding nations who were ruled by kings. So they clamored for a king of their own (1 Sam. 8:1-22).

This rejection was painful for God. But He heeded their cry and gave them a king — **SAUL.** Saul, like many of us, had ideas of his own. Before long, he flatly disobeyed God and was replaced by **DAVID** . . . a man after God's own heart (Acts 13:22). In the days of King David (cir. 1000 B.C.), all of Israel's enemies were subdued and the nation enjoyed peace in the land.

To David's son, **Solomon,** fell the task of building the first great temple for the Lord. It was as fabulous as wealth could make it. During Solomon's reign, the pomp and glory of Israel reached its zenith. The fame of Israel's glory spread far and wide (1 Kings 10:23, 24). In fact, the nation was financially exhausted in lavishing this glory on the monarchy. For nearly 3,000 years, Jews have dreamed of a rerun of the days of Solomon.

Modern Jews expect Messiah to establish a similar glory, exalting Israel above all other nations of the world.

TWO KINGDOMS AND TWO KINGS

With the death of Solomon, the empire was divided into two kingdoms. The northern TEN TRIBES split off into what was called Israel. The TWO southern tribes (Judah and Benjamin) were referred to as Judah (1 Kings 11:30-39). For another 300 years, the two kingdoms existed side by side, each with its own king. And not without a great deal of conflict between them.

As the Jews continued to reject God's laws and embrace the idols of the heathen, the Lord's patience ran out. He then undertook to discipline the divided kingdom. The northern kingdom was the first to feel His swat. It came in 721 B.C. when the king of Assyria besieged Samaria, the capitol of Israel. The ten tribes were taken captive.

After a 100 or so years had passed, Babylon, a new center of world power, arose just south of Assyria. Nebuchadnezzar, the king of Babylon, joined with the Medes to conquer Assyria and the TEN TRIBES were absorbed into the Babylonian empire.

But Judah, the southern kingdom of the Jews, had yet to feel God's switch. Her turn was next.

In 606 B.C., Nebuchadnezzar sent his armies against Jerusalem and the city was taken. The temple treasures and the nation's princes and mighty men were all carried to Babylon — among them, Daniel the prophet (2 Kings 25:8-17). Thus the TWELVE TRIBES were **reunited** in the Babylonian empire.

But Empires have a way of coming and going. In 539 B. C., Babylon was itself conquered by the Persians. Consequently the fate of the 12 tribes passed into the hands of the new ruler of Babylon — Cyrus. The Jews were chastised by God in Babylon for 70 years. During all these years out of their land, the Israelites learned a solemn lesson — **there is only one true God, the God of Abraham, Isaac and Jacob.** This was a lesson the Jews would never forget. Never again would they be found worshipping idols.

THE DISCIPLINED NATION
RETURNS TO ITS OWN LAND

In 536 B.C., Cyrus, ruler of Babylon, issued an edict ending the Jewish captivity. All 12 tribes of the Jewish people were allowed to return to the land and take with them the gold vessels of the temple (Ezra 1:1-11). Two years later, on the very same spot where Solomon had built that first magnificent house for God, the foundation was laid for another temple under the leadership of Zerubbabel (Ezra 3:8-13).

> **JEWS.** Have you noticed how I refer to the Israelites as Jews? After the division of the 12 tribes — 10 in the north and 2 in the south — the term JEW was applied to those in the southern kingdom of Judah. Technically the term means: "a man of Judah" (2 Kings 16:6). After the return from the Babylonian captivity, the word JEW began to be applied in a much broader form. All members of the newly reorganized nation were called Jews (Judeans actually). This was due, not only to the mingling of the tribes in Babylon, but because the religious hopes and ideals of the people were tied up with Judah. In Jesus' day, the name "Jew" was extended to members of the race scattered throughout the world.

The Jews were back in the promised land, but alas — **they didn't own it.** It would never be theirs again for almost 2,500 years. During that time, the control would pass from one empire to another. The Jews could DREAM of becoming a world power once again, under a Solomon-like king, but that's all it would be — **just a dream.** There would be no king to come their way —

until Jesus. It was God's intention that their hunger for a king would prepare them for HIS KING.

DANIEL SAW ALL THIS

Daniel the prophet, one of the noble youths carried into Babylon, was highly favored of God. He was gifted with regard to visions and interpretations. Most Christians know of him because of his deliverance from the lion's den. But prophecy students are intrigued by his interpretation of Nebuchadnezzar's dream and his visions which foretold the coming world empires . . . as well as the advents of Christ and antichrist.

By way of his visions, Daniel had seen the fall of the Babylonian and Persian empires (before they occurred), as well as the rise of the Greek and Roman empires. His predictions were so precise, it is possible to identify Alexander the Great and his conquest of the world. And beyond that to see the Roman Empire issue from one of Alexander's generals. Daniel's prophecies are remarkably specific.

In B. C. 63, Pompey's legions took Jerusalem from the Greeks, thus the city to which Jesus would come as KING OF THE JEWS, would be under Roman control. It's true an individual named King Herod was referred to as the ruler when Jesus was born, but he was simply a puppet king under the Romans. In Jesus' day, Palestine was nothing more than a Roman province.

WHEN JESUS ARRIVED

The Jewish prophets told of a coming king who would make Israel the greatest nation on earth. God had even gone so far as to promise King David that one of His descendants WOULD BE THAT KING. Literally hundreds of prophecies were made concerning this future king, right down to the very town in which He would be born — Bethlehem of Judea. Consequently, when Jesus was crucified and rose again and returned in the Spirit at Pentecost, no less than 513 Bible predictions were fulfilled.

In the heart of every Jew burned the hope of Israel's coming king. Childless women were scorned as having lost the chance to bear the Messiah. Every youngster was taught to believe that King/Messiah would come and restore Israel as the empress of the world. Therefore when Jesus, a carpenter turned Rabbi, spoke of DYING FOR SIN, He didn't fit that dream at all.

THE PEOPLE REJECTED HIM

Though Jesus displayed all the credentials of Messiah, particularly the HEALING SIGN (healing multitudes), the Jews couldn't bring themselves to believe He was the One they were waiting for (Luke 7:19-23). **They longed for a mighty conqueror, not a dying Lamb.** When Jesus said nothing about kicking out the Romans and rebuilding the kingdom, they couldn't possibly see Him as "the hope of Israel." So they rejected Him.

Fully aware that He didn't measure up to the Jewish dream, Jesus pleaded with the people, "If you don't believe because of my Word, at least believe because of my works!" (John 10:38). But it was of no use. ZIONISM— the dream of ruling the world — was too powerfully engrained in them. **Their passion for PHYSICAL PROMISES blinded them to the SPIRITUAL INHERITANCE coming to them through God's Son.**

SO JESUS MADE A PREDICTION OF HIS OWN

 "I am come in My Father's name, and ye receive Me not: if another shall come in HIS OWN NAME, him ye will receive" (John 5:43 KJV).

39

THE JEWISH STORY

40

To whom was Jesus referring when He said, "Another shall come?" You know — ANTICHRIST, the false messiah due to appear in the last days. You've heard plenty about him. He is clearly going to be the man of the hour. God, you see, is STILL chastening the Jews for their rejection of His Son. 1,900 years of being scattered throughout the world was only **phase one** of their punishment. Their final chastisement will come at the hands of antichrist. His persecution of the Jews will make Hitler's pogroms seem like children's games.

The rejection of Jesus, their **true** king, makes the Jews vulnerable. It is an inexorable law — when anyone rejects the true, he sets himself up for the false. **With the Jew's rejection of the TRUE MESSIAH, they have set themselves up for SATAN'S SUPERMAN.** And will he promise to fulfill their dream? And how! Coming as he will, in the power of the devil, his MIRACLES will dazzle them. They will be saying to themselves, "When Messiah comes, will He do more miracles than this man?" (John 7:31).

THE FIRST PHASE HAS MOVED SLOWLY

Forty years after Jesus completed His earthly ministry, the city of Jerusalem was again destroyed. Once more it was the Romans, this time led by Titus. In A. D. 70, the city was levelled, with Jews scattered every place. They were buried, so to speak, among the nations of the world. In country after country, they endured persecutions as the various nations either banished them or sought to eliminate them.

REMNANT PRESERVED. Consider again God's promise to Abraham — the nation issuing from his loins was to inherit a land which has never entirely been in the hands of the Jewish people. That promise remains to be fulfilled. Therefore if God is to keep His promise, the nation has to be preserved. She has yet to receive the land and her king.

41

It is GOD'S PROMISE, not the faithfulness of the Jewish people, that has preserved Israel. Any other nation would have disappeared from the earth forever, but God's commitment to Abraham makes it impossible to wipe out the Jew. No matter what it takes, God has to see that this nation one day receives the PHYSICAL PROMISE. Bear in mind she has already forfeited the SPIRITUAL PROMISE.

Jerusalem was to see more battles as the land passed from the Romans to the Persians in 614 A. D. Still more wars transferred it to Arab hands. By 700 A. D. the Arab Empire (Mohammedan) stretched from Spain to the borders of India, with its influence having a profound effect on the face of Jerusalem (the Mosque of Omar, for example). The Crusaders seized the city for a time, but the Turks wrestled it from them. It was to stay in Arab hands for 800 years.

In the years 1500 to 1800, the land fell into disuse. There were few Jews in Palestine, perhaps as few as 1,500. In 1865 there were only 18,000 people in Jerusalem, 9,000 of them Jewish. Then, around the turn of the 20th Century, Jewish persecutions flared again around the world, causing many to think of a national homeland.

The longing to return to the land was articulated by a man named Theodore Herzel (1897) in a pamphlet called, "The Jewish State." From that time on, the passion for a national home became increasingly intense. By 1914 there were 90,000 Jews in Palestine, but the land was still in Turkish hands.

As Jews drifted back to Palestine, Isaiah's dream began to come true. Orange groves and productive farms sprang up. A piece of land was staked out for a city. (It blossomed into Tel Aviv.) A Jewish miracle was in the making. In November of 1917, the "Balfour Declaration," a 117 word document, sparked Jewish hopes around the world. In effect, it pledged the resources of the British Empire to secure a home for the Jews in Palestine.

THE DRY BONES RATTLE

On December 11, 1917, a British officer walked into Jerusalem and accepted the city from the Turks. With Jerusalem now in their hands, the British could make good on their promise. The Jews were on the road to an independence they hadn't seen since 606 B. C. For nineteen centuries they had suffered humiliation and persecution, but now it appeared they were on the way to becoming a nation again.

No surprise to the prophet Ezekiel.

When Ezekiel was down in Babylon, he had several prophetic visions. One had to do with the rebirth of the nation. In this vision, the Spirit of the Lord carried the prophet to a valley full of dry bones. He stood him where he could survey the sight, then asked . . . "Son of man, can these bones live?" To any sane person that was a ridiculous question. But the prophet was wise enough to reply . . . "Thou knowest."

Then God commanded him to do a weird thing — speak to those dry bones and prophesy over them. It must have struck the prophet as a senseless act, but he obeyed. As he did, strange noises reached his ears. First there was a shaking as the bones began to come together. (That must have blown his mind.) Then he saw flesh and skin begin to form over those bones and cover them. Finally, on command, the four winds blew and " . . . breath came into them, and they lived, and stood upon their feet, an exceeding great army" (Ezek. 37:10).

SURPRISE. Who wouldn't be surprised? Ezekiel was mystified until God explained what it was all about. Those

43

DRY BONES LIVE!

Foreign Office,
November 2nd, 1917

Dear Lord Rothschild,

     I have much pleasure in conveying to you, on behalf of His Majesty's Government, the following declaration of sympathy with Jewish Zionist aspirations which has been submitted to, and approved by, the Cabinet.

     "His Majesty's Government view with favour the establishment in Palestine of a national home for the Jewish people, and will use their best endeavours to facilitate the achievement of this object, it being clearly understood that nothing shall be done which may prejudice the civil and religious rights of existing non-Jewish communities in Palestine, or the rights and political status enjoyed by Jews in any other country"

     I should be grateful if you would bring this declaration to the knowledge of the Zionist Federation.

Facsimile of the Balfour Declaration of 2nd November 1917

44

bones, the prophet was told, represented the WHOLE HOUSE of Israel; and this was God's way of saying He would cause them to come out of their graves and would bring them back to their own land (Ezek. 37:12). What Ezekiel saw was a preview of the restoration of the nation in the END TIME. Actually the bones were NOT BURIED, but scattered throughout the valley. Ezekiel did not see bodies rising from graves, as one thinks of a resurrection. The word "graves" was used merely to give the picture of Jews as buried among the nations. The nation was figuratively "dead" and buried in the graveyard of the world.

● Ezekiel's prophecy began to be fulfilled with the Balfour Declaration in 1917. (Though some rattling was surely taking place when Theodore Herzel kindled the dream of a national home for the Jews.) But it would take two world wars before sinew and flesh and skin would come upon those bones. Even then, they would **still be in the valley** . . . as they are at this moment. The "valley" symbolizes the suffering and humiliation still awaiting the Jews. Phase Two of God's punishment is still ahead of them.

In 1920, the Allies delegated Palestine a British Mandate and the door was thrown open for Jewish immigrants to return to the land. One would think it would be downhill for the Jews from then on, but it was not to be. The huge influx of Jews soon frightened the Arabs who had been living in Palestine for centuries. Though they had done little to improve the land themselves, the Arabs resented the industrious, ingenious Jews.

The British, who had pledged themselves to see both sides (Arab and Jew) treated fairly, found no way to restrict the desperate avalanche of Jews. Hitler's shadow was spreading across Germany and millions of Jews began to anticipate their fate. Try as they might, the British couldn't stem the influx of Jewish refugees.

45

After 25 hopeless years of trying to keep peace in the holy land, the British gave up.

THE NATION RISES TO ITS FEET

MIDNIGHT — May 14, 1948. The British mandate ends. By noon the next day, Jews in Palestine declared themselves a nation. They called it — "Israel." Twenty minutes later (per international dateline) President Truman, in Washington, dramatically announced recognition of the Jewish State. Ezekiel's vision was fulfilled. The dry bones were standing up . . . ALIVE . . . **but still in the valley.**

And what a valley! Within hours after the Jewish state was proclaimed, Arab forces began dropping bombs. The Arabs were determined to rid the land of its 710,000 Jews. With the U. S. and Russia backing Israel, the Israelis gained the upper hand and an armistice followed. The Arabs still had control of OLD JERUSALEM with its revered fragment of the old temple wall.

● The armistice didn't last. In 1956, Nasser called for a holy war against Israel. Equipped with Soviet weapons and under a unified command, the Arab armies moved into the Sinai and "round two" began. It was short and dramatic, with the Israelis again teaching the Arabs a lesson. A cease-fire was invoked after the U. S. and Russia put pressure on the Jews once more.

KING'S TEMPLE AREA RECOVERED

Smoldering Arab resentment exploded once more in 1967 to bring about the SIX DAY WAR. Egypt launched an all out attack, against which the Israelis retaliated with lightning speed, soundly defeating the Egyptians. Old Jerusalem was snatched from the Jordanians and Syrians. **The site where Solomon had built "a house for the Lord," was back in Jewish hands.** A quarter-million Jews streamed into the Old City and headed for the wailing wall. All parties accepted a United Nations cease-fire, but it was a shaky peace at best.

● For 25 years, the newly risen nation stood in the valley with hardly a chance to catch her breath. The Arabs, it seemed, were determined to drive her into the sea. On October 6, 1973, she again suffered a massive Arab attack. This time she was completely caught off guard as her people were celebrating their most holy day — Yom Kippur. It looked bad for a time. But God's Word to Abraham was now being fulfilled. That made the difference.

When a cease-fire was declared some 18 days later, an amazing military situation had developed. Close to **12,000 Israeli troops and 200 tanks were on the west side of the Suez, deep inside Egypt.** The Egyptian Third Army was trapped. That's when Mr. Brezhnev reached for the "red phone." Thus we've come full circle to the scene in the Oval Office when Mr. Nixon pushed the "alert" button.

THE SHAKY MIDEAST

The United States worked hard, seeking to effect a peace agreement between Egypt and Israel. The Camp David Accords, while easing the tension a bit, did not quench the resentment smoldering in the hearts of Palestinians. Trouble could flare up at any time. Observers fear a serious outbreak could involve the major powers in a showdown, for each has vital interests in the area. It's almost as if the Lord were purposely keeping the pot boiling.

47

PROPHECY IN THE MAKING? An **American president** (born-again Jimmy Carter) cheers the wonder of diplomacy he wrought at Camp David: a design for peace in the Middle East — and a bear hug between **Arab and Jewish leaders** (Anwar Sadat and Menachem Begin) in 1978.

WHY NO PEACE?

Ah, that brings us to another fascinating point of prophecy.

To the JEWISH MIND, peace is necessary for the little nation to develop her resources and get ready for her KING. If God has kept His Word with respect to the land, He will also keep His Word with respect to Israel's King. Many Jews are looking for THE KING. Even though the Jewish people have returned to the land in unbelief, the ZIONIST HOPE burns hotter everyday. They know they're going to have a kingdom and a king... **even if they have to bring both into being with their own hands!**

That's not what God has in mind however. Peace between Arab and Jew has a very different meaning to Him. When a peace agreement is finally reached (even though a precarious one), another element of Ezekiel's prophecy will be fulfilled. Through the prophet, God revealed He would bring GOG out of the north **only when His people dwelt safely and securely in their land.** The present unrest is simply God's way of controlling the timing, as Ezekiel says:

 " . . . in the latter years thou shalt come into the land that is brought back from the sword, . . . against the mountains of Israel, which have been always waste: but it is brought forth out of the nations, and they shall DWELL SAFELY ALL OF THEM" (Ezek. 38:8 KJV).

In two other places in the same chapter, this timing is stressed, WHEN HIS PEOPLE DWELL SAFELY (vss. 11, 14). Watch the news headlines. When you read of the signing of a workable Jewish-Arab peace treaty, listen also for growls from the Russian "Bear." Then WATCH OUT — the prophetic moment will be at hand. The **red phone** in the Oval Office will ring again.

THE PROPHETIC MOMENT

Right on schedule, the Lord will bring the "Bear" out of the north against the mountains of Israel. Committed to the defense of Israel, the United States will challenge the aggressor. But this time the Soviets won't back down. With their strategy geared to a FIRST STRIKE, we can anticipate nuclear blows against every military target of our armed forces. While it will be crippling, it may not wipe out our ability to retaliate.

RETALIATE. At this writing, the U.S. has 31 Poseidon submarines, with roughly half of them on patrol at any given time. In the event of a FIRST STRIKE by the Russians, two of our submarines carry enough warheads to destroy more than 200 Soviet cities of 100,000 population and larger. Inasmuch as these subs are relatively invulnerable, they could really hurt the Russians . . . provided they catch them outside their civil defense shelters. In any event, the Bear would feel God's wrath against her homeland as well as against the mountains of Israel. Whether our president would order a retaliatory strike is another matter.

The Soviets will certainly caution us NOT to retaliate with our nuclear subs. Their warning will have teeth, for they will have plenty of warheads aimed at our population centers and industrial centers. However, if we do elect to retaliate (and I think we will), both Russia and the U. S. could be reduced to 3rd rate powers . . . or less . . . within hours.

On the other hand, it is possible, because of our Pro-Israel position, the Lord may intervene to spare our people in some way. However, since our nation is itself overdue for judgment, we probably should prepare for the worst.

But you ask, why would God want to neutralize Russia and the U. S.? Ah, that's another vital piece of God's plan.

IT CREATES A POLITICAL VACUUM

Can you picture the world situation with the two major powers suddenly impotent? Right now the world is divided, east against west. The military standstill has been used of God to maintain the status quo. But with the two major powers suddenly neutralized . . . and China only beginning to awaken . . . a political and military vacuum would exist. You know how nature hates a vacuum. Who do you think will step into that vacuum? Right — a remarkable genius and miracle worker — ANTICHRIST! His appearance on the world scene will be right on schedule, God's schedule.

How do you suppose this SUPERMAN will look to the Jews? Like a king? Yes, a super king. Bear in mind how vulnerable they are, how susceptible they'll be. **Having rejected the TRUE KING (Jesus), they'll be ready for Satan's substitute (antichrist).** When people reject what God offers them, the devil devises a substitute to match their longings. The substitute king Satan has in store for Israel will be an amazing world ruler who will appear to be everything a Messiah should be.

NOW YOU KNOW WHAT GOD IS UP TO

He has brought His people back into their own land, but they have **returned in unbelief.** They still don't want Jesus. They're just as stubborn about that as they were 1,900 years ago. The fact that they have "come home," doesn't mean they have "seen the light." **They're still not interested in a Savior. They want a political king who can restore the glory of Israel.** Consequently they are RIPE for antichrist.

God will let them have THEIR king, just as He let them have SAUL centuries ago. His unique way of chastening Israel for rejecting His Son will be to let her have the desire of her heart — antichrist.

Little does Israel suspect what awaits her at the hand of this man. You wouldn't think a human king would be able to sell himself to Israel as her Messiah. But wait until you see how he pulls it off. That's next.

51

I AM NOT ANTI-SEMITIC

Like the apostle Paul, "My heart's desire is that Israel might be saved" (Rom. 10:1). God has given me a love for the Jew, probably because of the great debt we Christians owe God's people. But I must state the facts as they are. As you read of the dreadful things in store for the Jew, and find me saying they are due to stubbornness and rebellion, you may think I am anti-Semitic. I am not. I have shed tears over this very thing. Israel, as a nation, has REFUSED the **spiritual promises** of Abraham (salvation and the Holy Spirit), desiring only the PHYSICAL PROMISES (the land, the kingdom and an earthly king). Israel forfeited the spiritual promises by rejecting Jesus. The church has inherited them . . . a church made up of **both** Jew and Gentile (Gal. 3:26 -29). **So while my words seem harsh at points, bear in mind my longing is for Jews to come to their real Messiah — JESUS.**

Chapter Three

We Want
Superman!

Are you old enough to remember the rise of Superman? He first appeared as a comic strip character in the newspapers. (When I was a boy, I'd race for the paper every afternoon to see what Superman was up to.) Then came the Superman comic books. His fame continued to grow as more people came to know him via the TV series, *THE ADVENTURES OF SUPERMAN.* His fame climaxed in a motion picture that showed what he could do — on a wide screen.

What is there in man, do you suppose, that makes him dream of being stronger than a locomotive, faster than a speeding bullet? **It is because the world is in such a mess that it will take a "superman" to straighten things out.**

While the bulk of mankind doesn't know it, you and I know that **Jesus alone is the answer to our messed up world.** Strangely enough, though, people keep on dreaming of a heroic individual who is so powerful and so wise he can solve global problems and move fast enough to give relief right now.

The world is in such a mess, leaders everywhere are looking for an outstanding individual, a "superman" who can heal world problems like magic. The devil has such a man waiting in the wings — **Satan's superman!**

● Sidney Harris, writing for the *South Bend Tribune,* made an insightful comment in his article entitled . . .

"WORLD CALLS FOR A LEADER, BUT WANTS A FALSE PROPHET!"

"People keep saying, 'We need a leader' . . . but that is not what they really mean. What most are looking for is not a leader, because a true leader tells us what we don't want to hear, but what we ought to hear. What we're looking for is neither a true leader nor a true Messiah, but a FALSE MESSIAH — a man who will give us oversimplified answers, who will justify our ways . . . in short,

we're invoking magic, we are praying for the coming of a WIZARD. What we're looking for is a leader who will show us how to be the same old man, only more successfully — and his ancient name is Satan." *

THE WORLD IS IN A MESS

You read the papers. You watch TV. You know the mess the world is in. Everywhere we look there is ruin; whether in the water we drink, the air we breathe or the ground we till. Everything man touches he ruins — from marriages to international relations. The earth groans under man's corruption. Those who believe modern education and advanced technology are making men better and better have to be deceived. They must be ignorant of the fallen human nature. Just look at the rampage of sin in our country:

Drugs and disease   Child prostitutes
Rape and child abuse   Exploding occultism
Pornography   Movie and TV filth
Homosexuality   Insane violence
Divorce   Spending madness
Rebellious children   Political corruption
Mental breakdowns   Inflation

. . . and the list goes on.

What is happening in the U. S. is being repeated in other countries. On top of that there are collapsing governments and terrorism, famines, earthquakes and drastic weather changes bringing drought. Sin is out of control. The nations can no longer cope. No wonder the creation cries for relief. It is reeling under the ruin heaped upon it by fallen man.

---

*South Bend Tribune, September 2, 1977

Yet, all is coming to pass as God's Word predicted it would:

 ". . . There will be terrible times in the last days. People will be lovers of themselves, lovers of money, boastful, proud, abusive, disobedient to their parents, ungrateful, unholy, without love, unforgiving, slanderous, without self control, brutal, not lovers of the good, treacherous, rash, conceited, lovers of pleasure rather than lovers of God" (2 Tim. 3:1-4 NIV).

The truth is — after nearly 6,000 years, man still doesn't know how to control himself. He can fly through space, triumphing over the law of gravity. But he can't conquer his own nature. As a result, the world in which we live is a mess.

GOD'S ANSWER TO THIS MESS

When human corruption reaches its climax, God will intervene. Since man is incapable of ruling himself, God's answer is His SUPERNATURAL KING JESUS, Who will exercise absolute rule over all the earth. At a precise moment in prophecy, He will return and establish a one world government. It will be government from the top down. It will not be a government of the people or by the people. It will be a DIVINE MONARCHY — yet run FOR the sake of the people.

Obviously I'm referring to the millennium, the 1,000 year reign of Christ on earth. We'll be discussing it later, but I mention it here as God's answer to man's inability to govern himself. With God's KING in command, the world will no longer be in a mess. Quite the opposite — it'll be a fabulous place to live. No more wars, no more crime. Plenty of prosperity and happiness for everyone. Life on earth will be bountiful under Christ's control.

• I wish I could tell you the next thing in prophecy is the return of Jesus and the establishing of this fabulous kingdom on earth. But I can't. The Jewish story isn't finished and it has to run its course. The Bible, as you know, is a Jewish book . . . and prophecy centers around the Jewish nation. **But the Jews have rejected God's answer.**

ISRAEL'S TERRIBLE SIN

Remember Pilate . . . and his predicament?

The Jews brought Jesus before him, accusing the Lord of capitol crimes. But when Pilate examined Jesus, he found Him to be innocent. Then the governor presented Jesus to the crowds, "I am bringing Him forth to you, that you may know I find no fault in Him." As Jesus stood there facing the crowds, Pilate exclaimed, "Behold the man!" (John 19:4,5).

When the chief priests saw Jesus, they cried out . . . **"Crucify Him! Crucify Him!"**

"What?" gasped Pilate, "Crucify your King?"

The priests answered, **"We have no king but Caesar!"** (John 19:15).

Convinced that Jesus was innocent, Pilate sought to release Him. Yet, fearing the Jews would make trouble for him at Rome, the governor turned the Lord over to them to be crucified, then washed his hands of the whole affair. In reply, the people shouted words which haunt the Jews to this day . . .

"Let His blood be on us and our children!" (Matt. 27:25).

• We know it was God's plan for Jesus to die this way. It was prophesied He would take the place of the

Passover Lamb and shed His blood for the sins of the world. But the Jews cared nothing for that. A perfect sacrifice for sin was the farthest thing from their minds. As far as they were concerned, they had gotten rid of a deceiver.

BUT THEY CRUCIFIED THEIR KING

Pilate tacked an inscription on the cross in the place where the criminal's crimes were usually posted. In full view of everyone the story was told in three languages...

"Jesus of Nazareth, King of the Jews."

The priests were furious. They demanded Pilate remove the notice. But he refused. Knowingly or not, he had posted the truth (John 19:19-22). In their blind passion, the Jews had crucified the very One God sent to make them a great nation. They didn't realize everything they longed for was fulfilled in Him. In killing the Christ, they dramatized another prophecy concerning them . . .

"We will not have this man to reign over us!"
(Luke 19:14).

Thus the Jews rejected God's answer to the world's mess.

SO GOD MUST DEAL WITH THE JEWISH HEART

It is said that when a Gentile sins, God strikes him once. But when a Jew sins, God strikes him twice. The reason, of course — he's had the greater opportunity. Now that isn't just a saying, for God's Word declares the same thing. Speaking through the prophet Jeremiah, God says:

 "At first I will recompense their iniquity and their sin DOUBLE; because they have defiled My land . . ." (Jer. 16:18 KJV).

The Lord knows the Jewish heart. He's had to put up with their rebelliousness ever since He brought the nation out of Egypt. It must have been brutal for God to watch the Jews reject their King, when He was so eager to pour out their SPIRITUAL INHERITANCE on them. How it must have torn His heart when they rejected His Son and crucified Him. Jesus was right . . . "Father they know not what they do" (Luke 23:34). The Jews couldn't possibly have understood the consequences of their act. For had they known the Scriptures, as they should have, they would have seen the DOUBLE

59

PUNISHMENT God had in store for them. And it's unthinkable they would have slain the Lord.

Let's look at that double punishment.

PHASE ONE: ISRAEL SCATTERED AMONG THE GENTILES

In raising their hands against Jesus, the Jews did a terrible thing. In 70 A. D., God raised His hand against the nation once more, this time using Titus as His instrument. If the Jews would use a Roman governor to crucify Jesus, God would use a Roman general to destroy their city and drive them from the land. The loss of the land ripped Jewish hope to shreds.

The Jewish dream was based on the land. To be torn from the land for 1,900 years was severe punishment. The land was an integral part of God's covenant with Abraham. The promises were tied to the land. **There could be no fulfillment of those promises apart from the land.** Therefore scattering them among the Gentiles was God's most effective way of shattering their dream, yet preserving a remnant that would one day inherit the promises.

JEALOUSY WAS PART OF THE PUNISHMENT

While scattered among the Gentiles, the Jews have suffered 1,900 years of jealousy. That, too, was part of God's plan. He meant for them to be jealous:

 "Did they stumble, I ask, to be lost altogether? Certainly not! By their error, salvation has come to the non-Jews (Gentiles) to make the Jews jealous" (Rom. 11:11 BECK N.T.).

But jealous of what, you ask? Well, the Jews lost more than their precious land when they rejected Jesus.

60

They also forfeited their **spiritual** inheritance. Did you know Pentecost was a **Jewish** promise? Indeed. God meant for His people Israel to receive the HOLY SPIRIT as their spiritual inheritance from Abraham. But their minds have been so taken with the PHYSICAL blessings of Abraham, they weren't interested in their spiritual inheritance.

SPIRITUAL INHERITANCE. You hear the expression, "Salvation is of the Jews" (John 4:22). It's true, but unfortunately most Jews will never be saved. The promises coming to them through ABRAHAM were **both physical and spiritual.** So great was their obsession for the PHYSICAL PROMISES, the Jews all but despised the SPIRITUAL PROMISES. They wanted to be a super nation with other nations bowing down to them. In the process they threw away their spiritual salvation (sons of God by the new birth; the indwelling Holy Spirit and eternal life). Their hearts were so set on a Solomon-like kingdom, they rejected the Son of God and blasphemed the Holy Spirit, the very One through Whom the promises are obtained. Once the Jews rejected the fabulous gift in Christ, God offered it to the Gentiles, thinking to provoke jealousy in the Jewish heart. So far that hasn't happened.

What the Jews rejected, the Gentiles have embraced. How it must irritate Jewish people to see Gentiles rejoicing in the name of Jesus, a denounced Jew . . . all the while claiming He is the Jew's own Messiah. So in scattering the Jews among Gentiles who worship Jesus, God gave them a good swat . . . where it would do the most good . . . in their jealous hearts.

But God Brought Them Back to the Land

It is a mistake to think God has brought the Jews back to the land to BLESS THEM. To the contrary, **He has brought them back to PUNISH THEM.** The DOUBLE PUNISHMENT continues. He must still deal severely with their hard hearts if He is to change their attitude toward His Son. This is why it is so important to observe **they have RETURNED IN UNBELIEF.** To this day, the Jews will have nothing to do with their true King — JESUS.

The 1,900 years of jealousy, persecution and suffering have done little to soften Jewish hearts. So you know it is going to take something special, something PAINFUL, something BITTER to break that stubborn attitude. Therefore God has brought His nation back to the land that He might deal with the Jews in the very place where they rejected their King, His Son. As must be obvious by now, phase two of their double punishment will be far more intense than anything they've suffered so far.

PHASE TWO: TRIBULATION
AT THE HAND OF ANTICHRIST

The prophet Daniel refers to antichrist with these words:

". . . the prince that shall come . . . shall confirm the covenant with many for one week (seven years): and in the midst of the week he shall cause the sacrifice and the oblation to cease, and for the overspreading of abominations he shall make it desolate . . ." (Dan. 9:26,27 KJV).

This is the passage scholars use when referring to Israel's acceptance of antichrist and her 7 year agreement with him. From the verse it is easy to see how the first 3½ years will be a HONEYMOON for Israel as she enjoys favored nation status. During this time, we can expect JUDAISM (the official religion of Israel) to be the official religion of antichrist's empire.

● At the end of the first 3½ year period, antichrist

will break his covenant with Israel. He will then step out, revealing his true colors — SATAN'S SUPERMAN! Having used the Jews to establish himself as the "savior of the world," he will make another shift and demand that all people worship HIM AS GOD (2 Thess. 2:4). The Jews will refuse, having been cured of that kind of idolatry through the Babylonian captivity. As a result, antichrist will turn against the Jews, persecuting them with insane fury, an episode Jeremiah calls "the time of Jacob's trouble" (Jer. 30:7). That will be the CLIMAX of Israel's punishment. This persecution (the second swat from God's switch) is calculated to CURE THEM of looking to anyone but Jesus as Messiah. Antichrist will be God's primary agent for breaking Israel's stubborn attitude toward Jesus.

Consider again the **TWO PHASES OF ISRAEL'S PUNISHMENT:**

- **PHASE I:** Scattered among the nations to be despised and suffer persecution and jealousy at the hand of the Gentiles (Rom. 11:11).

- **PHASE II:** Returned to their land in unbelief to accept Satan's superman — antichrist — as her king (time of Jacob's trouble. Jer. 30:7; John 5:43).

THE SATAN STORY

The devil has an incurable passion — he wants to be God — or at least equal with God. From ages past he has coveted God's throne. Scripture reveals he once led an angelic revolt against God in an attempt to seize the eternal kingdom. It failed (Ezek. 28:15; Rev. 12:4, 7-9). God could have destroyed him right then and there, but He is too wise for that. He now had something He could use. Consequently, the devil and those angels participating in his conspiracy were set aside as

63

fallen angels or demons (Jude 6; Matt. 25:41). Once God found sinful beings in His kingdom, a whole new program became possible.

● With sin available after Satan's fall, God could bring forth a race of beings with free wills and TEST THEM. For this He created the earth, made men in His own image and gave them FREE WILLS. God now had a perfect device for testing men. Once men were tested and proven faithful, God could safely commit Himself to them and plan on spending eternity with those who love Him.

Inasmuch as the devil and his demons were now useful to God, they were granted a reprieve, and even allowed to have a kingdom of their own (Eph. 6:12; 2 Cor. 4:4). That kingdom, though, would last only for as long as God needed them for testing purposes. After that, they and their entire kingdom would be cast into the lake of fire (Matt. 25:41; Rev. 20:10).

Consider the devil's freedom to approach Eve.

Successful in deceiving her, he then used Adam's affection for Eve to draw the first man into his coils. By getting Adam to disobey God and yield to his suggestion, **Satan gained control of the world**; that is, all the empires that would issue from Adam. **God, you see, had actually given the entire world into Adam's hands. So Satan, in tricking him out of it, LEGALLY acquired this world and all of mankind.**

Inasmuch as Adam was "not deceived," a valid transfer of authority occurred (1 Tim. 2:14). God has never once used force or acted illegally to retrieve the world from Satan. This is why the apostle Paul refers to Satan as "the god of this world" (2 Cor. 4:4). God recognizes his dominion and uses it for His divine purpose.

© Linda Lovett 1979

Successful in deceiving Eve, Satan then used Adam's affection for her to draw the first man into his coils. God had actually given the entire world into Adam's hands. So the devil, in tricking him out of it, LEGALLY ACQUIRED THE WORLD and all of mankind.

Consider the devil's freedom to approach Jesus.

One of the clearest evidences of Satan's authority is seen in Jesus' temptation in the wilderness. Familiar with the story? The Lord had fasted 40 days, allowing His flesh to subside, so that He could properly handle the awesome news announced to Him from heaven . . .

"Thou art My beloved Son in Whom I am well pleased" (Mark 1:11). We don't know what went on in Jesus' mind when He worked around His dad's carpenter shop and meditated on the Scriptures. He surely suspected something (Luke 2:49). However, when He was baptized in the Jordan by John the Baptist, He got the word . . . "You are My Son!" That is awesome news to lay on anyone. No wonder the Spirit led Him into the wilderness to adjust to the news and have His reaction to it TESTED.

Naturally, the devil would do all He could to turn Jesus aside from His mission, the work He had come to do. So he came to the Lord in all his kingly power to tempt Him; to see if He really believed what He had heard, that He was indeed God's Son. "If you are the Son of God," he challenged, do thus and so (Matt. 4:3). When that failed, he cleverly offered to GIVE JESUS the whole world . . . the very world He had come to save through His death. What subtlety! **Here was a chance to save the world WITHOUT going to the cross:**

 "And the devil, taking Him up into a high mountain, showed unto Him ALL THE KING-DOMS OF THE WORLD in a moment of time. And the devil said unto Him, 'All this power will I give thee, and all the glory of them: for THAT IS DELIVERED UNTO ME; and to whomsoever I will I give it. If thou therefore wilt worship me, all shall be thine!' " (Luke 4:5-7 KJV).

Note again, that was a **genuine** offer. Satan could honestly make such a proposal. He COULD give the world to Jesus, but it would be, of course, a sin-cursed world. Jesus **refused**. He had come, not merely to buy back the world, but to deal with its sin. **My point: Satan does have such power, for he is going to make this same offer to antichrist — AND HE WILL ACCEPT IT.**

© Linda Lovett 1975

To turn Jesus aside from His mission of redemption, Satan offered to GIVE Him the WHOLE WORLD — without going to the cross — if only Jesus would worship him. Of course Jesus refused. The point: Satan does have such power, for he is going to make this same offer to antichrist, and HE WILL ACCEPT IT.

The devil adapts to defeat.

He rolls with the punches, never backing away from his determination to overthrow God. Even now he is working on a remarkable scheme for rallying the world behind him for an all-out assault against the Lord when He returns. His plan will unfold in three stages:

1 He will bring onto the world scene a man whom he will establish as the "Emperor of the World." This man, of course, will be antichrist. He will be sold out to Satan and energized by his power. To get the world ready for this man, "THE SPIRIT OF ANTI-

CHRIST" has been working in the affairs of men, even as the "SPIRIT OF GOD" has been working in the hearts of men to get them ready for Christ. When things are just right (God controls the timing), this man will appear on the political stage (2 Thess. 2:3, 4; Matt. 24:23,24).

2 About mid-point in antichrist's reign, he will suffer a fatal wound (possibly assassinated) and die (Rev. 13:3, 12, 14). But his body will be resurrected, probably in three days to coincide with Jesus' resurrection. At this point, **Satan** will be in that body. **The devil will thus assume personal command of the world from inside the body of antichrist** (Rev. 13:3; 17:8). Immediately he will go to the Jewish temple in Jerusalem and present himself to the world AS GOD (2 Thess. 2:4). The devil's dream will be partially fulfilled if he can get the world to embrace him as deity, even though he is occupying the body of another world figure. (Later we'll see how he handles that little problem.)

3 His final act as ruler of the world will be to summon the armies of earth to battle against the Lord at His appearing. This is the battle of Armageddon (Rev. 16:12-16). Thus, in three clearly defined stages, the devil hopes to achieve what was denied him when the heavenly revolt failed. As long as God allows him to roam about freely, he will never cease trying to overthrow the Lord. His passion to be God is an incurable disease.

THE TIME IS AT HAND

Many prophecy students believe antichrist is in the world right now. And just as Judas was some time in preparation for the work he was to do, so is this man being groomed for the moment of his appearance.

68

• The devil has been waiting 1,900 years for another shot at the throne. All this time, his spirit (the spirit of antichrist) has been working behind the scenes to create in men an appetite for evil (1 John 4:3). You can be sure when antichrist does appear, his kingdom will be rotten to the core. With the way the world's passion for sin is being fanned today, things are about perfect for the "man of sin" to step in and take over.

Simultaneously, this same spirit has been doing all he can to hinder the Lord in the building of His church. Doctrinal quarrels and divisions are his speciality. The fragmented denominations of today are not God's doing. That's the **devil's** dirty work (1 John 2:18-22).

> **SPIRIT OF ANTICHRIST.** Christians live in enemy territory. This is the devil's world. You and I must live under the holy consciousness that we are watched, moment by moment, by an enemy of unimaginable power. The devil never sleeps nor slumbers, but is relentless in seeking to bring all or any part of our lives under his authority. He goes beyond what we normally think of as temptation to sin, to work his way into our everyday routines; into our business and the earning of our daily bread, our politics, our literature and entertainment. In all these things he seeks to take what is lawful and necessary and fashion it into a tool that will advance his devilish deceptions. We must recognize the effect of HIS SPIRIT throughout the whole of life on earth and determine within ourselves to carry the fight against him 'till death.

Now we can understand why Paul says . . . "evil men and seducers shall wax worse and worse . . . " (2 Tim. 3:13). The **spirit of antichrist** is working relentlessly to set the stage for Satan's man. Even so, the devil has to bide his time. He DOES NOT CONTROL the timing of antichrist's appearance. God does. **In no way is God going to allow the DECEIVER-KING to show up before God is ready for him.** That would foul up His plan for punishing Israel. So the rise of the future world ruler has been held in check, a truth the apostle Paul spells out precisely:

 "And you know what restrains him now, so that in his time he may be revealed. For the mystery of lawlessness is already at work; only he who now restrains will do so until he is taken out of the way. And then that lawless one will be revealed whom the Lord will slay with the breath of His mouth and bring to an end by the appearance of His coming" (2 Thess. 2:6-8 NAS).

See how clearly Paul speaks? God is definitely holding back the devil from producing his man. By what means is he restrained? The above text doesn't tell us. But elsewhere in God's Word it speaks of the MYSTERY OF GODLINESS (1 Tim. 3:16). We won't go wrong in assuming that God uses one mystery to hold back another, that the "mystery of godliness" is used to restrain the "mystery of lawlessness."

We also know the DEVIL is the prime agent behind the "mystery of lawlessness." Therefore we can assume God Himself is behind the "mystery of godliness." **This passage, then, is simply saying God is restraining the appearance of antichrist until He is ready for him.** And when He is ready, He will simply REMOVE THE RESTRAINT. Take away the "mystery of godliness," and the LAWLESS ONE will surely appear.

OTHER REASONS. Other passages give further reasons why God is restraining the appearance of antichrist. The "times of the Gentiles" must run their course. However, with Israel back in the land and the city of Jerusalem once more in Jewish hands, that time is drawing to an end (Luke 21:24). But there is more involved than punishing the Jews. God must also TIME the sequence of events to coincide with the LAST MAN TO BE SAVED. There is, you see, a specific number of people making up the church, the body of Christ. And since people must be saved during the age of the Holy Spirit, that age cannot end prematurely. Therefore antichrist's appearance must be TIMED PRECISELY to bring all these events together on schedule. Not one tribulation event will be left to chance.

I think it's safe to assume that Satan's man is alive and well on planet earth and is being groomed for his appearance to Israel.

HE'LL COME WITH CREDENTIALS

Antichrist will be a master salesman, a charmer, hard to resist. He will perform miracles so powerful and so convincing, they will **appear** to surpass the works of Jesus. He will appear to raise the dead and call fire down from heaven. And because he employs familiar spirits, he may be able to **counterfeit** resurrections of world famous people.

The apostle Paul speaks of antichrist's credentials in this manner:

 "The coming of the lawless one will be in accordance with the work of Satan displayed in all kinds of counterfeit miracles, signs and wonders, and in every sort of evil that deceives those who are perishing. They perish because they refuse to love the truth and thus be saved. For this reason, God sends them a powerful delusion so that they will believe the lie and so that all will be condemned who have not believed the truth, but have delighted in wickedness" (2 Thess. 2:9-12 NIV).

From the first century, the "spirit of antichrist" has been working steadily, conditioning people to LOVE

71

EVIL. The modern appetite for sex and violence, as well as greed and corruption, demonstrates how well he has done his job. Consequently, when SATAN'S SUPERMAN shows up, not only will Israel want him, but so will the rest of the world.

THE NATIONS WILL BE READY FOR HIM

Consider the great concerns facing the world today:

☆ Economic chaos   ☆ Pollution of every kind
☆ Nuclear annihilation   ☆ Overpopulation
☆ World-wide famine   ☆ Lack of leadership

A group of top international businessmen and brains has been putting heads together to see what could be done to prevent a universal catastrophe that would destroy the human race.

In 1974, this group, after receiving a study done by M.I.T. (The Massachusetts Institute of Technology), concluded that the world system as we know it, will soon collapse unless a way can be found to UNITE MANKIND. The concensus—A ONE WORLD GOVERN-MENT is the only answer. That nothing short of a super world-ruling government can prevent cosmocide. Ever since that conclusion was reached, some of the most powerful men in the world have committed themselves to bringing it about.

If you could hear these leaders talking, you'd be shocked at their words. In the face of a possible nuclear holocaust, they are saying the only hope for world survival is for a talented and powerful man to take complete control — in other words . . . a SUPERMAN! Isn't that amazing! Right in line with the prophetic word, the trend today is toward a one world dictatorship. Yes, the **world** will be ready for him.

72

APOSTATE CHRISTIANITY
WILL BE READY FOR HIM

The story of the church is as sad as the history of Israel. In Pentecostal days (when the church was beginning), the church was a glorious thing, a lovely picture of the Holy Spirit working through God's people as they upheld the purity of the apostles' teachings. But that has long since passed.

When Paul was establishing churches among the Gentiles, he saw great unity among them. For a time it was precious, but that too passed away. The faithful apostle never saw their failure, but he warned them of the corruption that would creep in. It remained for the apostle John, who outlived them all, to see the incoming tide of iniquity that was to shape the story of the church until the Lord would return.

Today, we're approaching the **maturity** of that evil which was only then getting started. We are on the threshold of the latter days. The standing of the church has long been forfeited. We no longer have to warn of the incoming corruption, we must now face up to the ruin it has brought.

When I speak of apostate Christianity, I am **not** referring to born-again believers, but those organized institutions the world views as THE CHURCH, religious structures made up of unconverted people who profess to be Christians, but are not born of the Spirit.

The devil's aim has been to get as many unsaved people into the church as is necessary to rob her of her power and vision. We have now arrived at the place where the apostasy has become highly visible as different leaders depart from the Word of God. Many religious leaders now **deny** the authority of the Scriptures and **ignore** the fundamentals of biblical Christianity. The

73

doctrine of the Trinity is **rejected** along with the virgin birth and the personality of the Holy Spirit. The death of Christ has **no atoning value** to these people, but is held up as an example of devotion and self-sacrifice.

I could list more basic truths either scorned or explained away, but you've heard it all before. What this is all pointing up to is this — **in the world today we have religious leaders striving to present a UNITED FRONT to the world.** That would be great if it were based on Christ as the only Savior, and the Bible as the only authoritative rule of doctrine. But that's not what this movement is all about.

The modern ecumenical movement is prepared to SACRIFICE TRUTH in an attempt to collect all and any of the various groups under a single banner. Without realizing it, they are paving the way for the FALSE PROPHET, who will head up the religious department of antichrist's kingdom. So what we have is a FALSE CHURCH clamoring for a WORLD-WIDE ORGANIZED RELIGIOUS BODY . . . doing its part to set the stage for antichrist.

ECUMENICAL. Will you again note I am **NOT** referring to evangelical Christians. Although I think we must agree they are not immune to these tendencies. Where is the fire, the passion, the vision and faith of our early fore-bearers? We may be orthodox in doctrine, but often our hearts are cold and our love for Christ half-hearted. Obedience to the Word is partial and our separation from the world is incomplete. Some great evangelical churches with glorious histories are dead in their witness — because "the love of many grows cold." So while there have been visitations of revival here and there . . . and certain ON FIRE ministries remain, the situation with the church as a whole, is pretty sad. A host of religious leaders will be ready for a miracle worker who promises to step in and do the job for them.

ISRAEL WILL BE MORE THAN READY

We have already seen how the Jews, having rejected their true king, the Lord Jesus, will be powerfully attracted to Satan's DECEIVER-KING. Think how long this nation has dreamed of a king. Do you think this man will look good to them? And how. Coming in the power of Satan, he will seemingly fulfill many messianic prophecies — backing his claims with astonishing miracles. Why, the Jews will rush to embrace this man as Messiah.

Emotion as fierce as pain seizes a Jew in prayer shawl worshipping at the wailing wall in Jerusalem as he longs for the Messiah of Israel. Having rejected their true Messiah, Jesus, the Jews will rush to embrace Satan's man — **antichrist**.

Then recall Satan's dream and his plan to bring to power the "Emperor of the world." **When you connect the devil's dream with the Jewish dream of being the "Empress of the world," there is no way to keep this union from taking place.** When it happens, Jesus' word will be fulfilled . . . "Another shall come in his own name, and him ye will receive" (Jo. 5:43).

See now how God has arranged for the **double punishment** of the Jews? Don't you get the feeling He has everything under control? Of course. That's the point of prophecy.

THE STAGE IS SET FOR SATAN'S SUPERMAN

☆ His rise will be swift.
☆ His eye will be on Israel.

Fully aware of God's PROMISE to the Jewish nation, he will seek to turn this to his advantage. Now that's clever. It takes a genius, when you are the enemy of God, to **turn the workings of God** to your advantage — but antichrist will have that genius. In fact, the world is going to be astounded at his political ingenuity. So hang on to your hat. That's next.

Chapter Four

Satan's Super Empire

"I'm going to tell you about the most incredible conversation I've had in my entire life!"

That's the way a pastor of a large church in California began his sermon on a recent Sunday morning. He had just returned from Florida aboard a 747 where he had an astonishing interview with a fellow passenger.

Someone mailed me a 12 minute tape of this pastor's remarks to his congregation. Before I could bring myself to take it seriously, I telephoned to make sure he had actually given such a report to his people. It was confirmed that the pastor had indeed traveled aboard the flight, seated next to a 58-year-old Jew who worked in the field of international loans. According to his words, the Jewish man had loaned SIX BILLION DOLLARS the very day he boarded the plane.

"What do you know of the European Common Market," asked the curious pastor, once the conversation was under way.

"I financed it!" the man replied, laughing.

"I can't believe what I'm hearing," gasped the preacher.

Whereupon the passenger produced a briefcase full of pictures of himself posing with various leaders of world governments.

"As a matter of fact," he continued, "I've just come from a meeting of leaders from all over the world in which we made decisions affecting the economy of this planet!"

The minister sat there dazed. Here was a man so wealthy it was impossible to identify with him. Yet, if all he was saying was true, a gold mine of information was stored in the fellow.

The preacher felt led to ask a penetrating question... "What is your real motivation in life?"

"My motives are two-fold," said the Jew earnestly. "Number one, I believe we must establish a ONE WORLD GOVERNMENT. There's no question about it. It's the only hope of the world."

"Number two, I want you to know I'm not for war or violence. I believe what we need is ONE WORLD RELIGION. In recent months I have been meeting with leaders of the various world religions where it was commonly agreed our only hope is for a one world religion. But can you guess the problem we're having?"

"What's that?"

"There are people in the United States who fight the idea of one world religion!"

The pastor had to conceal his amusement.

The man, it turned out, believed in God, yet knew nothing of Bible prophecy concerning antichrist, his one world government and one world religion. When he told the Jew everything he longed to see accomplished was predicted in the Bible, his comment was . . . "I'm going to have to pay more attention to that Book." But when the conversation moved to Jesus and His return, the man snorted . . . "Son, grow up!"

In sharing his feelings with his audience, the pastor confessed, "I sat next to this man utterly dumbfounded. My thoughts raced through the book of Revelation as he spoke. In my spirit I was asking, *'Lord, why are You letting me hear these things?'* "

"It seems to me, people," continued the pastor, "that a one world government is getting too close for comfort. Frankly I almost became a post-tribulationist yesterday!" While his pre-trib audience roared with laughter, you can be sure this pastor was reassessing his views on prophecy. Rapid fire changes in the world today are causing many Bible students to take another look at their prophetic stance.

NOT SO FAR OUT

A few years ago, the statements of the Jewish passenger would have been dismissed as the ravings of a lunatic. But times have changed. This pastor was rightly impressed. A new international order is in the making and signs of it are all around us. Even now, gas stations are offering fuel in litres. Why? The United States is converting to the metric system in order to merge with the rest of the world. Nations can no

79

longer go it alone, acting independently of each other. Things are moving swiftly toward a one world government.

Yesterday, as I stood in line at a drug counter, a lady in front of me hauled out a string of credit cards to pay her bill. They were assembled in a plastic device that unfolded like an accordian.

"What a novel way to carry your cards," I remarked, intrigued at the sight.

"Yes," she said, "the cards are so convenient, I don't carry money any more."

She was serious, even opening her purse for me to see. Sure enough. All she had was a few coins, which I suspected were for phone calls. I had read we were headed for a cashless society, but I didn't think of it as being this near.

Yet, I shouldn't have been surprised. Right now, many employees and social security recipients never see their checks. They are deposited directly into their accounts by EFT (electronic fund transfer). Come to think of it, my own modest retirement check from the Air Force each month doesn't come to me either. It goes directly to my bank. EFT is now a nationwide system. Many banks have "automatic tellers," computers allowing you to deposit, withdraw, transfer funds from one account to another — by means of a code number. By the end of the decade, EFT could become world-wide.

I recall another experience in a large chain department store. I wanted to use my credit card. The lady put the card in a machine that checked my credit in seconds. Nothing unusual about that. But when she told me I had been cleared by every one of their branches throughout the world, that was something else. It startled me to think I had been checked out on a GLOBAL BASIS.

To be sure — signs of an international order are everywhere.

THE POLITICAL TIMING IS RIGHT

The population explosion is turning this planet into a solid mass of people. Instant communications make it impossible for nations to act independently of each other. What affects one, now affects others. Besides, there are now global problems no one nation or group of nations can solve.

Brain trusts, made up of qualified men from all nations, are desperately trying to deal with these problems. And do you know what they are suggesting as a solution? BRING EVERYTHING UNDER A SINGLE LEADERSHIP! The same is true of the money people of Europe. Powerful voices are insisting the only way to stabilize trade, money and food distribution is to have it ministered by a **one world government.** Meetings devoted to bringing this to pass are taking place in key cities about the world.

Put that together with all one beholds in the news today — the shrinking world — a cashless society — everything reduced to a system of numbers — and leaders clamoring for a one world government . . . and what do you get? Like it says in the old song, "Another day older and deeper in debt," we're moving in only one direction — **setting the stage for Satan's superman — antichrist!**

• When people speak of a one world government, the question comes back . . . "Who's going to do the ruling?" Well, the "god of this world" controls the answer

(2 Cor. 4:4). The devil has been waiting for the world to ripen politically, so he could bring his man on the scene. **When things reach the place where world leaders are ready for a single ruler, there's only one man the devil wants in that spot — antichrist.**

THE REVIVED ROMAN EMPIRE

The **political** ripeness of the world is easy to see. We can watch it develop in the news headlines. Beyond that, activity within the old Roman empire will be like a signpost pinpointing Satan's man. Through this we'll be able to watch his rise to prominence.

The prophet Daniel was an expert on empires.

As you recall, he was one of four extraordinary Jewish lads transported from Jerusalem (the exile of 606 B.C.) and stationed in the palace of King Nebuchadnezzar. He was given special understanding with respect to dreams and visions (Dan. 1:17). Because of his interpretation of his own dreams and those of King Nebuchadnezzar, most prophetic writers agree that ROME will be revived to become an empire once more.

In the second chapter of Daniel, the prophet describes ALL OF THE EMPIRES scheduled to be on the earth up until the time of Jesus' return. The empires were pictured as AN IMAGE which King Nebuchadnezzar saw in a dream. It was a tremendous statue, larger than anything ever built by man . . . and so tremendous, it was terrifying even in a dream. The statue was constructed of different metals.

The head was made of fine gold and represented King Nebuchadnezzar's **Babylonian empire,** roughly 626 B.C. — 539 B.C.

The breast and arms were of silver and symbolized the **Medo-Persian empire,** 539 B.C. — 331 B.C.

82

The belly and thigh of brass depicted a third and larger kingdom — **Greece** — which would rule over more of the earth (331 — 323 B.C.).

The fourth empire, the mightiest of all, was pictured by legs of solid iron. Remarkably prophetic, those iron legs not only indicated the awesome strength of **Rome,** but also the powerful spread of her conquests and lengthy span of her empire, roughly 300 B.C. — 476 A.D.

ROMAN EMPIRE. By 68 B.C., the Romans had succeeded in taking over the disintegrating Greek empire. Before long its IRON RULE moved northward to England, westward to Spain and south to Africa and Israel. Then Rome assumed control of the countries bordering the Mediterranean, all the way to the Euphrates river. The map (p. 87) shows what is referred to as the prophetic world empire. Inasmuch as it was so vast, the empire existed in two parts, hence the TWO LEGS of the image. The center of governmental authority was in Rome, but the Eastern Division, consisting mostly of the old Greek empire, had Constantinople as its capitol.

As one continues down the legs, he comes to the TEN TOES. But they are a mixture of iron and clay, hence not very strong. That's not a good mix. This is why the prophet said, "The kingdom shall be divided" (Dan. 2:41). Who but Daniel, under divine inspiration, could have foretold the breaking up of the mighty Roman empire (Iron empire) into **unstable** nations? It came to pass just as he predicted.

During the fourth and fifth centuries A.D., the empire began to be divided as several distinct barbarian kingdoms within her midst gained independent power. These kingdoms, which later developed into the nations of Europe, have ever remained divided.

83

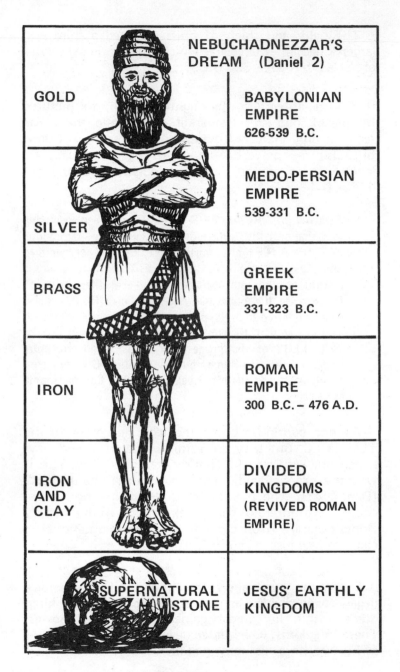

	NEBUCHADNEZZAR'S DREAM (Daniel 2)
GOLD	BABYLONIAN EMPIRE 626-539 B.C.
SILVER	MEDO-PERSIAN EMPIRE 539-331 B.C.
BRASS	GREEK EMPIRE 331-323 B.C.
IRON	ROMAN EMPIRE 300 B.C. – 476 A.D.
IRON AND CLAY	DIVIDED KINGDOMS (REVIVED ROMAN EMPIRE)
SUPERNATURAL STONE	JESUS' EARTHLY KINGDOM

• Yet the Iron empire was not to be wiped out. That is the significance of the TEN TOES of Daniel's image. Even though Roman power was to be shattered, Daniel prophesied it would continue to rule in its fragmented condition. That's what happened. The broken pieces of the Iron empire began to accumulate colonies about the world. As one studies European history, he sees how the great colonial powers: Spain, England, France, Germany, Belgium, Portugal, The Netherlands and Italy, are merely huge chunks of the old Roman empire.

Daniel further prophesied these colonial powers themselves would suffer crumbling, that is, be stripped of their colonies and **finally rejoin in an alliance that would constitute the REVIVED ROMAN EMPIRE.** Thus the IRON EMPIRE would not be wiped out completely. From the TEN TOES would come a new union in the last days. In this manner, the Iron empire was to continue until Jesus returned. **It is out of this revived Roman empire that antichrist will come** (Dan. 7:7, 8).

> **FOUR EMPIRES ONLY.** By way of this vision through Daniel, God was revealing that there would be four — and only four — universal world powers until the coming of the Lord. Various monarchs, dictators and emperors have risen seeking to conquer the world. Spain tried and failed. Napoleon tried. Hitler and others have also tried. But none have succeeded, for God has determined there would be four and no more.

• After Daniel describes the image down to its toes, a time element is introduced in which God speaks of another kingdom being established on earth, a kingdom set up by God Himself. A kingdom that is indestructible. This is described in the final scene of the King's dream (Dan. 2:44, 45).

In his dream, Nebuchadnezzar was staring at the image for some time, when suddenly a SUPERNATURAL

STONE came flying through the air and smashed the entire statue. This stone, cut out of a mountain "without hands," struck the image on its TEN TOES with such force, the whole statue crumbled into tiny fragments and was blown away. It simply disappeared!

Then this same supernatural stone expanded itself into a mountain and continued to mushroom until it filled the whole earth (Dan. 2:34, 35). The action of this "stone" (symbolic of Jesus' kingdom) pictured the destruction of antichrist and his armies, as well as the establishment of Jesus' dominion over the earth (Dan. 7:13, 14).

● Bible scholars agree that Rome must be revived in the form of a ten nation alliance before antichrist can appear. And when he does, **he will ascend politically to become the supreme ruler of the TEN TOES (nations).** Therefore it is biblically proper to refer to the revived Roman empire as antichrist's kingdom.

> **TEN TOES.** As a point of interest, the nations making up the European Economic Community or the Common Market, have their headquarters in Brussels, Belgium. In front of the building are ten flagpoles of the ten member nations. On March 25, 1957, six nations met at the Vatican to sign the "Treaty of Rome" — THE EUROPEAN COMMON MARKET WAS BORN! Effective Jan. 1, 1958, the charter members were Belgium, France, The Netherlands, Italy, Luxembourg and West Germany. The remaining four are Great Britain, Denmark, Ireland (joining in 1973), and Greece (to be installed by Jan. 1, 1981).

A good number of premillennial authorities feel the European Common Market, shortly to become ten, constitutes the TEN TOES of Daniel's image. They could be wrong, but it certainly fits the prophecy to a tee. I'm ready to go along with them on this. If these authorities are correct, **we can expect a political genius to rise from the midst of this coalition of powers any time.**

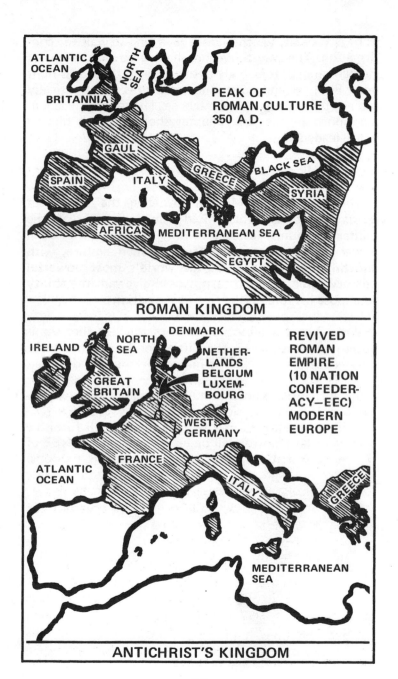

PEAK OF
ROMAN CULTURE
350 A.D.

ATLANTIC
OCEAN

NORTH
SEA

BRITANNIA

GAUL

SPAIN

ITALY

GREECE

BLACK SEA

SYRIA

AFRICA

MEDITERRANEAN SEA

EGYPT

ROMAN KINGDOM

REVIVED
ROMAN
EMPIRE
(10 NATION
CONFEDER-
ACY–EEC)
MODERN
EUROPE

IRELAND

NORTH
SEA

DENMARK

NETHER-
LANDS
BELGIUM
LUXEM-
BOURG

GREAT
BRITAIN

WEST
GERMANY

ATLANTIC
OCEAN

FRANCE

ITALY

GREECE

MEDITERRANEAN
SEA

ANTICHRIST'S KINGDOM

In any event, we shouldn't have long to wait for confirmation. The way things are shaping up within the old Roman empire, **it is likely antichrist is in the world right now.** Political and economic conditions are practically perfect for his rise to prominence. The military vacuum mentioned in the first chapter should launch him to world leadership.

THE APPEARANCE OF ANTICHRIST

The war in the Mideast involving the two great powers, Russia and the United States, should create the military vacuum necessary to bring him to power. **Such a war would leave the revived Roman empire, with antichrist at its head, as the world's most powerful military force.** This, in turn, would give him the ability to impose his rule on the rest of the nations.

With Russia making no secret of the fact that she is out to rule the world, it is little wonder she has to be crushed before antichrist can become the world leader.

But just WHO is antichrist? He's a man, a king, whom the prophet Daniel said would rise after the TEN NATIONS were rejoined. His first move that will furnish a clue as to his identity will be his **conquest of THREE of the member nations:** "As for the ten horns (nations) out of this kingdom, they are ten kings; and another (out of this group) will arise after them, and he will be different from the previous ones and will subdue three kings" (Dan. 7:24).

Daniel speaks further concerning the power of this man:

 "His power shall be great, and he shall cause fearful destruction, and shall succeed in what he does, and destroy mighty men and the people of the saints. By his cunning he shall

88

make **DECEIT PROSPER under his hand, and in his own mind he shall magnify himself. Without warning he shall destroy many . . . "** (Dan. 8:24-25 RSV).

Observe that he shall "make deceit prosper." We know the master of deceit — Satan. So let's trace the pattern. The strategy of the devil will be to offer the world (which is his) to the one who will worship him. Among the rulers of the TEN NATIONS of the revived Roman empire he will find such a man: one whom he will endue with the foulness of hell and the power to execute it on earth.

Keep in mind this is an INDIVIDUAL. He is a political entity, having dominion over peoples, tribes and nations. Thus he is NOT a system nor a kingdom, as some have suggested. Only MEN are worshipped, not systems.

WHO IS ANTICHRIST?

We can expect a political genius to rise from the midst of the revived Roman empire (European Common Market).

INDIVIDUAL. Some have attempted to identify antichrist with individuals of antiquity, whether Antiochus Epiphanes, Nero, Judas or an early pope. But someone from the past, someone completely out of touch with our times and practices, cannot fill the bill. There is no hint that Satan supernaturally educates this man with respect to politics, war strategy, commerce, industry or finance. And there is certainly nothing about death and resurrection that would equip anyone for world-wide leadership. These men of the past never saw a telephone or a TV, never rode on a jet liner or dreamed of an atom bomb. It is impossible to conceive of intelligent people claiming leadership for a man 2,000 years behind the times. Besides, the "little horn" description given by Daniel, denotes the emergence of a hitherto obscure personality.

In his rise to power, antichrist will pose as a man of peace, one who is holy as well as stately. We first see him in the 6th chapter of the Revelation. There he appears in symbolism of a rider on a white horse. A crown is on his head, signifying kingship. In his hand he carries a bow, representing his power to make war, but no arrows. He won't need them. Armed with supernatural charm and military forces behind him, he won't have to fire a shot.

He will unite the 10-nation confederacy, and offer solutions to all the problems of the world. But he won't settle for **political** control only. That's not his ultimate goal.

SATAN IS READY FOR HIS NEXT STEP

For Satan to gain control of the world, it must not only ripen politically — it must also ripen RELIGIOUS-LY.

This is what the man on the plane saw. It is what others will begin to see very shortly. This is what our leaders have missed. The devil, you see, has been on top of this for centuries and he's been steadily working to bring about the ripeness he needs.

Why does religion have to ripen? In the next chapter you'll meet the amazing answer.

Chapter Five

Satan's Superchurch

Down through the centuries, men have been haunted by the idea of a revived Roman empire. Back in 800 A.D., when the pope crowned Charlemagne Holy Roman Emperor, the pontiff was no doubt dreaming of the days of Constantine and the power that came to the church under his reign (312-337A.D.). He was hoping for a rerun, thinking the newly crowned Charlemagne might do the same. But his dream vaporized when Charlemagne died 14 years later and his kingdom was divided among his sons.

In the 10th century, the dream was rekindled when Otto the Great sought to establish the Holy Roman Empire and Vienna was the seat of authority. While it lasted for hundreds of years, that dream also came to an end in 1814. Later the Hapsburgs tried once more. But the dream was never really achieved, though never forgotten.

THE DEVIL KNOWS SOMETHING
OUR LEADERS HAVE MISSED

Satan understands something that leaders like Napolean and Hitler, who momentarily consolidated the power of Europe, overlooked. **Europe can never be united on a purely military basis.** Nor can greed for money do it. Secular leaders, such as the Communist rulers of Eastern Europe, prove that walls and barbed wire do not produce a unified government. There can be no government unity unless the **hearts of the people** are behind their leaders.

Before there can be a United States of Europe, there has to be a common motivation, a common bond or glue among the peoples of all the states. **THAT GLUE IS RELIGION.** Only the church can bring people of various nationalities to the place where they will **happily submit** to the authority of a single government. Only the church can deliver the hearts of the people to the state.

Knowing this, the devil has been working BEHIND THE SCENES to bring the world to **religious** ripeness. **He knows there can never be a one world government, without a one world religion.** Therefore we must consider Satan's strategy for bringing the world to religious ripeness. When we understand that, we'll know exactly how antichrist will come to power.

SATAN'S AGE-OLD STRATEGY
FOR RELIGIOUS RIPENESS

There are really only two churches in the world — the church of Jesus and the church of Satan. We know when Jesus' church was born — at Pentecost. But the organized church of Satan had its official beginning more than 2,000 years before Christ.

• On the plain of Shinar, not far from the location of the Garden of Eden, the entire population of the world huddled together. They all spoke the same language and were determined to remain together. To insure against being scattered, they proposed to build a tower (Gen-11:4). Referred to today as the "Tower of Babel," it rose to a probable height of 600 feet or more. At the very top was a room designed to house their gods, which many scholars identify as the "host of heaven."

> **GODS.** While these gods were nothing more than hand-carved idols, they represented more than that to the people. They sensed a spirit was behind their gods, even though they didn't know him personally. That spirit was Satan. Having been deposed from his high place in heaven, Satan has never lost his desire to be worshipped. If he could not be worshipped in heaven, then he would seek the worship of men on earth. But since he operates as a spirit-being and not in a body, men cannot see him. However they can FEEL his spirit and his power. In response to that, they created idols and worshipped them. In this way, Satan has been worshipped ever since men began to make idols and bow down to them. Of course this can't satisfy the devil's passion, and before he is through, he means to have the world at his feet, worshipping him as the only true god.

The people of that day had as their leader a wicked man named Nimrod, the great grandson of Noah (Gen. 10:8-10). From secular history and tradition, we learn that Nimrod married a woman by the name of Semerimus, who was every bit as evil as himself. Knowing the true God had promised a Savior would one day come into the world, this woman seized upon that promise and claimed her first born son, Tammuz, was the fulfillment of the prophecy. The knowledge of the coming Savior was, of course, handed down from Adam.

THE MOTHER-CHILD CULT

From that point on, Satan inspired Semerimus to

establish a religious system that exalted HER AND HER SON as objects of worship. **Thus began the MOTHER-SON cult which was to spread over all the world and down through history.**

You are familiar with the story of how God confounded the language of the people gathered about the tower (Gen. 11:5-9). Separated by language differences, the people parted company and began to scatter over the face of the earth. As they moved about, they took with them the mother-child worship system already ingrained in their lives.

• When Abraham was a boy in Babylon, this was the religion of his country. He was born not far from where the Tower of Babel was erected. From Babylon, this satanic religion spread along the trade route to Phoenicia, where instead of Semerimus, they were called Ashteroth and Tammuz. From there the cult went north into Asia Minor and south into Egypt. The Egyptians called the two — Isis and Horus. The Greeks referred to them as Aphrodite and Adonis. And when the cult reached Rome, they were worshipped there as Venus and Cupid.

In this way, Satan's powerful religion kept pace with the spread of civilization. It kept people linked to him BY FAITH, even though they didn't realize it. To the devil's mind, if they didn't worship him (through a false system), they might be inclined to worship the true God. That he wanted to avoid. Still, he was wise enough to know there had to be an element of truth in his religious system. He knew people had to believe salvation would issue from their faith.

So he led Semerimus to claim that worshipping her and her son would bring the salvation of one's soul. He inspired her to assume the title. . . "Queen of Heaven." People worshipping her were unknowingly worshipping the devil. Even though it was coming to him indirectly, Satan was nonetheless receiving worship. He knew he would have to bide his time. However the day will come when he will be in a position to command the entire world to worship him as God.

TRADITION. The story of Semerimus varied widely among the different religions. In general, though, tradition relates that Tammuz was killed while bear hunting, but was raised out of death 40 days later. Every year after that, temple virgins would fast for 40 days as a memorial to his death and resurrection. Following the fast, the feast of Ishtar (Easter) was celebrated, during which colored eggs were exchanged and eaten to symbolize the resurrection of Tammuz. Simultaneously an evergreen tree (Christmas tree) was displayed and a yule log burned. Special cakes were baked with the letter "T" on them (hot cross buns), and these were eaten in the name of Tammuz before the people. It is obvious that modern Christianity has not been entirely immune to the influence of Satan's church.

SATAN WORSHIP IN ANCIENT ISRAEL

When the children of Israel came out of Egypt and headed for the promised land, Satan's religion was waiting for them. It flourished under the name of Baal. It wasn't long before the Israelites "forsook the Lord and began to worship Baal and Astaroth" (Judges 2:11-13). This form of idolatry continued throughout the history of the nation, climaxing in the days of wicked King Ahab and Queen Jezebel (1 Kings 16:31-33).

Finally the abominations were so rife, God determined to punish His people by sending them into captivity in Babylon. Yet He didn't do this without first raising up Jeremiah and Ezekiel to warn them. In the words of these prophets we can see how thoroughly the Jewish people were caught up in the mother-child worship:

"Then He brought me," said the prophet, "to the door of the gate of the LORD'S HOUSE which was toward the north; and behold, there sat women weeping for Tammuz" (Ezekiel 8:14 KJV).

Imagine that! Carrying on for the son of Semerimus at the very gate of God's temple. So terrible were these abominations to God that He said to Jeremiah . . .

 "Therefore pray not thou for this people, neither lift up cry nor prayer for them, neither make intercession to Me: for I will not hear thee. Seest thou not what they do in the cities of Judah and in the streets of Jerusalem? The children gather wood, and the fathers kindle the fire, and the women knead their dough, to make cakes to the QUEEN OF HEAVEN. . ." (Jer. 7:16-18 KJV).

No wonder God sent them into captivity. The 70-year bondage in Babylon served to cure the Jews of their idolatry. Never again would they acknowledge any god but the God of Israel. But that doesn't mean they would obey Him or submit themselves to His Word. But at least they were through worshipping idols.

SATAN'S CHURCH AT ROME

In Jesus' day, the satanic religion had saturated the lives and leadership of the Romans. The influence was so permeating, the caesars were not just crowned as rulers of the empire, but were also given the title. . . PONTIFEX MAXIMUS — high priest. High priest of what? Satan's church. These rulers of the world were steeped in the religion that began at Babel. So true was this, that the apostle John attached the name "BABYLON" to this church at Rome:

96

"And upon her forehead was a name written, MYSTERY, BABYLON THE GREAT, THE MOTHER OF HARLOTS AND ABOMINATIONS OF THE EARTH" (Rev. 17:5).

A whore, as you know, prostitutes herself. And a church that prostitutes itself is one that is willing to mingle with any doctrine or belief in order to gain converts and make a name for itself. John was obviously speaking prophetically, looking toward the day when Satan's church at Rome would cohabit with all the religions of the world.

CHRISTIANITY — A TEMPORARY HINDRANCE

When Jesus' church (built upon faith in His shed blood) got started, it had to rise in the face of the powerful satanic religion already entrenched in Rome. Christianity was a threat to the devil's plans, for if it were to get going on any scale, it could slow down his schedule. So he fought it tooth-and-toenail.

For 300 years Satan brought the full power of his church at Rome against Jesus' little church that began at Pentecost. The persecutions were fierce, awful. Yet, for every believer who died at the hand of Satan's men, more believers rose to take his place. It was obviously the wrong tactic. The use of force against the church was like kicking a bonfire to put it out. It actually caused the movement to spread. In time the devil realized that approach was futile.

JUDAISM. What of Judaism in the meantime? It is **dead.** God created Judaism as a TEMPORARY worship system for His people Israel. And when Jesus died on the cross, its job was done. The rending of the temple veil from top to bottom signaled the end of Judaism (Matt. 27:51). God later declared it obsolete, **replacing it with faith in Jesus** (Heb. 8:13; 9:15,26; 10:9,10). The fact that there are

97

still synagogues throughout the world is evidence only that the Jews refuse to worship another God, even though they will have nothing to do with Jesus. **True Christianity is the fulfillment of Judaism.** That's why God set the ancient religion aside. **But Satan hasn't set it aside.** He has plans to REVIVE JUDAISM and use it, even as he has plans to REVIVE THE ROMAN EMPIRE and use it. Bear in mind that while God is through with Judaism, He is NOT through with the NATION of Israel. It is only their RELIGION that has been set aside.

THEN SATAN GOT A BREAK

In the year 312 A.D., according to Eusebius the historian, Constantine, with an inclination for the Christian faith acquired from his father, was leading his armies toward Rome. On a particular day, he beheld what he thought was a cross in the clouds. The Lord, it is said, is supposed to have manifested Himself to the emperor in a dream that same night. This resulted in his decisive conversion to Christianity.

Constantine then ordered his troops into a shallow river and immediately proclaimed all of them officially baptized Christians. Before summer was out, he triumphantly marched into Rome with the cross of Christ emblazoned on the shields of his troops. **Shortly after the conquest of the city, he declared Christianity the OFFICIAL RELIGION OF ROME.**

OFFICIAL RELIGION. With Christianity declared the official religion of the empire, the pagan church at Rome was immediately "Christianized." That is, the priests of SATAN'S CHURCH became "instant Christians," enjoying a new status. The emperor endowed the church with position and wealth, exempting the priests from military duty and granting them vast powers. The ruling body became an elite corps and the Roman church was born. This would

98

now be Satan's OFFICIAL RELIGION for it provided him with a way to create a ONE WORLD RELIGION. He would now make his religion "Christian," but with elements of the cult of Tammuz mingled with the gospel. Of course, there would be GENUINE CHRISTIANS within this church, but they would be so feeble in their understanding, they would not realize they were involved in a satanic system.

It wasn't difficult for the Roman priests of the cult of Tammuz to adapt their system to the new religion. It was easy for Satan to show them how to shift their MOTHER-CHILD worship scheme, to that of a MADONNA-CHILD system. With this slight adjustment, they could continue without interruption. All they had to do was add the holy water sacraments and other trappings of the satanic church to the simple gospel, and they had it made.

So instead of fighting Christianity, as he had for 300 years, the devil slyly elected to "go forward and join the church." Now that method worked. And how it worked. 1,200 years of "DARK AGES" followed during which the light of evangelical Christianity was reduced to a flicker.

SATAN SUFFERS A SLIGHT SETBACK

Something happened in the 16th century that rattled the devil's cage. In 1517, that faint glimmer of evangelical Christianity suddenly burst into flame when Martin Luther ignited a revolt against the church at Rome. But the revolt was only partly successful. Masses of Protestants were suddenly free to read the Word and worship God as they pleased. Yet few bothered to do so. Millions remained with the Roman church. Those who came out, emerged with the clergy/laity distinction still clinging to them. The result was a LARGE MASS of idle believers, with a few professional clergymen trying to do all the work of the Lord. Such a program was doomed to fail.

The Lutheran revolt (The Protestant Reformation), which held such promise, fizzled into failure. As a result, there has never been a single organized church of TRUE BELIEVERS on earth since the early centuries. Instead, we have numerous denominations bulging with "wheat and tares" mingled together. Most modern believers are so mild in their faith, it is impossible, in many cases, to distinguish between those who are born of God and those who are not.

The best we can say for the protestant church, is that here and there . . .sprinkled across the denominations . . . are those who truly love Jesus and are born of His Spirit. However, even that is upsetting to Satan. Why? These believers, are for the most part, the CREAM of God's family. They are consistently reaching out in the name of Jesus.

Despite the large numbers reported by the various denominations, the actual count of TRUE CHRISTIANS has to be very small. The Lord was aware of this when He spoke of the "few" who would enter by the "straight and narrow gate" (Matt. 7:14).

So while over 460 years of Protestantism have been a hindrance to Satan, and he regrets losing a few million souls, it hasn't crippled him in any way. He can handle it. In fact, he has a plan for overcoming this annoyance. Even now he is working to regather the splintered groups back under the banner of Rome.

REUNITING SATAN'S CHURCH

In 1948, the year Israel was declared a nation, an interesting development was taking place in Protestantism. The first assembly of the WORLD COUNCIL OF CHURCHES met in Amsterdam, Holland. The purpose? To bring together two separate streams of an ecumenical movement that got started right after World War I.

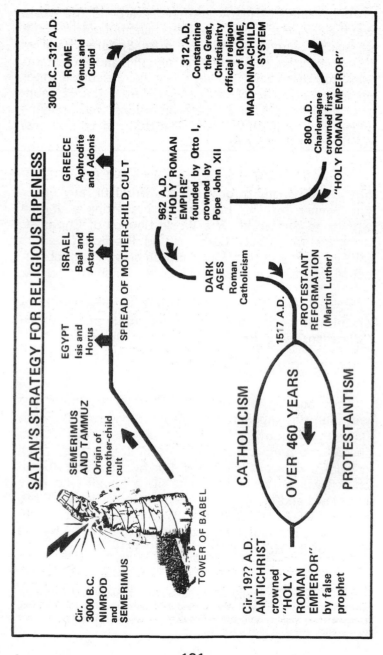

SATAN'S STRATEGY FOR RELIGIOUS RIPENESS

Cir. 3000 B.C. NIMROD and SEMERIMUS

TOWER OF BABEL

SEMERIMUS AND TAMMUZ
Origin of mother-child cult

EGYPT
Isis and Horus

ISRAEL
Baal and Astaroth

GREECE
Aphrodite and Adonis

300 B.C.–312 A.D.
ROME
Venus and Cupid

SPREAD OF MOTHER-CHILD CULT

312 A.D. Constantine the Great, Christianity official religion of ROME, MADONNA-CHILD SYSTEM

800 A.D. Charlemagne crowned first "HOLY ROMAN EMPEROR"

962 A.D. "HOLY ROMAN EMPIRE" founded by Otto I, crowned by Pope John XII

DARK AGES
Roman Catholicism

1517 A.D.
PROTESTANT REFORMATION
(Martin Luther)

CATHOLICISM

OVER 460 YEARS

PROTESTANTISM

Cir. 19?? A.D.
ANTICHRIST crowned "HOLY ROMAN EMPEROR" by false prophet

101

In the mind of many churchmen around the world was the notion that all the various denominations should be regathered under a single authority. **So forces were set in motion, calculated to bring Catholics and Protestants back together again.** However, we can be sure it never entered the minds of the delegates from the 42 countries represented, that their ambitions were playing squarely into Satan's hands. The devil, of course, was sponsoring this meeting.

Before long, we're going to hear a call from ROME inviting Christians throughout the world to rally under one banner for the purpose of presenting a unified witness to the world. The World Council of Churches, composed of BOTH Catholic and Protestant leaders by this time, will be a key factor in bringing this about, while the real spearhead will be a charismatic* pope.

Whole denominations will shift *en masse*. Entire organizations will "sign up." A multitude of professing "Christians" will flock to the one world church.

But some won't fall for it.

Those born-again believers who KNOW GOD'S WORD will shun this superchurch. They'll recognize it for what it is — the work of Satan. They'll want no part of it. And there'll be born-again Catholics in this group who'll recognize what has happened. By this time, the Roman church will be an inhospitable place for all who truly love Jesus and cling to the Word of God. Then we'll see some TRUE ECUMENICITY, as genuine believers, Catholic and Protestant, are also banded together — **by the GLUE of the Holy Spirit (1 Cor. 12:13)!**

------

*Inasmuch as there is a "charismatic movement," I should explain that the word "charismatic" is used here to describe a person with great charisma, a magnetic personality and compelling personal appeal. It is not a reference to one endowed with spiritual gifts.

KNOW GOD'S WORD. Sadly though, we can predict there will be some genuine Christians who will not be grounded in the Word to the place where they can recognize what is going on. There'll be no way they can stand firm in the face of this movement. They'll go with the crowd and be swept into the superchurch. The Holy Spirit will have to guard them, for they belong to the Lord. But they'll never suspect they're being used to establish Satan's one world religion. To their minds, this will be the GREAT REVIVAL they heard was coming. They'll be totally unaware of its purpose: **delivering the hearts of the people over to a one world government.**

WHO'LL RUN SATAN'S SUPERCHURCH?

In the 13th chapter of The Revelation we're introduced to TWO BEASTS, not just one. The **first beast** (vss. 1-10) is clearly the **antichrist.** The second, referred to as **"another beast,"** is a DIFFERENT MAN raised up by Satan to help antichrist to come to power. This man is a **religionist** (vss. 11-12). Elsewhere in The Revelation, the apostle John describes him as **"the false prophet,"** for he will be a **counterfeit** religionist. This is the significance of John's words. . . "It has two horns like a LAMB and it spoke like a DRAGON." (A real wolf in sheep's clothing).

Now and then various evangelical personalities express the conviction a great revival will occur in the end time. I'm sure there'll be such a revival, but it won't be of the Holy Spirit. **It will be satanic.** As various denominations and associations swarm to the superchurch at Rome, so will countless individuals. It will seem as though Christianity has finally caught fire on a worldwide scale. So widespread will be this "revival," multitudes will be fooled into thinking it is the real thing. The power of this revival will be spectacular.

But how can Christianity GLUE the ten European nations into a unit? Ah, by drawing the HEARTS of the people to a powerful RELIGIOUS LEADER. The nations of Europe are predominately Roman Catholic and many of the leaders are even now looking toward Rome for leadership. The present pope, John Paul II, is calling for the "spiritual unity of Europe." On his historic trip to Poland in June of 1979, he dropped a thunderbolt on audiences . . . **"Europe,"** he said, **"cannot cease to seek its fundamental unity and must turn to Christianity . . . and Christianity must commit itself to the formation of the spiritual unity of Europe."***

It won't take "all the king's horses and all the king's men" to put the Roman empire back together again. All it takes is one pope with a glue bottle labeled "RELIGION." Now I'm not saying that Pope John Paul II is the "false prophet." He may be only a forerunner. But it will take "POPE POWER" to glue the Roman-based ten nation confederacy together. And what better way to express SPIRITUAL unity than with a UNITED STATES OF EUROPE!

A NEW ROMAN EMPEROR

It is approaching the end of the 20th century. People are crammed into St. Peter's Square, Vatican. Cameras, sending TV pictures worldwide by satellite, are trained on a man on the podium. The pope, dressed in his finest, appears before the cheering crowd and stands next to the man waiting on the podium. He raises his hand for silence. Then he picks up the royal crown. He asks the man to kneel. Holding the crown over the bent man's head, the pope cries,

"With this crown I anoint you HOLY ROMAN EMPEROR of the United States of Europe!"

The pontiff sets the crown on the man's head. He

---

*U.S. News and World Report, June 16, 1979.

rises to his feet and faces the crowd. A thunderous ovation drowns out the pealing bells. The days of Constantine have returned. Antichrist has come to power with the false prophet's blessing. The newly united Europe is economically and militarily more powerful than either the U.S. or the U.S.S.R.!

BEWARE OF THESE TWO MEN!

One is a religious figure (the false prophet), the other is a political leader (antichrist). The false prophet helps antichrist come to power by using Catholicism to create a common bond among the 10 European nations (EEC). By preaching the doctrine of a UNITED STATES OF EUROPE, the false prophet will prepare the nations for antichrist's call. When he steps out and says, "I will lead you and make you a Catholic empire," they will be ready to follow. The Roman church will enjoy the blessing of antichrist as a reward for aiding him in coming to power.

RELIGIOUS BABYLON — SATAN'S SUPERCHURCH

This is the devil's church the apostle John describes in the 17th chapter of Révelation:

 "So he carried me away in the spirit into the wilderness: and I saw a woman (the devil's church) sit upon a scarlet colored beast (antichrist), full of names of blasphemy, having seven heads and ten horns" (vs. 3).

There is unanimous agreement among scholars that the beast to which John refers is antichrist, and the seven heads are the seven hills of Rome. Verse nine of this same chapter clearly states, "the seven heads are seven mountains," identifying the city of Rome. This is a rather clear prophecy relative to the union of antichrist and the satanic church based at Rome. **The point: the ten nations** (ten horns of the beast or ten European countries) **with antichrist at the head, are definitely working together with the woman** (church) **of the city of the seven hills.** By this, the apostle is showing us how essential is the GLUE OF RELIGION to the reuniting of the old Roman Empire. It is this gluing of the ten nations that makes possible the United States of Europe.

BUT THIS CHURCH WILL BE SHORT-LIVED

In Revelation 17, the apostle John sets forth this church in all her glory. But her glory is NOT that of the Lord. The "harlot," as John calls her, gets her thrills by indulging in idolatry, witchcraft, sorcery, and supernaturalism. Anything she desires, antichrist will see that she gets. Money will pour into her coffers through her unholy dealings. But her royal robes will be covered with blood, the blood of those true saints of God who refuse to join in her religious revelry.

But **this** religious Babylon is headed for destruction.

In this same chapter, John tells us the reign of the harlot church is short-lived. **When he is through with her, antichrist and the ten kings with him, will hate the woman and attack her, leaving her "desolate and naked, and shall eat her flesh, and burn her with fire"** (17:16). But isn't that often the fate of harlots? Don't they usually suffer rejection and cruelty at the hands of those who use them?

> **HER FATE.** Some students reading chapters 17 and 18 of Revelation, feel only ONE BABYLON is in view. In my opinion, these two chapters are discussing TWO SEPARATE BABYLONS and two distinct destructions. In chapter 17 we clearly see RELIGIOUS BABYLON, the superchurch. Observe that she is HATED by the kings of the earth and destroyed by them (Rev. 17:16). In chapter 18, we have a POLITICAL AND COMMERCIAL BABYLON, whom the kings of the earth LOVE, because she makes them rich. They are shocked at her demise, for she is destroyed by God's judgments (Rev. 18:5,8). It is important to see how one Babylon is LOVED and the other HATED by the kings of the earth. **Very clearly we have two Babylons destroyed at two different times.**

WHY WOULD SATAN DESTROY HIS OWN CHURCH

There is only one thing the superchurch can do for antichrist — **bring him to power.** Once that has been done, **the church will be of no further use to him.** In fact, it will be in his way. Why? The next step in Satan's plan is to have antichrist acclaimed as MESSIAH OF ISRAEL. So the church has to be disposed of — and fast.

Can you imagine the effect this will have on the billions of people who have come to regard Christianity as the official religion of the empire? Why, it would be like reversing the Colorado river to have the world ruler suddenly declare . . .

"CHRISTIANITY IS ALL WRONG! JESUS WAS A FALSE PROPHET! GOD HAS GIVEN BUT ONE FORM OF WORSHIP TO MANKIND AND THAT IS OLD TESTAMENT JUDAISM!"

But this is exactly what he will do.

And he doesn't have to be nice about it.

As far as the devil is concerned, the more ruthlessly the shift is made, the better. The gloves are off now. He's nearing his goal. Anything that will create confusion and chaos at this point will serve his purpose. To make the effect as devastating as possible, the FALSE PROPHET will get into the act. Imagine the consternation when the HEAD OF THE SUPERCHURCH (the pope) echoes the words of antichrist. . ."Christianity is all wrong!"

> **SHIFT.** The false prophet will play a significant role in engineering the shift from Christianity to Judaism, a change which is not as drastic as it sounds. Remove Jesus from Catholicism and you can see at once the numerous similarities between O.T. Judaism and Catholicism, i.e. beenies, priestly intercession, decorated robes, swinging incense, mass/sacrifice and ornate services. On the surface the change will seemingly occur overnight, but in actual fact, it will be carefully worked out by antichrist and the false prophet with the cooperation of the various branches of the superchurch. As other religious leaders join in the announcement, the effect will be staggering, bewildering. When all this is accompanied by the worldwide TV programs showing how Judaism is God's ONLY revealed form of worship, the assault on Christianity will be horrendous. Jesus will be denounced as a false teacher and His divinity discredited. The supernatural fireworks of the false prophet will be so astounding, the world will assume heaven is behind him. This repudiation of Christianity will be swift and brutal.

● The demise of the superchurch must occur once antichrist is through with it. **Christianity will be outlawed almost immediately.** Shameless persecutions will be ordered against those who continue to stand up for Jesus. Can you fathom how this will shatter the spiritual foundations of those who had no hint it was coming? It'll be devastating to their faith. This, of course, is what Satan wants. It'll make it easier for him to lead befuddled "Christians" out of Christianity and into Judaism.

WHEN IS SUPERCHURCH DESTROYED?

Superchurch, worldwide Christianity, is destroyed AFTER antichrist comes to power, for he needs the church to unify the TEN NATIONS of Europe. Yet it must be BEFORE he makes his covenant with Israel. The reasoning is simple. Antichrist's arrangement with Israel is more than a scheme for helping the Jews survive in the midst of an Arab world. **He plans to USE JUDAISM (even as he has used Christianity) in getting the world to acknowledge him as God.**

THEREFORE THE DESTRUCTION OF THE CHRISTIAN CHURCH WILL OCCUR BEFORE THE TRIBULATION. REMEMBER WE ARE SPEAKING OF ORGANIZED CHRISTIANITY (THE INSTITUTION), NOT THE ORGANISM. IT IS INDESTRUCTIBLE (Matt. 16:18).

THE SHIFT TO OLD TESTAMENT JUDAISM

Just as antichrist revived an **old empire** (The Roman Empire) to give him a POLITICAL BASE, so will he revive an **obsolete religion** (Judaism) to give him a RELIGIOUS BASE. I expect antichrist to embrace Judaism personally, passing himself off as a committed Jew. Once the superchurch is destroyed, he will announce that Old

Testament Judaism is the official religion of his empire. The next step will be to have himself accepted as the Messiah of Israel.

SUMMARY OF THE SITUATION

The world is swiftly rushing toward a one world government, with a single individual exercising rule over the nations. The devil has his own idea as to who should be Holy Roman Emperor — antichrist, of course. To bring this to pass, Satan makes use of some knowledge that world leaders are overlooking — RELIGION has the power to deliver the hearts of the people to the state. Thus the IRON and CLAY nations of Europe, which normally will not adhere to each other, CAN BE GLUED TOGETHER WITH RELIGION.

We can expect a huge religious system, the superchurch, based at Rome, to mushroom anytime now. This system will be the GLUE for welding the TEN NATIONS (Common Market) together. The Bible tells us that as soon as this great system is of no further use to antichrist, he will destroy it. When he reaches the height of his political power, the superchurch will be AN OBSTACLE in his path to the throne of God (2 Thess. 2:4). Therefore it has to go.

The apostle John describes the destruction of this huge religious system, to which he gives the names, **"BABYLON THE GREAT"** and **"MOTHER OF HARLOTS"** (Rev. 17:5). Her destruction is by the hands of the very nations she glues together for antichrist.

DESTRUCTION. The timing of the destruction of the superchurch is based on our observation that Revelation 17 and 18 are speaking of TWO DIFFERENT BABYLONS and two separate destructions. Readers should check these chapters to see for themselves how one is loved by the kings of the earth and the other is hated by them. Since there are

110

two destructions, I place the destruction of **RELIGIOUS BABYLON** (destroyed by the ten kings) BEFORE the tribulation and the destruction of **COMMERCIAL** BABYLON (by the hand of God) AT THE END of the tribulation. It is common for Scripture to blend events seen by the prophets before they occur. It is called, "The Law of Double Reference." While there is some mingling of ideas, the separate destructions stand out very clearly. This is a powerful key to the interpretation.

With the superchurch destroyed, antichrist will make overtures to Israel. He will settle the Arab/Israeli dispute to the utter satisfaction of the Jews. The false prophet, with great signs and wonders, will offer him to Israel as her Messiah . . . **and the Jews will buy it.** Totally unaware of his true identity, the Jews will believe the long awaited kingdom has arrived. But that idea won't last long . . . as we'll see . . . next.

PLEASE DON'T BE OFFENDED . . .

if I step on a few toes. Keep in mind I am sharing insights as I understand them. I am doing my best to fathom what the Holy Spirit is saying through the Scriptures and events in the world. I will be off on some things, for no man has all the truth. But I will also be accurate on some things, for the Spirit has called me and is helping me. So as you read, constantly check for the witness of the Spirit. You'll find He will use this book to arm you against the deceptions of the last days, even though I may have misread him on a point or two. It is not my purpose to malign or discredit any persons now living, whatever their spiritual heritage.

Chapter Six

The Pied
Piper Of Israel

Remember the Pied Piper of Hamelin and how he rid that city of its mice? And when the townsfolk refused to pay him as agreed, he led the children out of the village and away from them? The children were so spellbound by his music, they followed him, oblivious to where he was taking them.

Well, that piper was a piker compared to Satan's man.

Antichrist will mesmerize multitudes with his incredible power. He will mount the greatest display of supernatural fireworks this world has ever seen. His miracles will dazzle the hearts and minds of superstitious multitudes. The Jews in particular will follow him, like children behind the piper. They'll be so blinded by his wonders, they won't realize where he's taking them. But you'll know.

THE PIED PIPER OF ISRAEL

Once the superchurch is out of business, the world ruler will be free to execute the **second step in Satan's plan — wooing the hearts of the Jewish people.** It is the devil's ambition to have the Jews accept antichrist as their Messiah. **After that, one final step remains — presenting himself to the world as the only true God.**

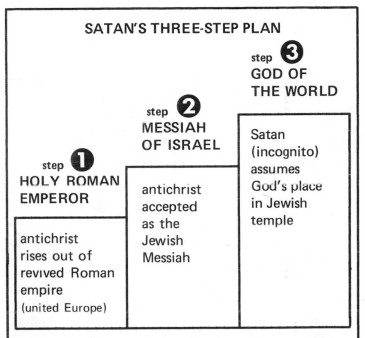

SATAN'S THREE-STEP PLAN

step **3**
GOD OF
THE WORLD

step **2**
MESSIAH
OF ISRAEL

step **1**
HOLY ROMAN
EMPEROR

antichrist
rises out of
revived Roman
empire
(united Europe)

antichrist
accepted
as the
Jewish
Messiah

Satan
(incognito)
assumes
God's place
in Jewish
temple

By now you're getting a feel for Satan's 3-step plan for obtaining the worship of the world. Let your mind click like a camera. Snap the shutter on those 3 steps, leaving an image in your memory. That way you'll remember the three great movements of the end of this age: 1. **the formation of the superchurch which solidifies Europe and brings antichrist to power;** 2. **antichrist accepted as the Messiah of Israel;** 3. **the worship of the world.** These steps are the keys that unlock the scenario leading up to the Lord's coming.

FINAL STEP. We must not think of antichrist as some individual who operates on his own. He is clearly SATAN'S MAN . . . for the devil himself is the guiding genius behind all of his moves and wisdom. This satanic superman is coming "after the working of Satan with all power and signs and lying wonders" (2 Thess. 2:9). From the day the devil was defeated in his attempt to seize God's HEAVENLY THRONE, he has been determined to occupy God's EARTHLY THRONE. To achieve this, he is going to USE A MAN (antichrist) to pave the way for Satan worship . . . so that one day the devil will have the whole world bowing at his feet.

● It's obvious antichrist must approach Israel carefully. This nation learned an unforgettable lesson in Babylon 2,500 years ago. **She will never accept anyone as Messiah unless she is convinced he comes from God.** He must have the right credentials. Consequently, antichrist will have to move carefully, slyly and scripturally.

JEWISH ANTICHRIST? Would the Jews accept a Gentile as Messiah? Hardly. With the nation itself founded upon God's promises to Abraham, it was her destiny to bring Messiah to the world. **Messiah must be a Jew.** Moses was specific in saying that one from their midst, one of their own brethren would be Messiah (Deut. 18:15). Therefore if antichrist is not Jewish, he will certainly have to CLAIM JEWISH DESCENT. That's all it will take, for what Jew today can trace his roots? Everything was mixed up during the Babylonian captivity. For that reason, antichrist can easily claim to be Jewish. If he choses to say he's from the tribe of Judah, who can prove him wrong?

First he will come to Israel **politically,** settling the Arab dispute in her favor. Beyond that, he will promise to restore Israel to her former glory, per the days of Solomon. If you were a Jew and the ruler of the world (who claimed to be Jewish) said he felt called to exalt your nation to a glory surpassing the "good old days," wouldn't you WANT TO BELIEVE HIM? Of course. It would thrill you to think the kingdom was at hand. Well, that will be antichrist's irresistible bait — the fulfillment of the national dream.

The Jews won't suspect a thing. But you and I know antichrist will never exalt Israel for nothing. He's after something. He's worming his way into Jewish hearts, expecting before long to be their acclaimed Messiah. However, since he has been primarily a **political figure** up to this point, it will take some doing for him to be embraced as the **spiritual leader** of the nation. But he's got a terrific campaign manager — the false prophet.

> **FALSE PROPHET.** The only reason antichrist allows himself to be identified as a Roman Christian is to exploit the religious unity of Europe. When the organized Christian church is destroyed (please remember that antichrist and his 10-nation alliance do this), the Jews will be impressed with antichrist's part in her destruction. He couldn't have been a genuine Christian if he gave orders to wipe out Christianity. The Jews will believe his claim that he took on the GUISE OF A CHRISTIAN merely to secure that destruction. He will explain that it was the best way to make Judaism the official religion of the world. The false prophet will make the same claim. He will affirm that even though he held the TOP POSITION in the Christian church (probably the pope), it was for the sole purpose of unifying Europe to bring the Messiah (antichrist) to power. Once the super-church is destroyed, antichrist and the false prophet will both declare themselves to be Jews.

ANTICHRIST'S CAMPAIGN MANAGER

 "For the Jews require a sign..." (1 Cor. 1:22).

The Lord Jesus knew only too well the Jewish passion for signs. They hurt Him enough with their demands for proof of His claims. **"Except ye see signs and**

wonders," He said to them, **"ye will not believe"** (John 4:48). We could just as easily turn that around and say, "If a person comes along with enough signs and wonders, you'll believe anything he tells you." That's the implication.

You can be sure the false prophet, now posing as a great exponent of Judaism, will know how to exploit this Jewish weakness. If it's signs they want, it's signs they'll get. He'll perform the most dazzling feats imaginable. Listen to this . . .

>**"Then I saw another beast (the false prophet), coming out of the earth. He had two horns like a lamb (very religious outwardly), but he spoke like a dragon (the authority of Satan)... and he performed great and miraculous signs, even causing fire to come down from heaven to earth in full view of men. Because of the signs he was given the power to do on behalf of the first beast (antichrist), he deceived the inhabitants of the earth . . . "** (Rev. 13:11,13, 14 NIV).

With signs of this caliber performed by the false prophet on behalf of antichrist, the people will be in awe. They'll remember how Elijah did a similar thing, calling down fire from heaven to confound the priests of Baal (1 Kings 18:17-40). With miracles of this magnitude, this exciting personality will deceive the people into believing he is from God.

SATAN'S "JOHN THE BAPTIST"

It will be the task of the false prophet to prepare the way for antichrist, even as John the Baptist prepared the way for Jesus.

The priests and Levites asked John, "Who are you?"

116

The same questions will be put to the false prophet. "Are you Elijah? Are you the Prophet?"

Unlike John who answered "No," he will declare ...

"I am the Prophet, the voice of God. The kingdom of heaven is at hand. 'Make straight the way of the Lord.' I have come to anoint the Messiah of Israel!"

And all the world will be listening to Satan's "John the Baptist," "Moses" and "Elijah" all rolled into one (John 1:19-28).

SELLING THE SUPERMAN

As soon as the false prophet has been accepted as from God, the way will be clear for him to begin a most important role — **wooing Israel to antichrist.** How will he do it? In extolling the world ruler and his love for Israel, he will speak of antichrist's passion to help the nation achieve her proper place in the world. As a token of antichrist's sincerity, the first issue to be raised will be the Arab business. "You watch," promises the false prophet, "he will settle it in Israel's favor!"

Right on cue, antichrist will announce a dramatic settlement of the Palestinian problem. The Arabs won't like it, but the wiley ruler will honor the LAND GRANT God made to Abraham. The new boundaires of Israel will range from the river of Egypt to the Euphrates river (Gen. 15:18). **Once the Jews see him uphold the Abrahamic Covenant, they'll be convinced he is Jewish and believe his promises to restore Israel's glory.**

As ruler of the world, he'll have the power to dispossess the Arabs with a single decree. He won't hesitate to do anything that helps to accomplish his objective. If he has to disfranchise a few million Arabs, what is that to him? At this point, all he cares about is getting the Jews to believe he is ready to fulfill the Zionist dream.

"BEHOLD THE MAN!"

Imagine how the tiny nation will quiver when the false prophet makes the electrifying announcement . . .

"BEHOLD THE PRINCE OF ISRAEL" (Ezek. 44:2, 3).

The result will be explosive. An ecstatic populace will rush upon this charming, powerful man, ready to begin a kingly procession to Jerusalem. 1,900 years earlier they wanted to do the same thing with Jesus after He had miraculously fed them. However, He knew they were only interested in their bellies, not their sins. So He withdrew from them (John 6:15, 26).

Now this man seems to be everything they expect in Messiah. But antichrist will be clever in the way he accepts their acclamation. Let's suppose he says to the Jews . . .

"Let's not be hasty, brethren. You don't want to put the wrong man in office. So let's make sure we're in God's will. I'll tell you what I'll do. I'll accept the leadership of Israel for SEVEN YEARS. That will give us time to make sure I'm God's man for the job. Agreed?" (Dan. 9:27)

Agreed? And how. The Jews will seize this moment as Israel's golden hour. The national hero will be stuffed into a limosine (no donkey this time) and the procession will head for Jerusalem. Instead of palm branches strewn in his path, confetti will rain down on this man. TV cameras will telecast the glorious event to the world. Antichrist will love every moment of it. His heart will swell with pride as he makes his acceptance speech. A sharp contrast to the way Jesus entered Jerusalem (John 12:12-15).

HUMILITY

JOHN THE BAPTIST

clothed with camel's hair and skin

JESUS CHRIST

Riding on a donkey

PRIDE

FALSE PROPHET

(high priest) finest garments

ANTICHRIST

Riding in a limo motorcade

At the same time, **the newly accepted "prince of the people" will announce the shift of his headquarters (political and religious) from Europe to Jerusalem.** Why not? Isn't Jerusalem the "city of the Great King!" (Matt. 5:35). With this action, the key verse of Daniel's prophecy will be initiated . . .

"And he (the prince) shall confirm the covenant with many for one week (seven years)..." (Dan. 9:27).

COVENANT. Will the events actually take place as I have set them forth above? We can't be sure at this point. The Bible simply tells us that antichrist makes a covenant with Israel for 7 years. To go beyond this, we must put two-and-two together, and work with pieces of the prophecy puzzle. There is no way for me to claim NEW REVELATION as I write this book. We don't need it. All God wants us to do is put circumstances and His Word together, and then look to Him for light. In these days, when we have more pieces of the puzzle to work with, the picture is getting clearer. However, should it turn out what I have written is accurate, it won't be because I possess special knowledge. I do not. It will simply be God's working through me, as He has in the past, to give His people the help they need. So if I happen to be on target, it will be God's doing, not mine.

MESSIAH OF ISRAEL

" . . . when the Messiah comes," they said, "is it likely that he will perform more signs than this man?" (John 7:31 NEB).

Those words were on the lips of many when Jesus appeared in the temple after healing a man born blind. And this is what many will be asking when antichrist is installed as "PRINCE OF THE PEOPLE." Working with the false prophet, he will perform healings on a grand scale, possibly eliminating the need for hospitals in Israel. The Christian evangelists who served in Jesus' name will seem powerless by contrast.

What's more, **he will see to it that the temple is rebuilt and the sacrifices resumed.** He's going to need that temple later on, so it will be urgent business to get the Old Testament system cranked into operation again. He'll make a point of saying the Galilean Carpenter was a mere pretender and the religion based on Him was not of God.

By restoring Judaism to full operation, he will seek to demonstrate that God HAD NEVER set aside the Mosaic system, for the real Messiah had not yet come into the world. He'll get no opposition from the Jews. They'll love this. To them, this man will be deliverer, healer and king, all rolled into one. An inescapable conclusion will dawn on the Jewish mind . . . "THIS HAS TO BE THE MESSIAH!" And when they come to the false prophet, asking . . . "Is this man the Messiah?", the answer will be "Yes."

MESSIAH. In no way does antichrist seek to pass himself off as Jesus — but as THE CHRIST. Christ is a Greek word for Messiah. He would like to remove the name of Jesus from the minds of men. His ambition is to convince men he is the TRUE CHRIST that is to come.

HIGH PRIEST OF ISRAEL

But why ask the false prophet? By this time the former pope (?) will be the **high priest of Israel.** His supernatural powers will make him stand head and shoulders above any other religious leader of the world. His credentials will automatically qualify him for the post. So, with the eyes of the world watching via the news media, he will anoint the world ruler as the long awaited Messiah of Israel. The proclamation will echo throughout the nations . . .

"THE MESSIAH HAS COME AT LAST! THE KINGDOM OF HEAVEN HAS ARRIVED!"

Antichrist is anointed MESSIAH by the false prophet (high priest) to the tumultuous roar of Israel — "We want this man to rule over us!" The union of this MAN and NATION fulfills Jesus' prophecy, " . . . **another shall come in his own name, him ye will receive**" (John 5:43)!

Judaism will be declared the official religion of the world and the honeymoon will be on for the Jews. They will believe the long-awaited "millennium" has arrived!

SATAN'S "MILLENNIUM" — FOR JEWS ONLY

The joy in Jewish hearts will be indescribable. To their minds, the kingdom has come and Israel will soon be exalted as the supreme nation of the world. With her "prince/messiah" displaying unparalleled wisdom in foreign policy and prospering the nation with his economic genius, the Jews will be convinced the golden age has arrived (Micah 4:1, 4; Isa. 60:12-18; Isa. 35:1, 2, 7). **Only those believers who know their Bibles will realize this is a FALSE millennium.**

More significantly, antichrist will devote himself to Judaism, using all of his satanic skills to create the illusion he really is Messiah.

To make sure his credentials stand unchallenged, antichrist will appear to be very biblical. He'll insist everything be done according to the Law of Moses. To erase any doubt in Jewish minds regarding his identity, he will become personally involved in the sacrifices (Ezek. 45:22; 46:12). He will count on his vigorous participation to reinforce the impression that he is dedicated to the ways of God. He will pass himself off as a committed believer in the Law and the Prophets.

SACRIFICES. For fascinating reading, take another look at Ezekiel 44-46 in the light of what I have just said. Notice the "PRINCE" in particular and observe how he is told NOT to thrust out the people or take their lands (46:18). But here's the real tipoff — **he is seen making a SIN-OFFERING for himself!** (45:22). Could you possibly believe this is Jesus? No way. He offered Himself for us! He is OUR sacrifice. This is NOT Jesus referred to here, but

123

ANOTHER "PRINCE." Again we have a case where prophetic events are mingled and the LAW OF DOUBLE REFERENCE must be invoked. There are references here to the TRUE millennium, but there are also references to the FALSE millennium as well. From this portion, we see antichrist will be very religious, taking part in the temple program as though he really were Messiah.

THE GREAT "FALLING AWAY"

"Christianity outlawed!"

"Judaism — official world religion!"

These will be the headlines after antichrist is exalted as Israel's "prince." The New Testament will be banned. The Old Testament will be required reading throughout the world. Why? It sets forth Judaism as the ONLY DIVINELY APPOINTED religion in the world. Antichrist will want people familiar with it, since it will make all he does appear solidly biblical.

True believers will have to go underground.

With Christianity outlawed and Judaism the official religion of the empire, the stage will be set for the GREAT "FALLING AWAY" of which Paul speaks:

 "Let no man deceive you by any means: for that day (the coming of the Lord) shall not come, except there come a FALLING AWAY first . . ." (2 Thess. 2:3 KJV).

For the moment, see if you can picture what it might be like to live in a world where everything Christian is denied and denounced. Consider how open identification with Jesus will bring persecution and death. On the other hand, picture Judaism flourishing, outwardly enjoying the blessings of God . . . or so it seems. The Jewish people will be so happy, clearly prosperous.

124

Antichrist, in an apparently magnanimous gesture, will insist that Judaism has been "set as a light unto the Gentiles" (Isa. 42:6; 49:6). **He will open the door for all men of good faith to come and be a part of the Jewish family.** Judaism will no longer be exclusive. "Let's have a Jewish world," he'll say. **"Let's really be ONE PEOPLE under the CHRIST of Israel."** That will sound attractive to so-called "Christians."

> **ONE IN CHRIST.** Remember, this will be highly deceptive, for there is nothing believers treasure more than their ONENESS WITH THE LORD. The devil is tricky with words. He is happy to use the word "CHRIST," since it is the Greek word for the Hebrew word "MESSIAH." Inasmuch as antichrist will be passing himself off as the Jewish Messiah, he will uphold the CHRIST IDEA. But the name of JESUS is something else. He hates that name. The Carpenter of Nazareth will be denounced as an impostor. Consequently we can expect antichrist to lift up the CHRIST, inviting the masses to become involved in his brand of Judaism.

THE STAMPEDE TO JUDAISM

"Christians" everywhere will behold what appears to be God's blessing on the Jews and want to get in on the outpouring. In some places it will be like the "gold rush of '49" — crowds of professing "Christians" in a dash to join Judaism. The number is certain to be great.

> **THIS IS WHAT THE APOSTLE PAUL HAD IN MIND WHEN HE REFERRED TO THE GREAT FALLING AWAY — HORDES OF "CHRISTIANS" FORSAKING CHRISTIANITY FOR JUDAISM.**

Closed churches throughout the world will reopen as **synagogues.**

When the stampede is over, there'll be few genuine believers above ground. Once the world becomes politically Jewish, it will be dangerous for true Christians (those born of God's Spirit) to reveal their identity. They'll have to go underground. But as they do, it will refine the church. Christianity is cheap now. It costs nothing to be identified with Jesus. But in that day, when it can cost a man his life, there'll be a clean separation of "true possessors" from "false professors."

THE TRIBULATION — PART ONE
(The first 3½ years)

Bible students everywhere agree antichrist's covenant with Israel marks the beginning of the tribulation. It will be a time of severe testing for all who dwell upon the earth. The tribulation is a colossal event which must occur before the Lord's return. Jesus was definite about that:

 "Immediately AFTER THE TRIBULATION of those days . . . they shall see the Son of Man coming in the clouds of heaven with power and great glory" (Matt. 24:29,30).

But what IS the tribulation?

THE FINAL SEVEN YEARS OF THIS AGE
(70th Week of Daniel)

THE TRIBULATION

FIRST 3½ YEARS	SECOND 3½ YEARS
ANTICHRIST MAKES COVENANT WITH ISRAEL	Middle of the Week	SECOND COMING OF THE LORD JESUS CHRIST

It is the final seven years of this age (some say the last 3½ years) with antichrist in charge of the world. The seven year period will end with the visible return of the Lord. This seven year period is divided (by most scholars) into two parts, with the first 3½ years referred to as "THE TRIBULATION" and the last 3½ years designated "THE GREAT TRIBULATION."

THE 70TH WEEK OF DANIEL

This interval of the last seven years is identified by students as DANIEL'S SEVENTIETH WEEK — a term you should get used to. Any serious work on prophecy must take Daniel's SEVENTIETH WEEK into account, for the passage unfolding this prophecy is considered to be the most important, most amazing single prophecy in the entire Word of God (Dan. 9:24-27).

Why a seventieth week?

● One day, as Daniel was praying in Babylon, it was revealed to him that . . . "70 weeks are determined upon thy people and upon thy holy city to . . . " and the angel Gabriel went on to describe five things that were to be fulfilled during the 70 weeks (Dan. 9:24). Those five items included the **first coming** of Jesus to deal with sin and His **second coming** to establish a righteous kingdom on earth.

It was further revealed that 69 weeks (scholars agree a prophetic week equals seven years) would pass from the issuing of the commandment to restore Jerusalem (after the Babylonian captivity) to the first coming of Jesus (Dan. 9:25). This prophecy of 69 weeks was literally fulfilled. It was exactly 69 weeks of years (483 Jewish years, which have less days per year than our present calendar) from the edict to rebuild (cir. 445 B.C.) to the time Jesus offered Himself to the Jewish nation as her king (cir. 32 A.D.).

But then something happened.

127

DANIEL'S 70 WEEKS (Dan. 9:24-27)

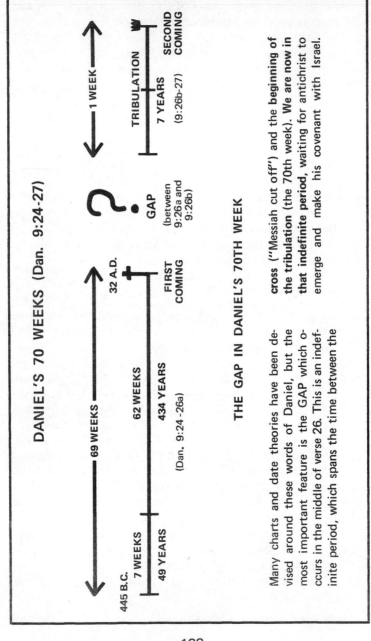

THE GAP IN DANIEL'S 70TH WEEK

Many charts and date theories have been devised around these words of Daniel, but the most important feature is the GAP which occurs in the middle of verse 26. This is an indefinite period, which spans the time between the cross ("Messiah cut off") and the beginning of the tribulation (the 70th week). We are now in that indefinite period, waiting for antichrist to emerge and make his covenant with Israel.

The Jews crucified their king. The prophetic clock stopped ticking.

Consequently a "break" occurred between the 69th and 70th week of Daniel. That break has lasted for almost 2,000 years. **However the day we see antichrist make a covenant with Israel, we'll know the 70th week has begun** . . . and the tribulation is upon us.

ISRAEL'S 3½ YEAR "HONEYMOON"

However, for the nation Israel, the first half of Daniel's week (the first 3½ years), will be a "honeymoon." With her "prince" the ruler of the planet, she'll enjoy a FALSE MILLENNIUM as the empress of the world.

While Israel is enjoying her 3½ year "honeymoon," the rest of the nations are in for tough times. They're going to resent having to yield their sovereignty to a Jewish prince. Judaism, unlike Christianity, is THEOCRATIC, i.e., religion runs the government. When the Christian superchurch was in operation, it left room for separation of church and state. The antichrist was a POLITICAL RULER with his headquarters amidst the ten nations (in Vienna?), whereas the religious leader, (the false prophet) had his headquarters at Rome. Consequently, Judaism will not be the GLUE Christianity proved to be. Instead of unifying antichrist's empire, Judaism will tend to fragment it.

NOT GLUE. Antichrist will have his hands full trying to compress the Gentile nations into a tiny Jewish mold. After all, Judaism has been a minor religion, full of strange customs, ancient practices and restrictive rules, a far cry from the superchurch with its watered-down message. A diluted Christianity was perfect for surrendering the hearts of the people to the state, since it left room for national independence. But for the nations to yield their **political**

129

reigns to a SUPER JEW and live under Jewish rules, is something else. Most of the nations will not like it. The Arabs, for example, would rather die first (they probably will die). And other countries will find Judaism totally unacceptable. It will be one thing for antichrist to proclaim Judaism the official religion of the empire, another to make it stick.

TRIBULATION OF THE GENTILES

Will antichrist tolerate rebellion in his kingdom? No way. Cloaked in the pious garb of the Jewish Messiah, he may look like a peaceful man of God, but under that cloak lurks a sinister, ruthless, vicious heart, bent on self-exaltation. Up to this point, antichrist has made a peaceful conquest of the world. It was easy, because the nations swallowed his promises and plans for peace. **But when various countries resist his dream of a Jewish world, it is going to bring out the WORST in him.** Then we'll all see him for what he is.

The "prince of the planet" will deal with rebellion with surprising force. It won't be beyond him to crush opposition with atomic weapons. Should he resort to overkill, the earth will be in for some devastation. But what is that to him? He's more interested in a world bowed at his feet than he is in productivity. By this time, he'll be through playing Mr. Nice Guy. People will do things his way — or else. And if he wipes out A FOURTH of mankind in the process, that's a cheap price as far as he's concerned.

DEVASTATION. Observe how antichrist's plan to compress the world into a Jewish mold inaugurates the first half of Daniel's 70th week . . . the **tribulation of the Gentiles.** The trials brought on the world by antichrist's fierce retaliation will be those described under the first four seals in John's vision of the Revelation (Rev. 6:1-8). The opening of these seals brings forth **The Four Horsemen**

130

of the Apocalypse: 1.) antichrist astride the WHITE HORSE peacefully conquers the world, 2.) but when he seeks to impose his Jewish dream, there is rebellion in his empire. This brings war (THE RED HORSE), 3.) employing weapons that destroy land and change weather. The result is famine in many places (THE BLACK HORSE). 4.) In all, it spells death for one-fourth of mankind (THE PALE HORSE).

• Will the Jews go along with their "prince's" ruthless retaliation? Indeed. Even during their "honeymoon," they will be ruthless, too. The sacrificing of a few Gentile (dog) nations, would easily be tolerated if it would unify the Jewish kingdom. The Jews have always looked on Gentiles as "uncircumcised outcasts" and the slaughter of a billion of them would be regarded as proper retribution for Hitler's slaughter of a few million Jews.

HOW DOES GOD FEEL ABOUT THIS?

As far as the Lord is concerned, the world is ripe for judgment. The fury of antichrist vented against the nations fits God's timing perfectly. This evil man may THINK he's the product of his times, but actually he is an instrument of God's judgment. **Even before antichrist could appear and begin his political ascent, God had to undertake a specific action that would make it possible. It was necessary for God to release the DIVINE RESTRAINT holding back the tide of evil.** Remember how Paul spoke of this:

 "Now with regard to the coming of our Lord Jesus Christ and our gathering together to meet Him . . . there are two things which must take place before that day can come: the wholesale departure from the faith (the falling away) and the appearance of the lawless leader (antichrist) who will be sin personified . . . You also know what RESTRAINS

HIM . . . for the one responsible for restraining the tide of evil in this world, will continue to do so until God tells him to release the brakes and stand aside. Evil will then begin to accelerate (snowball) in the world" (2 Thess. 2:1, 3, 6, 7 Lovett's Lights).

Throughout the centuries, God has been restraining evil in this world. **The human heart is so full of wickedness, that had not God done this, the human race would have disappeared from the earth long ago.** Consequently God has assigned A RESTRAINER to hold back the tide of evil. While this "Restrainer" is not identified by name, we assume He is the Holy Spirit. Earlier we saw how the "mystery of iniquity" was being held back by the "mystery of godliness." In the passage above, the apostle Paul advises us the "Restrainer" is a person.

However, even with the "SIN BRAKES" applied to slow down the progress of evil, sin has nonetheless ripened to the point of judgment. **To bring about that judgment, THE RESTRAINER need only take His foot off the "sin brakes" and let sin snowball.** Then **man** will bring plenty of punishment upon **man.** Thus, the release of the restraint, is itself a form of punishment.

The acceleration (snowball effect of sin) will be more swift than any might suspect. In my opinion, God is even now giving this command and we are presently witnessing a SPEED UP of natural and moral decay. The stage is rapidly being set for antichrist. Everything is shaking loose. Things are coming apart at the seams. The headlines indicate the advent of antichrist is almost at our door.

DECAY. With the "sin brakes" released, the effects of evil will snowball. Not only can we expect mental and moral pollution, but the natural world is in for a beating. The earth, as you know, is under the curse of sin, too (Rom.

8:20-22). As sin accelerates, we can expect amazing changes in the landscape. Earthquakes of great magnitude will occur often. We can look for an increase in destructive hurricanes, tornados and volcanos. In the wake of these, weather patterns will shift. Vast areas will become desert. There will be widespread pestilence and death.

ANTICHRIST — GOD'S INSTRUMENT OF JUDGMENT

The Gentiles viewing the devastation will regard it as the world ruler's abuse of power. But the Bible student will recognize it as part of God's judgment upon an unbelieving world. He will understand how God has held antichrist in check until He was ready to use him as an instrument of punishment.

Outwardly the first 3½ years of the tribulation will look like the fury of antichrist directed against the Gentile nations. But you and I will know what it is really all about . . . the first of THREE JUDGMENTS set forth in the book of Revelation represented by SEALS . . . TRUMPETS AND BOWLS. The trumpets and bowls will follow later. Under antichrist, the world will reel under the judgment of the first four seals.

ISRAEL PROTECTED BY HER "PRINCE"

As wars, famine and death ravage much of the world during the first 3½ years of the tribulation, Israel will be prosperous and happy. Her prince will see that she remains immune to any devastation. The tribulation temple will be completed during this time. Israel's boundaries will be extended, further than in the days of Solomon. The land will be portioned among the tribes according to the ancient prophecies. Nearly everything foretold of Messiah will seemingly be fulfilled in the "PRINCE" as he exercises political and religious control of the world. The Jews, basking in his glory, will be exceedingly well off.

TALE OF THE TEMPLES

1. Solomon's
(cir. 1000 B.C.)

2. Zerubbabel's
(cir. 536 B.C.)

3. Herod's
(cir. 19 B.C.)

4. Antichrist's
(tribulation)

5. Jesus Christ's
(millennium)

Five temples are significant in the Jewish story: **1. Solomon's temple,** (cir. 1000 B.C.), symbol of Israel's glorious past; **2. Zerubbabel's temple,** (cir. 536 B.C.), a vastly inferior structure constructed by the Jews upon their return from the Babylonian captivity; **3. Herod's temple,** begun around 19 B.C., to replace Zerubbabel's building. It was a magnificent edifice in service in Jesus' day, but destroyed by Titus in 70 A.D.; **4. Antichrist's temple,** built either before or during the early part of the first 3½ years of the tribulation, but due to be destroyed by the final earthquake before Jesus returns; **5. Jesus Christ's temple,** built at the beginning of the millennium for Jesus' 1,000 year reign on earth. Ezekiel's passages referring to this temple also contain references to antichrist's temple (the tribulation temple) per the law of double reference.

● Once antichrist has gained control of the world and established himself as Messiah of the Jews, **Satan will be but ONE STEP away from his goal.** With his one world government and one world religion blended together in Judaism, the stage is set for his final move. His goal will be so close he can taste it — **getting the world to worship him as God.**

WORSE TROUBLE AHEAD

So far, we have discussed only the first 3½ years of the tribulation.

The next chapter is going to take us into the LAST HALF of the tribulation, the period known as "THE GREAT TRIBULATION." It is going to be tough . . . terrible . . . shocking. You'll have to lean on the Holy Spirit as we take up the startling things that are going to occur. You may find yourself facing things you've never heard before. So gird up your spirit and your mind.

Something astonishing is going to happen to Satan!

Something astonishing is going to happen to antichrist!

It will be easier to handle what you read if you keep in mind what we've seen so far.

SUMMARY OF THE SITUATION

We opened this chapter with the superchurch already destroyed by antichrist. This paved the way for him to approach Israel. He wants to be accepted as Messiah. The task of selling the antichrist to Israel falls upon the false prophet, the former pope (?) of the Christian superchurch. But it is not a difficult task. The tiny nation is eager to accept a supernatural Messiah who promises to fulfill her dream of ruling the world.

Shortly after antichrist (who claims to be Jewish) is embraced by the Jewish people, he will enter into a COVENANT WITH ISRAEL to serve as "PRINCE" for a period of seven years. This marks the beginning of the tribulation (Dan. 9:27). To show his enthusiasm for the job, Israel's "prince" will declare O.T. Judaism the official religion of the empire and invite the world to become Jewish.

A host of so-called "Christians," (now confused by the destruction of the superchurch), will be LURED into Judaism. Believing it to be scriptural (though abandoned by God) and awed by the supernatural powers of the false prophet, these "Christians" will stampede to Judaism. The apostle Paul describes this great shift as THE GREAT "FALLING AWAY" (2 Thess. 2:3). True believers will be persecuted and have to go underground.

While many "Christians" flock to Judaism, the nations are going to RESIST the idea. Most of them will not want to be in the Jewish fold. This will trigger the WRATH OF ANTICHRIST, leading him to use force in getting the nations to comply with his wishes. He wants a Jewish world. Devastation will follow in the wake of his use of force, thereby fulfilling the prophecy of the first four seals of the Book of Revelation (Rev. 6:1-8).

During the "tribulation of the Gentiles" when the nations are resisting the Jewish mold, Israel will bask in the blessings of her "prince." She will enjoy peace and prosperity during her 3½ year "honeymoon" (false millennium). In bringing his wrath on those nations resisting his wishes, antichrist will unknowingly become an instrument of God's judgment. His wrath will be the first of THREE JUDGMENTS due to fall upon an unbelieving world during the seven year tribulation period.

All right, take a deep breath. We're about to plunge into some of the most startling prophecy in the Word of God!

Chapter Seven

Satan Makes His Big Move

"Ladies and gentlemen, we interrupt this program to bring you a special news bulletin. It is our solemn duty to announce . . .

THE 'PRINCE OF PLANET EARTH' HAS JUST BEEN ASSASSINATED!"

THE WORLD IS STUNNED

Israel is in shock as headlines scream the news . . . **"Prince of Israel dead!"** How could such a thing happen? How could a man so powerful be slain? At this point, no one really knows the answer. It could possibly occur while antichrist is making a public appearance. Maybe someone close to him will stab him. Or again, perhaps he'll be shot while driving in a motorcade, as was President Kennedy. It's true that the apostle John speaks of his being fatally wounded with a sword, but guns weren't known in those days (Rev. 13:3,14).

Regardless of the method, antichrist is **killed.** And for many of the nations forced to submit to this SUPER JEW, it won't be sad news at all. In some places they'll heave a sigh of relief. But the relief will be short-lived.

ANTICHRIST'S SUPERNATURAL RESURRECTION

Antichrist doesn't **stay** dead. **HE RISES AGAIN,** likely in three days. That would be a nice touch. He could enhance his credentials, perhaps, by copying this feature of Jesus' ministry. One thing we know, he's out to establish himself as God (2 Thess. 2:1-4; Matt. 24:23,24).

How is he raised from the dead? **The false prophet, it seems, has a part in this as the one who heals him from his fatal wound** (Rev. 13:14). But this is **more** than a simple resurrection. The man who rises in that body is going to be different than he was previously. Why? Something NEW has been added. **There's SOMEONE ELSE dwelling in that body with antichrist.** Someone who needs a body very badly to carry out his ambitions. Can you guess who that other person might be? Right — **Satan himself.**

THE TRIBULATION — MIDDLE OF THE WEEK

Right at this time, midway through the tribulation, an event occurs in heaven that shows us how precisely God is in charge of things. A "star war" takes place in the spirit world. Ask yourself, how can a war occur in the heavenlies unless God orders it? The answer: it can't. This is how we know these events take place according to God's timetable.

"**And there was war in heaven, Michael and his angels waging war with the dragon. And the dragon and his angels waged war, and they were not strong enough, and there was no**

longer a place found for them in heaven (the spirit world). And the great dragon. . . the serpent of old, who is called the Devil and Satan, who deceives the whole world; he was thrown down to the earth and his angels were thrown down with him" (Rev. 12:7-9 NAS).

Did you see that! **Satan cast to earth!** What does that mean? Has he not been operating in the minds of men all this time? Of course. But he did so as the "prince of the power of the air," free to roam IN THE SPIRIT, enjoying a kind of omnipresence (Eph. 2:2). This is why he can read our minds and behold our thought-life. But once he's kicked out of the spirit-realm (heaven), he can no longer operate as the "prince of the power of the air." **He must now occupy a body and move around on the earth the same as the rest of us.** But WHICH BODY will he choose? **There's only one body he wants — that of the WORLD RULER — the slain antichrist.**

HOW THE MIGHTY HAS FALLEN!

Were you and I playing this game, instead of Satan, we'd let antichrist stay dead and simply rise in his body. To our minds, there'd be no point in bringing him back from the dead. Why not just use his body and leave him out of it? Ah. . . but we're not Satan. We don't think as he does, nor do we have his problems and feelings. He has reasons that wouldn't occur to us, until we consider his nature:

a. **Satan always thinks of himself AS GOD.** He wasn't content to be the "prince of the power of the air," let alone be found as a MAN, stuffed in a human body. To him, "GOD IS SPIRIT," and that's the way it ought to stay. It's hard for him to see himself operating in any fashion other than the way God operates. He's locked into that idea BY PRIDE.

139

b. It was very humiliating for Satan to be KICKED OUT of heaven. If he has to go around on earth stuck inside a body, he certainly doesn't want people recognizing him. That would be too painful. He knows they'd look at him, thinking to themselves, "How the mighty has fallen!" To have people chuckling inwardly, because the devil must now function (as a man) like the rest of us, would be more than he could stand.

c. Consequently, if Satan has to be in a body, he wants it to be SOMEONE ELSE'S BODY, one he can use as a MASK. No way will he allow himself to be exposed in person. And if he has to play a human role, he couldn't possibly accept a lower position than THE NUMBER ONE MAN IN THE WORLD. After all, he's been "the god of this world" (2 Cor. 4:4).

d. Raising antichrist from the dead gives him a chance to display resurrection power. And through this, make antichrist look like a god. At least, if he has to operate inside antichrist's body, he can come as close to PLAYING GOD as is left to him. No one will have to know about his masquerade.

e. The devil is actually a coward. He could never bring himself to face men on a one-on-one basis. He's afraid people would discover what he's really like — and laugh. It would tear him up should they exclaim. . . "Is this the man that made the earth to tremble?" (Isa. 14:12-17). A proud devil could never do that, so he must hide behind THE MASK OF ANOTHER PERSON. And that person is antichrist.

HOW SATAN WILL INDWELL ANTICHRIST

Can the devil really indwell a body already occupied by someone else? Of course. That's easy. All that is necessary is for the owner of the body to submit to him—

140

and IN HE COMES. Judas is a clear-cut example. Scripture states, " . . . Satan entered into him . . . " (John 13:27). Even though the devil entered Judas, the betrayer didn't cease to be Judas. He didn't become a different person. Though his behavior was controlled by the devil, he was still Judas and that's the way everybody knew him. Now who would be more yielded to the devil than antichrist, someone who is really the product of his own invention?

What is true of Satan is also true of his angels (demons). The angels that fell with him are also cast out of heaven. They too will have to find bodies, or go into the bottomless pit (Luke 8:31). Later in the tribulation we'll see hordes of them coming out of the abyss and doing just that (Rev. 9:1-11). Demon possession is a biblical fact. More than once Jesus had to order demons out of people, so that the individuals would be free of their domination (Luke 4:31-37; Mk. 7:24-30, etc.).

● Having another person live with us in our bodies is not unique. That's what **salvation** is all about. Jesus, Himself, indwells us — or we're not saved (Rom. 8:9b). The more yielded we are to our Holy Indweller, the more He directs our thoughts and actions. Hopefully we reach the place where we can say. . . "Not I, but **Christ** liveth in me!" (Gal. 2:20). Without argument, more than one person can occupy a single body.

In similar fashion, a man can surrender to Satan and say, "Not I, but the **devil** liveth in me!" If people can be indwelt by the HOLY SPIRIT, they can be indwelt by the UNHOLY SPIRIT. However, once the war in heaven takes place and Satan is cast out, he will only be able to indwell **ONE MAN**. That man has to be antichrist. Antichrist will be so yielded to the devil, Satan will be able to use his body as though it were his own. **Yet, he will still be antichrist.** His behavior will be different, of course. So different in fact, **he will be given another name —THE BEAST.**

141

THE HOLY TRINITY
(Acts 2:32,33)
GOD (FATHER)

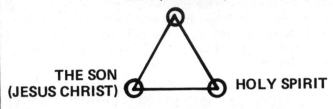

THE SON
(JESUS CHRIST)　　　　HOLY SPIRIT

VS. THE UNHOLY TRINITY
(Rev. 12–13, 19:20 – 20:2)
SATAN (DRAGON)

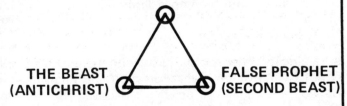

THE BEAST　　　　FALSE PROPHET
(ANTICHRIST)　　　　(SECOND BEAST)

Most Christians believe in the **HOLY** Trinity: consisting of **1. God the Father,** which no man has seen; **2. the Son (Jesus Christ),** who walked the earth in a physical body as God incarnate; **3. the Holy Spirit,** the unseen God Who indwells believers. We also believe these three are one.

But there is an **UNHOLY** trinity too: **1. Satan the dragon,** which no man has seen and who corresponds to God the Father; **2. the beast (antichrist),** a unique individual, born of a woman, but indwelt by Satan; **3. the false prophet,** also a man, a supernatural agency for the beast (antichrist), much as the Holy Spirit is a divine supernatural agency for the Son (Jesus Christ). In that day, when we have the BEAST indwelt by the DRAGON and aided by the FALSE PROPHET, we will have **"the unholy trinity"** on earth.

THE BEAST — SATAN INCARNATE

Just as Jesus was God incarnate when He was on the earth, the beast is Satan incarnate as he indwells anti-christ. Whereas God **voluntarily** became flesh to redeem mankind, Satan **involuntarily** becomes flesh to destroy it. (Col. 1:19-20; Dan. 12:11; Matt. 24:15; 2 Thess. 2:3-4). **In fact, the UNHOLY TRINITY will be on the earth at this point.**

SATAN'S BIG MOVE

Satan has been plotting and scheming for this day, ever since he tempted Eve in the garden and the world became his.

The Jews are stunned by the change in their "prince." He was so nice to them before he was killed. Now that he is risen, they are horrified by his actions. He is acting like a "beast." **With a single decree, he scraps the SEVEN YEAR COVENANT and orders the temple sacrifices to cease:**

 "And he will make a firm covenant with the many for one week, but in the middle of the week he will put a stop to sacrifice and grain offering . . . (Dan. 9:27a NAS).

The Jews can't believe their eyes as their one time benefactor **strides into the temple and seats himself in the MOST HOLY PLACE.** They cover their ears when **HE ANNOUNCES THAT HE IS GOD!**

 " . . . the man of lawlessness is revealed, the son of destruction, who opposes and exalts himself above every so-called god or object of worship, so that he takes his seat in the temple of God, displaying himself as being God." (2 Thess. 2:3,4 NAS).

143

How could their "prince" do such a thing? The beast has gotten all he wanted from the Jews and is through playing the "prince" of their Jewish game of Messiah. He desecrates all that is holy. We probably can't even guess the blasphemies and profanity he'll use in referring to the God of heaven . . .

 " . . . speaking arrogant words and blasphemies . . . against God to blaspheme His name and His tabernacle, that is, those who dwell in heaven." (Rev. 13:5,6 NAS).

The poor Jews will be in the dark, dumbfounded. But you and I'll know who this really is — SATAN INCARNATE! Egomaniac that he is, he'll want the whole world to see it, so it will be shown to the planet via satellite TV.

GOD OF THE WORLD

Except for the Jews (and believers), the **whole world** will go after the beast in wondering admiration. **Men will worship the dragon (Satan)** because he confers his authority upon the beast. They will worship the beast also, chanting, "Who is like the beast? Who can fight against it?" (Rev. 13:3,4).

Satan has finally reached STEP THREE in his plan to occupy God's earthly throne and demand the worship of the world. He has finally accomplished his goal of "I will make myself like the Most High" (Isa. 14:12-17). Let's review those three steps:

THE BEAST AND HIS IMAGE

If the Jews were dumbfounded by the shift in their "prince's" behavior, they'll choke on his next move. The beast orders a huge image made in his likeness. With the sacrifices ended, the false prophet discards his role of high priest. He is now charged with seeing that the people of the earth **"make an image to the beast** who had the wound of the sword and came to life" (Rev. 13:14b NAS).

But it doesn't stop there. **The false prophet has the power to GIVE LIFE to the image, enabling it to SPEAK.** We now have a statue that talks. Think of the people, in ages past, who worshipped gods they made with their hands . . . spoke to them . . . and wished they could answer. As we approach the second half of the tribulation, this is what is going to occur. What's more, the false prophet is going to have the responsibility of seeing that **everyone throughout the empire worships this image.**

Well, the false prophet knows how to accomplish that. Notice that he not only gives a voice to the statue so that it speaks, **he also gives LIFE to it so that it LIVES.** The 3-dimensional image will be magnificent, overpowering, possibly holographic, or a combination electronic and supernatural **wizardry.** The people will be obliged to supply the physical components, while the false prophet will use supernatural power to make it **appear** a living entity. Inasmuch as Jesus is expected to appear in the sky, the false prophet may even project the image using laser beams against the atmosphere. Then it would be like a BIG BROTHER watching from the sky. If this could be done, and I suspect it might, everyone on earth will be aware of its presence. It will make King Nebuchadnezzar's statue seem like a toy (Dan. 3:1-7).

THE WIZARD OF ZION

Remember the "Wizard of Oz" and how his citizens trembled at the sound of his voice? When they went into his presence, what did they behold? An awesome image, whose voice and demeanor made them shiver and shake. But when the secret was finally out, the person behind that image turned out to be a **timid old man,** in no way like the fierce sight on the huge screen. So will it be with the **image of the beast.** Remember, **the devil is a coward, much like the timid old man.** Satan needs to be the "Wizard of Zion." His ego forces him to use the **image of the beast** in order to speak directly to the people, **demanding that the world BOW DOWN to him.** Note the computer banks for keeping track of all those who worship the beast and receive his mark (Rev. 13:15-18, 20:4).

146

BUT WHY WOULD SATAN WANT
SUCH AN IMAGE?

The answer to that question lies in the devil's own nature, in his PRIDE. In using the personality of the beast AS A MASK, the devil still has to SHARE the glory and worship of the people with his servant antichrist, even though Satan indwells him. The devil doesn't like that. He prefers to have all worship directed toward himself, exclusively. But how can he separate himself from the beast without stepping out from behind his mask?

AH — BY MEANS OF A SEPARATE IMAGE. ONE THAT SPEAKS. ONE THAT APPEARS TO LIVE AND HAVE A PERSONALITY OF ITS OWN.

The decree goes out: anyone refusing to worship the image will be put to death (Rev. 13:15). As soon as people begin worshipping the image, Satan will have SEPARATED the worship from himself (dragon) and the beast. It is pure speculation on my part, but I have a hunch Satan will use the voice of the image and SPEAK DIRECTLY to the people. This would give him an added kick out of the whole thing.

IMAGE. This god, contrary to our God, will order graven images of himself to be made and distributed throughout the world. People may even have little statues to mount on the dash panel of their cars. It's likely to be a booming business, for Satan has always been one to merchandize religion. You can be sure people will also be encouraged to wear medallions of this image about their necks. It will appear on TV sets, probably between every program. We can be sure the devil will want his image plastered on walls and fences throughout the world. People can now forget about worshipping any other god. This will be the only religion allowed (Rev. 13:15).

147

SATAN NEEDS A FOOL-PROOF METHOD
BY WHICH HE CAN FLUSH OUT AND KILL
PEOPLE WHO WON'T ACCEPT HIM AS
GOD. SCHEMING MONSTER THAT HE IS,
HE COMES UP WITH AN INGENIOUS
IDEA . . .

THE MARK OF THE BEAST

 "And he caused all, both small and great,
rich and poor, free and bond, to receive a
mark in their right hand, or in their foreheads:
And that no man might buy or sell, save he
that had the mark, or the name of the beast,
or the number of his name" (Rev. 13:16,17
KJV).

Obviously some kind of a computer system will be
employed in keeping track of every man, woman and
child on this planet. A number, much like our social
security number, will be assigned to every individual.
Those worshipping the beast (or his image actually),
will be given a special mark to show their commitment
to him. By virtue of having this mark, they will be
allowed to hold jobs and do business in the stores.

COMPUTER. It's amazing how we Christians underestimate
our enemy. The average believer would be shocked if he
knew the data being collected on people at this moment.
One notable scientist affirmed that every driver's license
and social security number is already in the giant name
bank in Brussels, Belgium. It is under control of the common
market confederacy (EEC). In 1974, Dr. Hanrick Eldeman,
chief analyst of EEC, unveiled this gigantic self-programming
computer, programmed to give every person in the world a
number overnight. In order that no one loses his number,
Dr. Eldeman proposed a laser beam tatoo made in the
forehead or in the hand. The tatoo would be invisible to
the naked eye, but could easily be read through infrared

148

scanners. (The universal product code on items sold in stores may be a forerunner to this.) With this identification system, it would be easy to control who buys or sells. When the "beast" comes to power, we're going to be astounded at the thoroughness with which these people, dedicated to a single world government, have been collecting data on us. I'm not saying your name is in that file, but neither can I assure you it isn't. One thing is sure, we must stop being so naive about Satan's servants. They're good at their job.

So, having the "mark of the beast" is the same as worshipping the beast and his image as God. Those who do not accept the mark will not be able to buy or sell, and will be economic and social outcasts — "beast bums" — that is if they escape from being killed.

But this foolproof method is not without problems.

THE TRIBULATION — PART TWO
(THE SECOND 3½ YEARS)

Inside the body of the beast will be an angry devil. Furious over his defeat in heaven, he'll be ready to take out his rage on all earth dwellers — especially those who don't bow down to him. Thus we begin the second half of Daniel's 70th week (The Great Tribulation). This is why the SECOND HALF of the tribulation period will be far more terrible than the first 3½ years. There'll be a "roaring lion" inside the ruler of the world. Bible aware Christians will understand the reason for the difference in his behavior.

 "For this reason, rejoice O heavens and you who dwell in them. (The spirit world can relax with Satan and his angels gone). Woe to the earth and the sea; because the devil has come down to you, HAVING GREAT WRATH, knowing he has only a short time" (Rev. 12:12 NAS).

• Here's what it boils down to: people must choose between the WRATH OF SATAN or the WRATH OF GOD. If they go along with Satan and accept the mark of the beast, they escapé his wrath. But then they incur God's wrath, for He says anyone receiving that mark will suffer HIS WRATH (Rev. 14:9-11). On the other hand, if a person chooses to endure SATAN'S WRATH, for Jesus' sake, he will escape God's wrath. The wise person will choose to endure the wrath of Satan, for the devil can only kill the body (Matt. 10:28). On the other hand, "It is a fearful thing to fall into the hands of the living God" (Heb. 10:31; 12:29). Satan's wrath is temporary, lasting only months, whereas God's wrath is ETERNAL—HELL. No wonder John says . . . "Here is the patience of the saints" (Rev. 14:12,13).

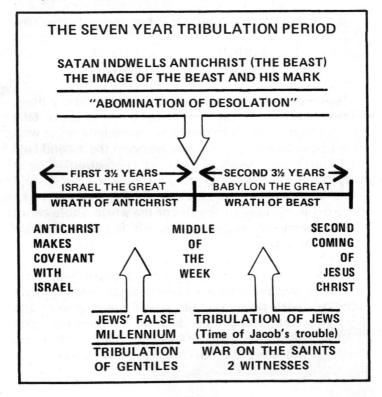

THE SEVEN YEAR TRIBULATION PERIOD

SATAN INDWELLS ANTICHRIST (THE BEAST)
THE IMAGE OF THE BEAST AND HIS MARK

"ABOMINATION OF DESOLATION"

←FIRST 3½ YEARS→ ←SECOND 3½ YEARS→
ISRAEL THE GREAT   BABYLON THE GREAT
WRATH OF ANTICHRIST | WRATH OF BEAST

ANTICHRIST   MIDDLE   SECOND
MAKES   OF   COMING
COVENANT   THE   OF
WITH   WEEK   JESUS
ISRAEL   CHRIST

JEWS' FALSE   TRIBULATION OF JEWS
MILLENNIUM   (Time of Jacob's trouble)
TRIBULATION   WAR ON THE SAINTS
OF GENTILES   2 WITNESSES

THE "HONEYMOON" IS OVER FOR THE JEWS

From where God sits, it is time for the Jews to enter PHASE II of their punishment — tribulation at the hand of the beast (time of Jacob's trouble). Remember that PHASE I was their scattering among the Gentiles to be persecuted by them. PHASE II begins with Israel's "prince" breaking the 7-year covenant. The man the Jews have embraced as Messiah is going to be God's instrument of punishment for rejecting Jesus. The "honeymoon" is over. They realize they've made a horrible mistake. Their "millennium" was not really a millennium at all.

The Jews may be stubborn and rebellious, but not stupid enough to worship an image. They've been over that road. They learned this lesson the hard way — the Babylonian captivity 2500 years earlier. Thus we can expect the Jews to make a **big turn**, denouncing the beast and exclaiming . . .

"No way can this man be Messiah! He is someone the prophet Daniel told us to expect . . . the 'abomination of desolation' " (Dan. 12:11).

DESOLATION. Desolation is right. This man, the beast (the title fits him), will seek to eradicate every vestige of Judaism. He will denounce the God of heaven, insisting he alone is worthy to be worshipped. He will fulfill John's word concerning him . . . "and a mouth was given to him, speaking great things and blasphemies: and power was given to him to continue forty and two months" (Rev. 13:5). In forbidding the worship of anyone but himself, the beast will create SPIRITUAL DESOLATION throughout the world. Mankind will now be in the grip of the satanic trinity. Not 777 (the Trinity of heaven), but 666, the trinity of man (Rev. 13:18).

What an awful moment for the Jewish people! How humiliating to realize they've accepted an IMPOSTER

AS MESSIAH! What fools they've made of themselves, boasting of their exalted position before all the world. Now they are not only embarrassed, they're spiritually bankrupt. The "abomination" has truly left them DESOLATE, with a great vacuum in their souls. Yet this is exactly what God had in mind for them. This is part of their punishment.

● As the Jews begin to resist the beast, he will turn on them with a fury that makes Hitler look like a sissy. Jeremiah describes this moment as the "time of Jacob's trouble" (Jer. 30:5-7). The Gentiles will take over the outer court of the temple, and trample the Holy City (Jerusalem) underfoot for 42 months, or the last 3½ years of the tribulation (Rev. 11:2).

The savagery of "the beast" will cut deeply into the Jewish population in a short time. Yet it is not God's will for the nation to perish through her mistake. He wants her to be caught in her folly (embracing anti-christ as Messiah) and realize what she's done, but He has to preserve some part of the nation to inherit the promises He made to Abraham (Joel 2:32; Jer. 30:11; Isa. 26:20). So God intervenes to spare a **remnant.** By supernatural means, **He seals Jews of each tribe against death.** That way a remnant will remain alive unto the coming of the Lord, permitting all the tribes to be represented in the millennial kingdom.

> **REMNANT.** In the Revelation, John tells us certain physical destructions of the earth are held back until 144,000 Jews are sealed, 12,000 from each tribe (Rev. 7: 1-8). Whether this number is actual or symbolical isn't clear. If all other Jews perish and that's easily possible, it will certainly be a small group left to go into the kingdom. Without doubt there will be some Jews, who, upon realizing their mistake, will turn to Jesus. Of course, they'll be martyred for their faith along with the blood-washed multitude (Rev. 7:9-15). **As for the 144,000**

(whether literal or not), **John tells us they flee to a place in the wilderness and remain out of reach of the BEAST for 1260 days** (Rev. 12:6; 14-16). This group of Jews is so divinely protected, the beast abandons his vendetta, to direct his rage against other targets.*

BUT WILL ONE OF HIS TARGETS BE THE CHURCH?

Jesus made one thing clear . . . "In the world ye shall have tribulation" (John 16:33). As long as Christians are in this world, tribulation will be part of God's plan for them, for without it, there is no way to develop patience (Rom. 5.3). So there's nothing unusual or abnormal about the church enduring tribulation. But when it comes to tribulation that issues from God's vengeance on an unbelieving world, can we expect the church to experience that kind?

When you consider the powerless condition of the church today; mingling with the world, no vigorous testimony, **you can't help but think it is going to take some kind of tribulation to get her ready for Christ's coming.** Here in the United States, at any rate, we clearly have the church at rest. It costs nothing to be a professing Christian in our country. But a church at ease is a phenomenon, not the norm.

The ease we Americans enjoy and the lack of tribulation has generated a host of evils within the church. **As one looks back over history, he can see how**

---

* Do not confuse the 144,000 of Revelation Seven, with those mentioned at the beginning of Revelation Fourteen. The latter are not Jews, but believers. They are clearly saved, "being the first fruits unto God and the Lamb" (Rev. 14:4). The 12 X 12 symbolism may have to be applied here as a Jewish expression for a "complete innumerable multitude." A careful comparison of the two passages reveals this is a different group from the 144,000 Jews of Rev. 7:5-8. Thus we have two groups of 144,000 mentioned, which in itself may indicate we should not take the number literally, but assume it refers to a good sized group.

the church has always flourished under trial. It refines her every time.

TRIBULATION FOR THE CHURCH, BUT NOT WRATH

The apostle John reveals the WRATH OF GOD is going to be poured out in the **final hours** of the tribulation. It will come in the form of the "seven last plagues" (Rev. 16:1). For that reason, nearly all prophetic writers (myself included) distinguish between the WRATH OF SATAN and the WRATH OF GOD. And with few exceptions, these writers insist **the church must NOT ENDURE THE WRATH OF GOD.**

There is some fuss over the exact timing of the last plagues, but the concensus is **they will NOT be poured out on the church. Why? The Lord Jesus bore the wrath of God for every believer.** He has already suffered this wrath in the Christian's place. Therefore it would be an act of unfaithfulness on God's part to visit His wrath on those Christians purchased with Jesus' blood. Hence unthinkable. Thus the church will be raptured before the 7 last plagues of God's wrath.

As for the church tasting the fury of the beast, many scholars feel it is absolutely necessary for her to endure SOME TRIBULATION if the "bride" is to make herself ready (Rev. 19:7).

THEREFORE IN THIS BOOK, YOU WILL FIND ME SAYING THE CHURCH WILL EXPERIENCE THE TRIBULATION (WRATH OF SATAN), BUT NEVER THE WRATH OF GOD.

WAR ON THE SAINTS

Once the beast turns from venting his wrath on the

154

Jews, he will go after the Christians, those true believers still on the earth.

 "And the dragon (Satan) was enraged with the woman (Israel), and went off to make war with the rest of her offspring, who keep the commandments of God AND HOLD TO THE TESTIMONY OF JESUS (Christians)" (Rev. 12:17 NAS).

With Satan no longer operating in the spirit world (which gave him access to men's MINDS), he cannot discern believers' hiding places by reading their minds. But he will use all of his power to discover them, and encourage BETRAYERS to dig them out wherever they can be found and kill them (Luke 21:16,17). He won't tolerate anyone who doesn't worship the beast or his image.

 " . . . and I saw the souls of them that were beheaded for the WITNESS OF JESUS, and for the word of God, and which had not worshipped the beast, neither his image, neither had received his mark upon their foreheads, or in their hands . . . " (Rev. 20:4 KJV).

There is a strong possibility that beheading will be the method of execution. Yet to do so, the beast must find believers. There may be a few nations who will drag their feet when it comes to cooperating with him. Not that they care so much about Christians, they just don't like the high-handedness and presumption of this man who calls himself "GOD" — even if he does have an image that speaks. So there will be a few believers alive on the earth when the Lord returns.

But, during the tribulation **most** of them will be slain after the beast comes to power. Martyrdom is nothing new to the Christian. The FIFTH SEAL of the Revelation shows the souls of ages past who had been slain because of the Word of God. They are in heaven, asking God . . .

" 'How long, O Lord, holy and true, wilt Thou refrain from judging and avenging our blood on those who dwell on the earth?'

And . . . they were told that they should rest for a little while longer, until the number of their fellow-servants and their brethern who were to be killed even as they had been, should be completed also" (Rev. 6:10, 11 NAS).

The last 3½ years of the tribulation will be the darkest hour for God's people. But there should be no hesitancy about the choice. There is no way a believer can accept that mark, no matter how he is threatened. Even if he sees his children tortured before his eyes, he cannot worship the image of the beast. The grace of God will empower him to resist (1 John 4:4). This should be settled in the mind of every Christian by the time he finishes this book. In fact, the second part of this book will help prepare you to endure the tribulation and be ready for the coming of the Lord.

SATAN'S WRATH — FORETASTE OF HELL

"And it was given to him to make war with the saints, and to overcome them: and power was given to him over ALL KINDREDS, AND TONGUES, AND NATIONS" (Rev. 13:7 KJV).

This man (the beast) will have unchallenged authority over all the globe. He will have plenty of power to make the nations do as he orders. The devil will use every trick in the book to extract worship from them, yet none of that worship will be from the heart. You can't

156

force people to love you, as the Soviets could testify. But what is that to Satan? As the father of hate, he cares nothing for love. He doesn't want it. He can't respond to it. He loves FORCE. It thrills him to use it. If it takes hobnailed boots on people's necks, that's fine with him. As long as they bow in submission, he doesn't care how they feel about him.

> **SUBMISSION.** The beast will use miracles, the mark and force — those three things, to bring the world to its knees before him. For some, miracles alone will be enough. For others, the need to feed their families will make them bow and accept his mark. Then there'll be those who'll submit only under force. The beast will be delighted to use whatever power it takes to humble the multitudes — even nuclear power, though it brings further devastation to the land, seas and inland waters. His supernatural displays and attempts to "alter the times" will affect the heavenly bodies (sun, moon and stars), bringing darkness to one third of the earth (Rev. 13:8; Dan. 7:25). If our planet suffered as antichrist tried to force the world's billions into Judaism, it will suffer even more as the beast forces its billions to bow before him as God.

● Can you imagine a world ruled by the PRINCE OF HATRED? It will be a foretaste of hell. The misery that will come to lives during the 2nd half of Daniel's 70th week will be indescribable. Fear and betrayal will be the character of the kingdom. The secret police (Gestapo) will be everywhere, scouring the earth for any refusing to worship the image.

Life will be rough for everyone, but worse for believers. They'll have a price on their heads, making it tougher to survive. Disease and pestilence will ravage the earth. Water will become more valuable than oil, as seas and rivers are turned to blood. With the land scorched, food will be scarce. Even so, there will be considerable commerce carried on by beast-owned enterprises throughout the world.

157

Those trafficking in beast-related items will do very well. But they'll be a minority. Most of the world's population will be reduced to the level of slaves. The tyranny of the beast will bring on a tribulation "such as was not since the beginning of the world to this time, nor ever shall be" (Matt. 24:21). Keep in mind that lawlessness is now unrestrained, the Lord having ordered the Restrainer to step aside (2 Thess. 2:7).

TRIBULATION. When you read John's account of the tribulation, you find him picturing it as three sets of judgments. The seven year period is spanned by visions of SEALS, TRUMPETS and BOWLS. Scholars are by no means agreed as to the relationship of these three visions, and there's even less agreement as to the timing of them. But I am struck by the fact that they all have one thing in common — WRATH. In the first 4 seals, ANTICHRIST vents his wrath against those resisting his call to Judaism. In the first four trumpets, the BEAST pours out his wrath on Israel, on believers, and on all who refuse to worship his image. Finally, the bowls CONTAINING GOD'S WRATH, are poured out on the beast and rebellious man. Christians will not experience God's wrath, for they are raptured prior to the emptying of the bowls.

POLITICAL BABYLON —
SATAN'S HEADQUARTERS

God's city becomes sin city.

In chapter five, we saw how ROME, as the headquarters of the false prophet, was **RELIGIOUS BABYLON**. We also discussed her destruction at the hand of antichrist prior to his alliance with Israel. Now, during the last 3½ years of the tribulation, we find JERUSALEM, as headquarters of the beast, is **POLITICAL/ COMMERCIAL BABYLON**. Thus we unravel the mystery of the two Babylons of the 17th and 18th chapters of John's Revelation.

THREE WRATHS OF THE REVELATION

ANTICHRIST'S WRATH	BEAST'S WRATH	GOD'S WRATH
(First 4 seals)	(First 4 trumpets)	(All 7 bowls)

In no way am I attempting an exposition of the book of Revelation. I seek, rather, to show how the THREE WRATHS of the book constitute God's judgment upon an unbelieving world. The **wrath of antichrist (seals)** devastates one fourth of the world, while **the wrath of the beast (trumpets)** devastates one third of the world. God uses these angry men as instruments of His judgment. **But God's own wrath (bowls)**, which is universal, does not come by the hand of men. It is administered by angels (Rev. 16:1). Those few Christians remaining on earth **will be raptured before God's wrath is poured out.** His wrath will last only a matter of days, otherwise "there should no flesh be saved" (Matt. 24:22). There is a mixing of the remaining seals and trumpets as they lead up to and merge with the 7 bowls (wrath of God).

JERUSALEM. Who would have dreamed God's city would one day become a "fountain of filth" before it becomes a "river of righteousness?" But that's how it is with Satan — he corrupts everything he touches. With Jerusalem as his capitol, we can expect the city to lead the world in lust. With great wealth flowing into her coffers, through her immoral traffic, she crowns herself with glory and honor. Sitting as a proud queen ("Babylon the Great"), she believes herself immune to destruction (Rev. 18:7). The apostle John, in describing this indulgent city, says she is a haunt of evil spirits and unclean birds. By this, he is telling us she becomes a cancer to the whole world. Her merchants traffic in immorality and every foulness associated with degenerate life-styles. Through this city, the world feeds out of the pit.

● Picture the beast with a world beaten into submission, ready to lick his boots. With fiendish pleasure he sits on his throne, watching the wealth of the world flow into his treasury as mankind is exploited for his profit. Those merchants of the world, trafficking in the weakness and depravity of men, all become rich. How they "love" the beast for the favors he shows them.

Can you see him watching his world on TV monitors? He rubs his hands with delight as people everywhere bow to his image, surrendering their wills to his foulness. However, it isn't as perfect as he'd like it. There are blotches on his satisfaction . . . Christians. He loves to see them executed. But it's tough to watch them die, proudly shouting the name of Jesus. And to see them prefer death to submitting to his demands infuriates him.

He knows that none of his followers would do that for him. He rules out of fear. But these believers have JOY on their faces as they give their lives for the Lord. He hates that, but he won't turn off the TV. He won't rest until every last Christian has been purged from his domain. It torments him to think there are those who count it a privilege to die for the Son of God. The Spirit calls them "blessed."

 " . . . Blessed are the dead which die in the Lord from henceforth: Yea, saith the Spirit, that they may rest from their labours; and their works do follow them" (Rev. 14:13 KJV).

So he sits there day after day fascinated, yet exasperated.

TWO THORNS IN SATAN'S FLESH

As the beast surveys his empire on TV, there's something else that gets him. Two men . . . right there in Jerusalem . . . continually speak out for Jesus and nothing can stop them. No matter what orders he gives or what methods are used, there is no way the beast can put them out of operation. They go on speaking out for Christ day after day. You can be sure the beast has a special monitor devoted to these men as he tries to come up with ways to silence them. The more they witness for Jesus, the madder he gets. They really bug him.

If the beast has power over the saints to make war against them and overcome them, **the Lord must take steps to see that some kind of an outspoken witness remains.** A lot of people are going to be saved out of this tribulation and a way has to be provided for them to hear the gospel. God meets this need by raising up two remarkable men. These two men are the mysterious witnesses of Revelation Eleven:

 "And I will give power unto my two witnesses, and they shall prophesy a thousand two hundred and threescore days, clothed in sackcloth" (Rev. 11:3 KJV).

161

TWO MEN. Some commentators feel these two men are symbolical of the church and Israel. And they might be right. But to my mind the language is too specific for them to be anything but two individuals. Who are they? Can we identify them in Scripture? I'm inclined to join those who believe them to be Moses and Elijah, both of whom made appearances after they had died. They were together with the Lord Jesus on the Mount of Transfiguration discussing His exodus from the world (Matt. 17:3). It is not likely these two men are the only evangelists in the world, but they are the only **indestructible** ones. As such, they stand as a testimony to the indestructibleness of Jesus' church (Matt. 16:18). These two men will serve as powerful encouragement to Christians all over as they hold up the Word of the Lord. They will be like searchlights piercing the darkness of the sky.

Concerning these two men, John says they will have "power to shut heaven, that it rain not" and "power over waters to turn them to blood . . . " (Rev. 11:6). You will remember how Elijah prayed and it didn't rain for three years. And Moses smote the Nile and it turned to blood. The parallel is so striking, that if the two witnesses are not Moses and Elijah, they are their antitypes. Observe also, how **they are empowered to minister throughout the second half of the tribulation, the entire 1,260 days (3½ years).**

What's more, these two men have the power to slay any seeking to harm them (Rev. 11:5). **Thus it will be impossible to silence their testimony.** You can imagine what that will do to the beast. You can also imagine the confidence it will give Christians the world over to have these living examples of God's power and presence.

The beast will give orders for their deaths, but no one will be able to slay them. This, plus their supernatural powers, will be effective in convincing hearers that Jesus is more powerful than the beast. It may look like the beast has the world in his hands, but these two witnesses will be proof that he doesn't. How embarrassing for the beast.

EMBARRASSING. It's not clear from the text whether the two witnesses spend the entire 1,260 days in Jerusalem or not. If they do, they'll be a continual embarrassment for the beast. He'll stay awake nights scheming ways to get rid of them. Inasmuch as they will be able to "smite the earth with all plagues, as often as they will," they will appear to have more power than the beast (Rev. 11:6). Their immunity to death will drive him wild. How many times will he come up with a "sure fire plan" to overpower them . . . stage it on TV . . . only to have them make him look bad in the eyes of the world. **These thorns in his side will be God's reminder that HE is running the show.**

THE BEAST'S DAYS ARE NUMBERED NOW

Time is running out for Satan. His 1,260 days on earth are coming to an end. The only reason God allowed him to set up an earthly kingdom was to give men a belly full of sin. On the surface, you'd think rational men would get fed up with filth, tired of living in a world of unrestrained evil. You'd think sin for breakfast, lunch and dinner would make them so sick of it, they'd ache for the joy and peace displayed in the faces of the martyrs.

Sick of sin? Impossible. God knows the human heart, how that it "is deceitful above all things, and desperately wicked" (Jer. 17:9). But does **man** know it? Does he realize he has an insatiable appetite for sin, and IN-FINITE CAPACITY for evil? Not for a second. So how do you convince an evil generation of its passion for wickedness? Simply. You put the MAN OF SIN in charge of the world and let him run it, or better — RUIN IT. That way everyone can witness the CONSEQUENCES of sin displayed on the stage of the world. But do these consequences frighten men? NO WAY — they love sin, even when it tortures them. Faced with a choice between God's righteousness and the devil's dirt, mankind chooses sin every time. If the tribulation does nothing else, it vindicates God's statement, "men loved darkness rather than light" (John 3:19).

● The devil is no dummy. He's aware of the ruin he's bringing to the earth. The thought of it delights him. After all, he is "the abomination of desolation." He gets his kicks out of creating desolation — **"even until a complete destruction"** (Dan. 9:27). Nothing pleases him more than making life intolerable on planet earth by means of his incredible power. What's his motivation for such destruction? He knows the Lord is going to intervene and snatch his kingdom from him. It's there for him to read . . .

 " . . . The kingdoms of this world are become the kingdoms of our Lord, and of his Christ . . ." (Rev. 11:15 KJV).

This is the real source of Satan's rage. He knows his time is short. **Operating inside the body of the beast, he is out to do as much damage as possible to both man and the earth.** If he is to go down, he wants to take as many as he can with him and leave the world in shambles. He wants Jesus to come to a totally devastated earth.

CULMINATION OF SIN ON EARTH

As the beast performs his abominable desolations, he degrades men by saturating their evil natures with the fire of desire. **He looses upon them hordes of demons able to torment men's souls with insatiable lusts** (FIFTH TRUMPET, Rev. 9:1-11). They hurt inside, so great is their passion for evil. And all the while they stupidly stare at the ruin heaped upon their planet. Why? They're like teen-agers hooked on dope. They're

164

SATAN — THE MASTER COUNTERFEITER
Note how Satan counterfeits
everything God does:

GOD	SATAN
HOLY TRINITY 1. God (Father) 2. Son (Jesus Christ) 3. Holy Spirit	**UNHOLY TRINITY** 1. Satan (dragon) 2. beast (antichrist) 3. false prophet
ANGELS	**DEMONS**
PROPHETS OF GOD (John the Baptist, Moses, Elijah, etc.)	**PROPHETS OF SATAN** (Joseph Smith, Buddha, Mohammed, Mary Baker Eddy, Russell, Rutherford, etc.)
SIGNS OF MESSIAH (healings, miracles, resurrections, etc.)	**COUNTERFEIT SIGNS** (healings, miracles, resurrections, etc.)
TRUE PRINCE OF ISRAEL	**FALSE "PRINCE"**
MILLENNIUM	**FALSE "MILLENNIUM"**
MILLENNIUM TEMPLE	**TRIBULATION TEMPLE**
WEDDING OF THE LAMB	**COVENANT WITH ISRAEL**
HONEYMOON WITH BRIDE OF CHRIST IN ETERNITY	**3½ YEAR "HONEYMOON" WITH ISRAEL**

JESUS CHRIST
  Prophet, Priest
  and King
	ANTICHRIST
	  king "prince" (Ezek. 45:22)
	FALSE PROPHET
	  prophet, priest (45:19)

JESUS
  God incarnate, came
  to redeem — voluntary
	BEAST
	  Satan incarnate, comes
	  to destroy — involuntary

SEAL OF GOD	**MARK OF THE BEAST**
JERUSALEM "The Holy City"	**JERUSALEM** "Babylon the Great"

so locked into their habit, they dare not upset the pusher who supplies them. Satan, like a drug pusher, is the evil supplier, promising men all the sin they can hold. But it is never enough.

NEVER ENOUGH. Man, made in the IMAGE OF GOD, is himself an INFINITE BEING . . . with an **infinite appetite.** He was designed to be satisfied by the **infinite God alone.** This is why nothing in this world can truly satisfy a person, whether sex, money, power or fame. Only the infinite God can satisfy our infinite appetites. Therefore Satan has to deceive people into thinking HE can satisfy their wants. However once they get started with him, they find themselves HOOKED by their own weaknesses. They keep wanting more . . . and he keeps giving more . . . but it's never enough. The satanic process is so blinding, people are kept from the knowledge that God is willing to give them the desires of their hearts, if only they will delight themselves in Him (Psa. 37:4).

The tribulation generation will be like that, drugged and dazed. These poor souls will view the desolation of their planet with feelings of helplessness. They will hate the beast for what he has done to them and their world, **yet they will not turn to God for forgiveness.** Clearly they prefer the ruin of the devil to the mercy of Christ. When that attitude becomes the universal choice — and it will — the world will be ripe for the wrath of God. If people stagger under the wrath of Satan, just wait until they feel the wrath of God!

THE TWO WITNESSES FINISH THEIR TESTIMONY

Finally a day comes when the work of the two witnesses is finished. (Of course, that will also mean the coming of the Lord is at hand as well.) The Holy Spirit apparently withdraws their powers, allowing the beast to **slay them.** Their dead bodies are left exposed on the streets of Jerusalem. Now THAT IS A SCENE THE

BEAST WILL DEFINITELY TELEVISE to his empire. The cameras zero in on those bodies and the picture is flashed on screens around the world. The event is declared a worldwide holiday (Rev. 11:7-10).

But the jubilation is short-lived. After three and a half days—to the consternation of those watching—an astonishing thing takes place. Those bodies stir. With TV cameras catching the action, the two men get to their feet. The video crews shake in their boots. Their cameras tilt upward, following the men **as they slowly rise and disappear in a cloud** (Rev. 11:11, 12). The beast is stunned! The whole world is shocked!

Those two men are not the only ones to rise.

IF YOU NOW BEHOLD THE TRIBULATION AS A TIME OF GETTING THIS WORLD READY FOR JESUS, YOU'VE LAID HOLD OF A SIGNIFICANT TRUTH. UP TO THIS POINT, NEITHER MANKIND NOR THE EARTH WAS READY FOR HIM. BUT NOW EVERYTHING IS IN READINESS.

The next chapter contains the BIG EVENT we've all been waiting for!

Chapter Eight

"Here I Come, Ready Or Not!"

"...98...99...100! Here I come, ready or not!"

How often did you shout that as a youngster? You were playing "hide and seek," covering your face while you counted. Your friends scurried to their hiding places. When you reached 100, you called out the warning and went looking for them with no concern for whether they were ready or not. Anyone who failed to conceal himself could be spotted and tagged . . . "Your it!"

So it is with the Lord's return.

We're in the final countdown, clicking off the moment of the Lord's return. And though we're approaching that day, the exact timing is known only to the Father (Mk. 13:32). We may confidently assume one thing — **the Lord WILL NOT return until the specific number of souls making up the church has been saved — that is,**

when the "bride of Christ" is complete. Since that day is unknown, the Lord's return will be as unexpected as a "thief in the night" (1 Thess. 5:2).

A thief gives no warning when he is about to enter a house. Neither will the Lord give warning when He is about to appear. Yet that day is not to overtake believers "as a thief," for the Lord has not allowed us to remain **ignorant** (1 Thess. 4:13-18; 5:4-6).

After suffering under the beast, our eyes will be scouring the heavens, anticipating the promised relief from the sky (2 Thess. 1:5-8).

ONE FELLOW WHO WON'T BE READY

Guess who's going to be caught by surprise!

The beast, of course.

A signal flashes to his command post. The camera crew covering the dead bodies of the two witnesses is calling . . . "Your majesty! Look in the monitor . . . quick!" The beast jerks to the edge of his seat. He stares in unbelief. Beads of perspiration appear on his brow as he watches the two witnesses rise to their feet. But that's not all. They keep on rising into the air, headed toward a peculiar cloud in the sky.

As the two witnesses reach the cloud, a deafening **SHOUT** rattles everything in the command post. The unbelieving world hears it too. "EVERY EYE" beholds what occurs next!

The sound didn't come from the TV monitors. It came from outside . . . **from the sky!** The noise, similar to the one heard on the day of Pentecost, turns every head skyward (Acts 2:2,6)! Leaping from his seat, the beast rushes to the window. His breath stops at the sight confronting his eyes! The sky is filled with angels. So numerous are they, they look like a cloud. And is that cloud bright. So bright, he must shade his brow to watch.

Then he catches sight of something that makes his blood run cold. There . . . at the center of the angels is the ONE PERSON HE DREADS MOST — the Lord Jesus Christ! When he sees the Lord, the beast knows exactly what is taking place. This is the moment he's been dreading, the time when "the Son of Man shall come in His glory and all the holy angels with Him . . ." (Matt. 25:31). With the exact time of the Lord's return hidden from him, he wasn't ready for it.

It's clear now what that SOUND (akin to a sonic boom, perhaps) was all about. It was the Lord Jesus SHOUTING the same words He uttered at the tomb of Lazarus . . . "COME FORTH!" His heart leaps into his mouth as the beast recalls the Scripture covering this event:

"For the Lord Himself shall descend from heaven with a SHOUT, with the VOICE of the archangel, and with the TRUMP of God: and the dead in Christ shall rise first" (1 Thess. 4:16 KJV).

The cloud suddenly becomes larger as the angels are joined by believers. In a flash, every person from Adam onward, WHO DIED IN FAITH, is at once a part of that crowd-cloud. They appear in glorified bodies that resemble, in many ways, the ones they had on earth. But they're definitely different, in that they're not subject to the law of gravity. Of course — they're SPIRITUAL BODIES (1 Cor. 15:44).

But that's only part of the action . . .

"Then we which are alive and remain shall be

170

caught up together with them in the clouds, to meet the Lord in the air . . . " (1 Thess. 4:17).

The beast DOES NOT know where every believer is hidden throughout his empire. If he did, he would have killed them, leaving none to be caught up with the Lord. But the Lord knows where His people are (2 Tim. 2:19). Consequently another sound is heard. This time it is the **VOICE** of the archangel.

In micro-seconds, EVERY LIVING CHRISTIAN is whisked from the earth to join the host in the sky! **This is the rapture of the church.** Now the **entire** family of God is gathered together with the Lord in the sky. Did not Paul speak of Jesus' coming and our GATHERING UNTO HIM (2 Thess. 2:1). This is it. I know it seems like a strange place for a family reunion, but you'll see why before long.

> **RAPTURE.** In the minds of many, the rapture is conceived as a large group of believers rising from the earth. However, the number is likely to be small. Most of the saints will have perished as martyrs. Even so, some will be scattered throughout the world in various hiding places. The rapture is a MOPPING UP OPERATION, with the angels gathering saints from the four points of the compass (Matt. 24:31). As recently as last year, isolated World War II Japanese soldiers, who didn't know the war was over, were found living inside a volcano rim. Once discovered, they were informed of Japan's defeat. Similarly, some saints will be preserved alive, isolated until summoned to the sky by the Lord's shout. The rapture will remove the last survivors.

RED ALERT IN BEAST'S HEADQUARTERS

Though unprepared, the beast is painfully aware the hour has come for Jesus to overpower him and seize his kingdom. Will he go down fighting? You bet — he has nothing to lose. However, he would like more time. With more time to prepare, he could make the forthcoming battle the greatest show on earth. As the Lord lingers in the sky, it seems the beast is going to get more time. Just how much, we're not sure. It looks like somewhere between 30 to 45 days (Dan. 12:11,12).

● You've got a question?

"Brother Lovett, do you mean to say the Lord is going to keep us with Him in the sky all those days, just to give the beast more time to get ready?"

Well that's only ONE of the reasons. A number of things are going to take place . . . not only on the earth, but in the sky as well. Hang on, it will unfold shortly.

THE RALLY IN THE VALLEY OF MEGIDDO

The beast springs into action. He presses the alarm bell in his headquarters, and three special ambassadors on standby alert scramble like jet interceptors. They have orders for the kings of the whole world to assemble in the valley of Megiddo — a place called Armageddon. The apostle John says they look like THREE FROGS.

That's his way of describing UNCLEAN SPIRITS. These three messengers streak to the kings of the earth, ready to foist ONE FINAL DECEPTION on mankind — the idea they can fight against the Lord — AND WIN!

For this task, the messengers will be operating under the combined authority of the dragon, beast and false prophet. They will be empowered to do miracles so eye-popping, the kings of the earth will be deceived into believing the suggestion (Rev. 16:13,14,16).

Does it puzzle you that the Lord would give His

172

enemies time to rally their forces against Him? Since He is coming to judge them, why not let them assemble in one place? Besides, the Lord is assembling His own army. Is not the sky filled with His soldiers? (Rev. 19:14).

> **ARMIES.** Though the beast has no precise knowledge of the day or hour of Jesus' return, he knows the Scriptures well enough to realize his time is short. For 3½ years, he has been developing his military might around the world. Once the alert is sounded, he must rally them to a staging area. It takes time, as you know, to field an army. They have to be mustered, fed, housed and equipped. A lot of supplies must flow together. The bigger the operation, the longer it takes. Using demonic agents to speed up the process, the beast will have his forces ready to meet the Lord at the end of the 30 or 45 days (?). He will expect to engage Jesus at Jerusalem, for that is the point of His final descent (Zech. 14:4). Megiddo (Armageddon), however, is the staging area.

As for the Lord, it will take Him but SECONDS to assemble His forces. It will be a supernatural operation. Given their spiritual bodies, His saints, MOVING AT THE SPEED OF THOUGHT, can assemble in a flash . . . in the "twinkling of an eye" (1 Cor. 15:52). With their bodies energized BY SPIRIT (rather than by food), no field kitchens or supplies are needed. Consequently the Lord will have His armies ready and waiting long before the beast can assemble his.

TIME TO KILL?

Does it seem as though we'll have a lot of time on our hands waiting for the beast to gather his forces? That we'll be milling around the sky, killing time while events ripen on earth? Not so. We'll be plenty busy.

● I sense this raises another question. All right, ask.

"Brother Lovett, you say the church will go through

the tribulation and be raptured just before God pours out His wrath upon the earth. Since many fine scholars insist the Lord will remove the church before the tribulation, could you explain how and why you came to this position?

A fair question. Before I answer, please remember I DO NOT seek to get people to believe as I do. I don't want a single reader to change his thinking because of what he reads here — **UNLESS it would help him put Jesus first in his life.** By themselves, doctrines are of little value. They are important only as they help us draw closer to Christ and exalt Him to His rightful place in our lives. If my views would help you do that better than the ones you now hold, by all means accept my thinking until you can find something better.

HAVING SAID THAT

Now for my answer. As many of you already know, I was raised in the C.I. Scofield ("pre-trib") tradition. My first real pastor believed in a pre-tribulation rapture,* and it was natural that he would school me as he believed. I devoured the Scofield Reference Bible, even to the place of accepting the SCOFIELD NOTES (printed right in the Bible) as inspired.

Beyond that, I memorized Larkin's charts and made

---

*The idea of a secret rapture, occurring seven years before the Lord's glorious return, is a fairly new teaching. No one ever heard of it before 1830. In recent times, Dave Macpherson, a gifted researcher, has presented documented evidence that a second coming in two stages was first put forward around the year 1830 by a young woman by the name of Margaret McDonald. Macpherson, who owns rare volumes exposing this matter, reveals how this Scottish lass received visions of a secret rapture before the tribulation. The girl made notes of her visions which fell into the hands of Edward Irving, the most famous preacher in England at the time. He began spreading the concept of a two-phase coming of the Lord's return far and wide. J.N. Darby (Plymouth Brethren) visited London and brought the idea back to the U.S., where Dr. C.I. Scofield picked it up and built it into his notes. The rest is history.

myself familiar with all the pre-tribulation authors and
their thinking. Believe me, I was totally saturated in the
tradition. I was a Scofield man, viewing the Word of God
through "Scofield glasses."

> **SCOFIELD.** In no way should my words be construed as
> belittling this godly man who contributed so much to my
> early growth as a Christian. I am satisfied that much of his
> work IS inspired of God. **And while I disagree with him on a
> few points, I do not allow that to diminish the high regard
> I have for him as an able student of God's Word.** I am too
> indebted to him to do such a thing. I would that all who
> profess to know Jesus would serve Him as devotedly as did
> our brother Scofield.

When it came time for me to go to Bible college and
seminary, I was steeped in pre-tribulationism. I could
defend the view rather skillfully from the Scriptures.
But that was before I learned you can build a case for
almost ANY VIEW from the Bible — if you come to it
with a preconceived idea and want to find it there.
That's the nature of the Word itself.

> **BUILD A CASE.** By now, I'm sure, you've discovered how
> easy it is to get an idea and then search out Bible verses
> that seemingly support it. The **cults** do this. They come
> up with their heresies and develop schemes of Bible verses
> to make the unsuspecting think their approach is biblical.
> Preachers frequently say, "The devil knows how to use the
> Word better than we do." Therefore as I explain how the
> Spirit shifted my thinking, I will not throw a system
> of verses at you. Instead, I will show how He altered my
> thinking with a few observations. All He did was draw my
> attention to a couple of things . . . and that was it.

HOW THE HOLY SPIRIT GOT ME TO DO MY OWN THINKING

Knowing I was a staunch "pre-tribber" and would

reject a frontal attack on my position, the Spirit dealt with me subtly. It's not that I'm stubborn (though at times I can be), but like anyone else, I hate to think I've been doggedly clinging to error. After being a "pretribber" for so many years, it was in me to "fight rather than switch." If you hold to the pre-trib view, you probably feel the same way.

So I'll simply share with you how the Spirit got me to take off my "Scofield glasses." Very clearly, I had been viewing the Word through his eyes. The Lord must have felt it was time for me to study this matter with MY OWN EYES. Interestingly enough, the first observations came out of the rapture passage itself. Here they are:

 THE FIRST OBSERVATION — "COMING"

I was working on LOVETT'S LIGHTS ON THESSALONIANS when I came to the familiar passage . . .

 "For this we say unto you by the Word of the Lord, that we which are alive and remain unto the COMING of the Lord shall not prevent (go ahead of) them which are asleep" (1 Thess. 4:15 KJV).

You recognize that verse, of course. Many Christians know it by heart. It's from the classic rapture passage which says we're going to "meet the Lord in the air." The Spirit drew my attention to the word "COMING." He then prompted me to take a look at it in the Greek. There the word is PAROUSIA. So I went to the lexicons and word-study books to see how this particular word was used in Paul's time.

In New Testament days a PAROUSIA (coming) was a remarkable event. It had to do with a king or ruler leaving his capitol to visit some remote part of his realm.

176

A "parousia" was a gala affair, one that called for all kinds of celebration. It was no small thing, you see, to have the emperor make a state visit to your area. It was usually declared a holiday with the people of the region invited to join the festivities.

In N.T. times a PAROUSIA (coming) was when a king or ruler came to visit some remote part of his realm. It was a gala affair, one that called for all kinds of noisy celebration. It was usually declared a holiday with the people of the region invited to join the festivities.

As I read a number of accounts of actual parousias occurring in Paul's day and saw how noisy and festive they were, I wondered why the apostle chose this word to describe the rapture. I had always thought the rapture would be a SECRETIVE THING, with only the saints aware of what was taking place. But if that were so, **why did this intelligent scholarly writer of so much of the New Testament choose a word that created such a noisy, public affair in the minds of his readers?**

177

That was a baffler. Far from being a secret, the word PAROUSIA indicated the Lord's coming was more like the premiere of a big budget movie — with the whole world invited to watch! That produced a hairline crack in my "Scofield glasses."

That did something to me. It generated a tiny seed of doubt in my pre-trib system. It led me to consider further checking — ON MY OWN.

● The next observation was also subtle, but it struck me with force. It's simple to be sure. But when I saw it — wow! See if it hits you the same way. It's in the next verse.

❷ THE SECOND OBSERVATION — "RISE"

 "For the Lord Himself shall descend from heaven with a shout, with the voice of the archangel, and with the trump of God: and the dead in Christ shall RISE first" (1 Thess. 4:16 KJV).

See the words . . . "THE DEAD IN CHRIST SHALL RISE FIRST!" It's the word "RISE" that seized me this time. I knew what it meant, and so do you — a RESURRECTION. I mean a physical, literal resurrection with people putting on bodies. As I pondered the word "rise," the Spirit fired a question in my mind . . .

"WHY WOULD PEOPLE NEED BODIES SEVEN YEARS BEFORE IT WAS TIME FOR THEM TO APPEAR WITH CHRIST?"

Do you catch the significance of that question? Why a resurrection 7 years **before** the day of resurrection? What possible use would anyone have for a body, if he were going right back into heaven where people can't use physical bodies? I don't know how you react to that, but I was stunned.

NO BODIES IN HEAVEN. The apostle Paul went to great lengths to explain that our heavenly FORM is totally unlike the physical body we wear on earth. He didn't for a minute suggest we'd be "unclothed," but instead, "clothed upon with our house . . . from heaven" (2 Cor. 5:2,3). The house from heaven is NOT a physical, but a SPIRIT FORM, one as perfectly suited to life in the spirit as our physical bodies are suited to life on earth. Do not confuse this SPIRIT FORM with the resurrection body, which is physical and fleshly and needed to appear with Christ in the kingdom (Col. 3:4; 1st John 3:2). The resurrection body is TEMPORAL, needed only for the earthly kingdom, but the spirit FORM is our ETERNAL house, which will serve us long after the resurrection body has done its job. At this point we have no idea what the heavenly form is like, except that it must be like "the form of God," since we are His image (Phil. 2:6).

Why did it bother me to have people receive physical bodies **seven years before they were needed?** Ah, glance up at verse 14 and you'll observe that all THE DEAD IN CHRIST have been with Jesus all along, some of them for centuries. Adam, Abraham, Moses and David — they had no physical bodies in heaven and got along fine without them. Why? Because they were **clothed with the heavenly form.** But now look at verse 14 . . . "even so THEM ALSO which sleep in Jesus will GOD BRING WITH HIM!"

See it? For all the centuries they were with the Lord, they had NO PHYSICAL BODIES. They didn't need them. **There's no place for physical bodies in heaven.** That being so, why would God suddenly give bodies to all these people SEVEN YEARS BEFORE it was time to appear with Him? Very clearly the only time departed saints will need physical bodies is when they are ready

179

to APPEAR with Jesus. Physical bodies are needed only for physical appearances.

> **BODIES.** Man, like God, is a spirit-being. But no one can see a spirit, at least not with physical eyes. Therefore if a spirit is going to be seen by men, he must put on some kind of a body. And if he plans to live on earth, he needs some kind of an "earth-suit" to get around in. There is no way to participate in physical life without a physical body. The Lord faced that problem. If He were to dwell among men, He had to have some kind of a body. Thus Jesus took on human form. And if "every eye" is to see Him when He returns, He must AGAIN take on a physical body. And if we're going to be seen with Him, we will also need bodies. But until it is time for Him to appear and for us to appear with Him, bodies simply aren't needed.

When I was teaching the pre-trib theory, I used to say the Lord descended to a certain level in the sky, gave resurrection bodies to the "dead in Christ," raptured the living saints, and the whole crowd went back to heaven for seven years. But now I had all these bodies on my hands. What would I do with them? When I was honest about it, I knew physical bodies could not participate in the spirit-realm.

As Jesus said to Nicodemus . . . **"That which is born of the flesh is flesh; and that which is born of the Spirit, is spirit"** (John 3:6). Flesh can no more mix with spirit, than thoughts can mix with sand. They are two different realms.

Isn't that a blockbuster! You can see why the question hit me so hard. I didn't have a way around the problem of giving bodies to people who couldn't use them. So I left it hanging on a peg while I went to the next verse, where the Spirit rocked me with another observation.

❸ THE THIRD OBSERVATION — "MEET"

 "Then we which are alive and remain shall be caught up together with them in the clouds, to MEET the Lord in the air . . . " (1 Thess. 4:17 KJV).

See the word . . . "MEET?" The Spirit prodded me to take a close look at it. It's a very precise word in Greek. Very interesting, too. It appears in two other places in the New Testament. When you see how it is used in those two places, you get a better idea how it is to be understood in the verse above.

I know you'll recognize the first case. It's the parable of the wise and foolish virgins (Matt. 25:1-13). The pertinent verse in that passage reads: **"And at midnight there was a cry made, 'Behold, the bridegroom cometh; go ye out to MEET him' "** (vs. 6). You don't have any problem understanding the word "MEET" here do you? Of course not. The wise virgins (those with oil in their lamps) went out to MEET the bridegroom and ESCORTED HIM BACK to the bridal chamber.

In his book, *Jesus Is Coming,* W. E. Blackstone, renowned scholar of a past generation, comments on the word "MEET" as it is used in the rapture passage: **"The Greek word here rendered 'to meet' signifies a going forth IN ORDER TO RETURN WITH."** Certainly that is the natural way to understand the midnight cry.

A more striking case is found in Acts 28:15. Here Paul is on his way to Rome to be tried before Caesar. As he approaches the Appi Forum and the Three Taverns, he is met by a group of Christians from Rome. **"They came to MEET us,"** says Luke. Please note that they met Paul and ESCORTED HIM BACK to Rome. By letting Scripture interpret Scripture, we get an understanding of what is meant by MEETING the Lord in the air. It is to escort Him to earth, not to disappear with Him in heaven.

I had always figured the Lord was going to make a GIANT U-TURN in the sky and our whole crowd would disappear into heaven for 7 years. Quite frankly I never could explain why we met in the sky, but I had accepted it without question. Now, however, when I found that the biblical usage of the word "MEET" forbade the U-TURN concept, the pre-trib theory was suddenly suspect.

With these three little words the Holy Spirit badly cracked my "Scofield glasses."

1. "COMING" (The spectacular parousia)

2. "RISE" (Resurrection of dead in Christ in physical bodies)

3. "MEET" (To escort Jesus to the earth)

A man can't work with shattered glasses, so I took off my "Scofield specs," satisfied the Holy Spirit Himself was weaning me from my dependence on this dear man and his system. **Without doubt, the Spirit was leading me to USE MY OWN EYES and let HIM show me what to expect in the last days** (John 14:26).

SO I TURNED TO OTHER PASSAGES

I wanted to see how some of the prophetic passages would look through "SPIRIT ANOINTED EYES." I scoured Matt. 24 and 25, Mark 13 and Luke 21, looking for some hint of a SECRET PHASE of Jesus' return. These chapters, as you know, contain Jesus' **direct answer** to the matter of His coming again. The only thing I could find was that He said He would return and gather His own . . . "Immediately after the tribulation of those days" (Matt. 24:29,30).

182

● Next, I went to Dr. Luke's book of Acts. There we are provided with a vivid picture of the way things will be when Jesus returns. Two angels, standing on Mt. Olivet (after Jesus ascended), said plainly that Jesus would come again . . . JUST AS HE HAD DISAPPEARED . . . that is, He would return personally, visibly and from a cloud (Acts 1:9-11).

According to these angels, the NEXT MANIFES- TATION of Jesus would be a glorious return with no hint of a secret rapture seven years earlier. I must confess I had never looked at that verse as a clear statement of what Jesus' disciples were to understand regarding the Lord's return. But there it was and my "pre-trib" system received another blow I couldn't handle. So I hung it on a peg too.

● Next, I turned to the apostle Paul. I already knew what to expect from this brother. As I came to his most direct words on the timing of the Lord's return, I could feel the Spirit beginning to break down my prejudice:

 "Let no man deceive you by any means: for it (that day) will not come except there come a falling away first, and that man of sin be revealed, the son of perdition" (2 Thess. 2:3 KJV).

As I studied that verse through "Spirit anointed eyes," I remember how I used to distinguish between the "day of the Lord" and the "day of Christ." For the first time I was willing to admit I was probably guilty of hair-splitting to defend a doctrine. Without question, these two terms are used interchangeably throughout the New Testament. So if I ceased my hair-splitting and took Paul's words at face value, he was clearly saying . . . THE LORD'S RETURN IS NOT IMMINENT.

Now what would I do? Would I hold to my pre-trib notions regardless, or admit the possibility that the **great falling away and the revelation of the man of sin had to occur before Jesus could return?** No preacher likes to think he's been teaching the wrong thing for years. It was hard for me to admit that, harder still to consider a shift. I guess I needed a final observation — one more thunderbolt.

BY NOW I WAS READY FOR IT

The Holy Spirit then took me to a section of the New

184

Testament where I felt the least comfortable as a pre-tribber — the Revelation. I had always puzzled over that vast multitude SAVED out of the great tribulation:

> **"After this I beheld, and lo, a great multitude, which no man could number, of all nations, and kindreds, and people, and tongues, stood before the throne . . . clothed in white robes . . . and one of the elders answered saying unto me, 'What are these which are arrayed in white robes? And whence came they?' And I said to him, 'Sir, thou knowest.' And he said to me, 'These are they which came out of the great tribulation, and have washed their robes, and made them white in the blood of the Lamb."** (Rev. 7:9 -14 KJV).

Who are these people washed in the blood of the Lamb?

How did I handle this as a pre-trib fan? Well, I simply explained these people were saved AFTER THE RAPTURE and were resurrected PRIOR to Jesus' descent. That way, He could return with ALL HIS SAINTS (1 Thess. 3:13). Having died as martyrs, they were scheduled to return with Him at His revelation. One of my pet phrases was: "In the rapture Jesus comes FOR His saints, in the revelation He comes WITH His saints." But it was never comfortable for me, for I also taught the Holy Spirit was removed from the earth at the rapture.

If you are familiar with the pre-trib view, you can understand my discomfort. It is generally held by pre-trib thinkers, that the Holy Spirit is taken out of the world when the church is raptured. This means no one could be born again in the sense you and I are born again. To explain how such a great mass of people could emerge from the great tribulation as BLOOD-WASHED

185

BELIEVERS, I would claim they enjoyed Old Testament salvation — saved in a fashion similar to Abraham, Moses and David, etc.

But even as I gave that answer, I would feel uneasy about it for two reasons:

1. I knew the Old Covenant had been superseded by the death of Christ, never to be revived (Heb. 7:11, 27; 8:13).

2. Those Old Testament saints were also in the SAME BODY with us (Heb. 11:40).

SAME BODY. While it's true the Old Testament believers were COUNTED AS RIGHTEOUS because of their faith, that didn't get them to heaven. They had to WAIT until Jesus came as the perfect sacrifice before actual righteousness could be IMPARTED to them (2 Cor. 5:21). Once Jesus finished His work at Calvary, Scripture says He descended "into the lower parts of the earth." This is where the Old Testament saints were waiting — in Abraham's bosom (Luke 16:22). From there, "when He ascended up on high, He led captivity captive" (Eph. 4:8,9). That is, He took the Old Testament saints from their waiting place into heaven. The way was now open. (Heb. 10:10,20) Before Jesus' death it was NOT OPEN (Heb. 9:8). In this manner, the Old Testament saints had their OWN PENTECOST before the New Testament saints had theirs. It is SPIRIT-BAPTISM that puts people into the body of Christ. Thus the Old Testament saints and the New Testament saints are baptized into the one and SAME BODY by the same Spirit . . . "for by one Spirit are we all baptized into one body" (1 Cor. 12:13).

GOD'S THUNDERBOLT — THE ONE BODY
CANNOT BE DIVIDED

As I looked at the tribulation saints through "Spirit anointed eyes," suddenly it hit me what I was doing —

dividing the body of Christ into **two classes** of believers! By creating RAPTURE SAINTS and TRIBULATION SAINTS, I was flying in the face of some of Paul's clearest teaching, "there is one body, and one Spirit, even as ye are called in one hope of your calling . . . " (Eph. 4:4-6).

Do you see what I was doing? I was, in effect, saying the tribulation saints were somehow UNWORTHY to be raptured with me. I was a true believer in the secret rapture and was therefore qualified to escape the tribulation, but these poor people had to learn the hard way by going through the tribulation. They didn't have my faith or understanding, therefore needed the tribulation to wake them up. Looking back, I can't believe I taught such a theory. But I did. What's more, I had them dying for a Christ THEY COULDN'T SEE — AND DOING SO WITHOUT THE HELP OF THE HOLY SPIRIT. Can you imagine that! I had them putting their trust in the unseen Lord to the place where they were willing to die for Him, rather than deny Him — **all without the Spirit's help.** What a shock when I finally realized what I was doing.

As I looked at those tribulation saints, I realized they satisfied the biblical qualification for entrance into the kingdom more perfectly than I. To strengthen his disciples, the apostle Paul repeatedly said ". . . we must through much tribulation enter into the kingdom of God" (Acts 14:22). What tribulation did I have? I thought about those of us anticipating the rapture, how we might be rescued from our electric blankets, fine cars and color TVs. Whereas those precious tribulation saints would suffer martyrdom. Did you know they have a commendation we don't have . . .

 "Blessed are the dead which DIE IN THE LORD from henceforth: Yea, saith the Spirit, that they may rest from their labors; and

their works do follow them" (Rev. 14:13 KJV).

If any group were special to God, it would have to be those dear saints, not us. As I thought how often I had implied these precious souls, due to be tried with fire, were not worthy to be raptured with our group and thus excluded from the blessedness awaiting us, I BLUSHED INWARDLY. I was embarrassed before God!

● That was the end of my DOUBLE VISION. No longer could I insist the body of Christ was divided into RAPTURE SAINTS and TRIBULATION SAINTS. **There was no way I could go on making God the author of such a division, when clearly He has no favorites** (Rom. 2:11). As I thought of those precious brethren laying down their lives for my Jesus, I couldn't take it any more. I set aside my "pre-trib glasses" for good.

But where did that leave me? What would I teach?

WHAT ABOUT THE MID-TRIB VIEW?

I felt I should take a look at the MID-TRIB position. At least it accommodated Paul's insistence that the "man of sin" had to be revealed before the rapture could occur. When I checked it out, I liked it in some respects. But it still left me with TWO FIRST RESURRECTIONS AND TWO LAST TRUMPETS. On top of that, we were still dividing the body into two classes of Christians — THE RAPTURE SAINTS and THE TRIBULATION SAINTS. Also, there remained the problem of giving resurrection bodies to the saints 3½ years before they could use them. No — the MID-TRIB position left too many serious problems unanswered.

THAT LEFT THE POST-TRIB POSITION

There was always one feature of the POST-TRIB

VIEW I couldn't stomach — the idea of God's people experiencing the **wrath of God.** To my mind, the whole thing collapsed right there.

But where else was I to turn?

If I could no longer teach that Christians were going to be raptured before the great tribulation, all that was left was the post-trib position. Perhaps my understanding of it was faulty.

So I took another look at the post-trib position, coming to it with two conclusions:

1. There has to be a rapture in order for those saints who are still alive to join Jesus and descend with Him (1 Thess. 3:13).

2. Yet those saints must not experience the wrath of God. Somehow they must be kept from the hour of trial, which shall come upon all the world. (Rev. 3:10).

Would the post-trib view accommodate these two elements? I wasn't sure that it would. Then it dawned on me! The rapture must occur JUST BEFORE God pours out His wrath on the earth! To push it back 3½ or 7 years is unnecessary.

NOAH'S STORY ILLUSTRATES
THE TWO ELEMENTS

My pre-trib training now paid off. I remembered how I used to teach that the story of Noah pictured the pre-trib position. But as I looked at Noah again, I saw that his story more perfectly pictured what the Holy Spirit was impressing on my mind.

The patriarch, you recall, was allowed to suffer the ridicule and harrassment of men for 120 years. It was ludicrous to build an ark when it had never once rained on the earth. But to obey his Lord, Noah had to endure this humiliation and tribulation right up till the moment God was ready to pour out His wrath. Only then did God seal him in the ark and lift him above the earthly scene. Then — when the judgment had passed — Noah was gently returned to the earth, settling on Mt. Ararat (Gen. 6-8).

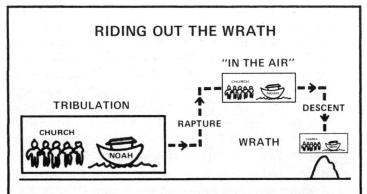

RIDING OUT THE WRATH

"IN THE AIR"

TRIBULATION

RAPTURE

DESCENT

WRATH

CHURCH   NOAH

CHURCH   NOAH

CHURCH   NOAH

Noah's experience typifies that of the saints. God leaves His people (like Noah) on earth to endure tribulation, but when He is ready to pour out His wrath, He calls His people out. At the rapture, the remnant of the saints will join Jesus in the sky. ALL THE SAINTS will be with Him as He takes vengeance on an unbelieving world. Once His enemies are punished and the world shaken and reshaped, we will descend with Him to Mt. Olivet. The Noah story is a perfect illustration, one which Jesus meant for us to understand (Matt. 24:37-39).

TRIBULATION — BUT NOT WRATH

The drawing indicates how the Holy Spirit led me to **separate** THE TRIBULATION from THE WRATH of God. Most Christians are aware that suffering is NORMAL for believers (Phil. 1:29; 1 Pet. 2:21, 3:14; 2 Tim. 2:12, 3:12; Rom. 8:17; John 15:18-20, 16:33).

For the church to go through the tribulation is totally consistent with this important concept of the Bible. While we cannot see believers enduring the WRATH OF GOD, the fact of our suffering tribulation is as biblical as can be.

> **TRIBULATION.** Throughout history God has refined His people through suffering. From Nero until now, there's nothing new about tribulation for Christians. This entire age is one of trial for believers — as God said it should be. It's hard, here in "easy living" America, to believe that suffering is proper for God's people. But the Bible makes it patently clear we are **"not only to believe on Him, but also to suffer for His sake"** (Phil. 1:29). The early church was taught to expect suffering with no relief promised UNTIL THE LORD WAS REVEALED FROM HEAVEN (2 Thess. 1:4-8). Check that passage and see if it doesn't say the church will suffer persecution right up to the very moment God is ready to pour out **His wrath** on an unbelieving world.

Where did that leave me?

When I put the facts together, it suddenly dawned on me that I was NEITHER a PRE-TRIB, MID-TRIB NOR POST-TRIB believer. **I was a PRE-WRATH believer!**

A PRE-WRATH BELIEVER

Near the end of the great tribulation, God will pour out those seven bowls (vials) of His wrath (Rev. 16:1). But you and I WON'T be here. We'll be raptured **just before** that happens. Very clearly the world will suffer the wrath of God **AFTER** God's people are raptured. This position solves the problem of trying to avoid tribulation, which is necessary for God's people, yet affirms that God will keep His children "from the hour of trial" (Rev. 3:10).

191

THE PRE-WRATH RAPTURE

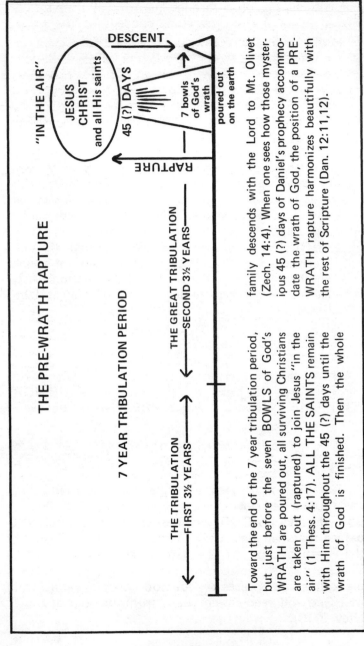

"IN THE AIR"

DESCENT

JESUS CHRIST and all His saints

45 (?) DAYS

7 bowls of God's wrath

poured out on the earth

RAPTURE

7 YEAR TRIBULATION PERIOD

THE TRIBULATION —FIRST 3½ YEARS

THE GREAT TRIBULATION —SECOND 3½ YEARS

Toward the end of the 7 year tribulation period, but just before the seven BOWLS of God's WRATH are poured out, all surviving Christians are taken out (raptured) to join Jesus "in the air" (1 Thess. 4:17). ALL THE SAINTS remain with Him throughout the 45 (?) days until the wrath of God is finished. Then the whole family descends with the Lord to Mt. Olivet (Zech. 14:4). When one sees how those mysteripus 45 (?) days of Daniel's prophecy accommodate the wrath of God, the position of a PRE-WRATH rapture harmonizes beautifully with the rest of Scripture (Dan. 12:11,12).

"A PRE-WRATH CHRISTIAN!"

How I liked those words! At last the Holy Spirit had brought me to a position that was comfortable, exciting and accommodated nearly every objection. You can see how this view might easily heal a lot of divisiveness racking the church.

TEST ALL THINGS BY THE SPIRIT

Can you see how my mind was shifted by the Holy Spirit? He led me, as I have shown, from one observation to another. But that does not mean He wants you to do the same.

In sharing my experience, **I've tried to avoid imposing my views on others.** I seek to be sensitive to the Holy Spirit, stating my views firmly and without double-talk. I think it is important that I speak out clearly. At the same time, though, I realize there are brethren who've probably forgotten more prophecy than I'll ever know. I wouldn't presume to teach them.

But if you, dear reader, have scratched your head over this matter or felt undecided about it, I would trust the Lord to make my testimony a help to you. If my words lead you to a settled view . . . praise the Lord. Even so, **I'd like my spirit to be such, that even if you don't agree with me, you love me and appreciate what I am trying to do for God's people.**

● Three things are going to occur while we're in the air with Jesus. Can you guess what they are? I'm sure you'll find them fascinating. They are in the next chapter.

Chapter Nine

Big Business In The Sky!

When we paused to discuss my shift in rapture views, we were with the Lord in the air — expecting to be there possibly as long as 45 days. The beast had frantically dispatched his demonic emmisaries to summon the kings of the earth to Megiddo. That has to take time — weeks anyway. While the forces on earth are gathering for battle, what will we be doing in the air?

BUSINESS MEETING IN THE SKY

The meeting in the sky involves more than pleasure. There are business matters to be cared for as well. **Three** are scheduled for the time we're waiting with the Lord in the air:

1. **The judgment seat of Christ.**

2. **The marriage of the Lamb.**

3. **The last trumpet.**

❶ THE JUDGMENT SEAT OF CHRIST

The judgment seat of Christ is, without doubt, the most frightening moment of the believer's life. Paul calls it "the terror of the Lord" (2 Cor. 5:11). Rightly so, for it is at this time that our earthly lives are evaluated. This is the FINAL EXAM for our time on earth. Exams are always scary, but this is the daddy of them all — THE BIG ONE.

 "For we must all appear before the judgment-seat of Christ, that each one may be recompensed for his deeds in the body, according to what he has done, whether good or bad" (2 Cor. 5:10 NAS).

Wow! None of us likes to be examined. When you consider this is the absolute final . . . with our whole future at stake . . . well, it just has to be the most important event we'll ever face.

You've heard the motto:

**"Only one life, 'twill soon be past;
only what's done for Christ, will last."**

This motto is fulfilled at the judgment seat of Christ. This is where we learn WHAT WILL LAST! In other words, here we receive our ETERNAL REWARD. It's the word ETERNAL that makes this moment so fearful. You see, there are no second chances in the Christian life. As they say in the TV commercial . . . "You only go 'round once in life" (See Heb. 9:27).

Believers who squander their earthly opportunity living for self or family will be sorry. Their record at this judgment will be miserable. **And when you consider we receive our ETERNAL ASSIGNMENTS at this judgment, that translates into our ETERNAL JOB WITH**

JESUS. Once the Lord assigns us a position or rank, it will be PERMANENT . . . final . . . forever!

Those spending their time seeking comforts, security and pleasure, will find they have FORFEITED THEIR ONE CHANCE to qualify for a fabulous job with Jesus. I don't know about you, but to me that's frightening! It means our future is in our own hands.

> **JUDGMENT SEAT.** Do not confuse the judgment seat of Christ with the great white throne judgment (Rev. 20:11). These two judgments are separated by 1,000 years. The great white throne is for the UNSAVED of all ages from Adam onward. (We'll be discussing that in chapter eleven). The judgment seat of Christ is for CHRISTIANS ONLY. At this judgment you and I will be judged for our persons and our works, **not** for our sins. They were judged at Calvary. Since Jesus bore the GUILT of our sins, they do not enter the judgment picture (Rom. 8:1-4). **The basis of our judgment is what we've DONE FOR Christ** (with the opportunity He's given us) and how much we've GROWN to be like Him.

When the MASTER examines our lives, He'll be weighing our faithfulness and motives. Since He died for us, He has every right to expect to be NUMBER ONE, coming ahead of family, fame and fortune. Those who forego the goodies of this life, to invest themselves in Jesus, will be thrilled with His reward. Why? They've proved He can depend on them to PUT HIS INTERESTS AHEAD OF THEIR OWN. That's what all leaders look for in people. Thus they will receive the TOP JOBS and be the BIG SHOTS in the world to come.

And what is our reward?

The rewards we receive from Jesus will be our future tasks or assignments in His kingdom. The Lord keeps books. He watches our performance every moment.

196

Basing His judgment on our actual record, He knows precisely where we'll fit best in His program. Consequently He has a spot ready and waiting for each of us.

● How long will it take the Lord to complete the reviews and appoint us our places in His administration? I think it occurs INSTANTLY — the moment we join Him in the sky! In a split-second, we not only know our eternal assignment, but the RANK that goes with it — a rank we'll hold forever (Rev. 11:18).

While the assignment occurs in micro-seconds, I'm sure we'll need time to check out our jobs and get acquainted with the people who'll be working with us. That's one of the things we'll be doing while we're waiting in the sky. It's my opinion that by the time we're ready to DESCEND WITH THE LORD, we'll already be in our slot in His government.

> **RANK.** While all of us are loved the same by the Lord, not all of us will have the same rank or privileges. While there is no respect of persons with God, there will definitely be HIGHER RANKING and LOWER RANKING positions in the kingdom. That's what the judgment is all about (Luke 19:17,24). There's no point in a judgment unless it is to determine the believer's position in Christ's administration. Calvary gets us to heaven. But our WORKS earn for us our job with Jesus. The point: anyone who desires to be close to Christ in His kingdom had better get serious about serving Him NOW. It will be TOO LATE to qualify for anything once this earthly life ends (Heb. 9:27).

② THE WEDDING FEAST (MARRIAGE OF THE LAMB)

When I say feast, does your mind picture a banquet hall with food piled high on tables. Sorry, but there won't be any food at this feast. The resurrection body won't need food. It is energized BY THE SPIRIT, re-

197

quiring NO FOOD for fuel. Oh, it can eat food, and drink, but it won't be needed to keep things going. At this feast we'll be feeding the SOUL rather than the body. It will be a FEAST OF FELLOWSHIP, a feast of satisfaction. In my opinion, the real food of heaven — IS PEOPLE. Our hunger of soul will be entirely satisfied by the family of God.

At the wedding feast we'll meet Jesus first of all. Think how your soul will devour HIM! Imagine being in His embrace and having Him say to you . . . "It's great to get MY hands on you at last! Let ME hold you for a moment!" And then to feel those arms about you. Huuuummmmm. Perhaps He'll want to personally introduce you to Adam and Eve, Abraham and David . . . and so on. For dessert, He might bring you to those friends and relatives who preceded you in death. Wouldn't that be a fabulous feast for any soul? And how.

But this is also a **wedding**. This is the day Jesus gets "married." Right there in the sky, He takes "Miss Church" — all true believers — as His bride. This will be the most gala wedding in all of history! All the angels will be in attendance. Even the world will be called to witness the wedding of Jesus and "Miss Church." He wants "every eye" to see it!

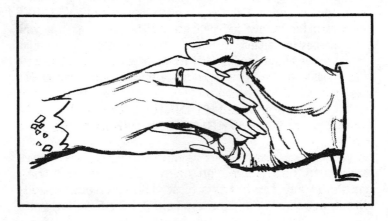

John's words are reminiscent of a society reporter as he tries to describe the event:

"Again I heard what sounded like a vast crowd, like the noise of rushing water and deep roars of thunder, and they cried:

 'Alleluia! The Lord our God, sovereign over all, has entered into His reign! Exult and shout for joy and do Him homage, for the wedding-day of the Lamb has come! His bride has made herself ready, and for her dress she has been given fine linen, clean and shining.'

(Observe: Fine linen represents the righteousness of God's people).

Then the angel said to me, 'Write this: Happy are those who are invited to the wedding-supper of the Lamb!' " (Rev. 19:6-9 NEB).

In all this, who do you think will be the happiest of all? Ah — the Lord Jesus. This is HIS DAY. He's been waiting a long time (as we reckon time) to receive His bride. He has loved her to the death, yet He couldn't get His hands on her as long as the faith program was in operation. But once that program ends, He can gather His bride to Himself and experience the JOY THAT WAS SET BEFORE HIM! (Heb. 12:2).

Can you picture Jesus reveling in honor and praise of those who really love Him and deeply appreciate His sacrifice for them? Imagine how He will feel surrounded by those who can't do enough to make sure His satisfaction is complete. When He looks on those who have PUT HIM FIRST, the Lord will weep for joy. This will be the biggest day in His whole life! You and I will stand there beaming with delight . . . even if tears of joy are streaming down His face. We'll know we brought Him that joy!

Don't be afraid to use your imagination on this. Picture Jesus with joy exploding all over His face! Imagine Him LOOKING AT YOU and thrilled with what He sees! Won't that be the greatest moment in your life? And then to have our MASTER express His *agape* love with BEAR-HUGS will be glory for us! Jesus is scheduled to be the HAPPIEST MAN IN THE WORLD . . . as the Word says:

 "Therefore God, Thy God, hath anointed Thee with the oil of gladness above Thy companions!" (Heb. 1:9b NAS).

Now you know what that verse means. It's referring to the day the Lord greets you in a face to face encounter. You're going to bring Him the greatest joy He's ever known.

The wedding in the sky.

Jesus is returning as the KING OF KINGS. He's coming to inherit the "throne of His father David" (Luke 1: 32). So King Jesus and His future queen ("Miss Church") deserve this extravagant ceremony that uses the sky for a wedding hall. Admittedly this is an unusual place for a marriage, but haven't we come to expect the Lord to be unusual and original? Of course. Besides, what's wrong with letting the rest of the world see what it has missed. They could have all been here, but they spurned His invitation (Matt. 22:1-14; Luke 14:16-24).

MARRIAGE. I don't mean to suggest the holy nuptials are limited to our brief time in the sky. That's too short. Only the wedding ceremony occurs there. This will be followed by a 1,000 year reception (wedding feast) on earth. During the millennium He will share His kingdom with His bride. Yet, even that is too brief. After all, this is an ETERNAL UNION. The real honeymoon LIES BEYOND the millennium. As long as the Lord is in the ROLE OF A SON, and we continue to occupy with earthly things, **the marriage is not yet fully consummated.** Observe how John (clearly struggling for adequate words) continues to see the church STILL AS A BRIDE after the 1,000 years have ended (Rev. 21:2). Without doubt, the UNION and LIFE for which we were intended can only begin when God is finished with PROGRAM EARTH. Only an eternal honeymoon will satisfy an ETERNAL GOD.

❸ THE LAST TRUMPET

The THIRD thing that happens while we're with Jesus in the sky is the sounding of the last trumpet. And you know what that means:

> **"And the seventh angel sounded . . . (and look at this) . . . and the nations were enraged, AND THY WRATH CAME, and the time came for the dead to be judged, and the time came to give their reward to Thy bondservants the prophets and to the saints and to those who fear Thy name, the small and the great (note the ranks), and to DESTROY those who destroy the earth"** (Rev. 11:15, 18 NAS).

Look at all the stuff packed into verse 18:

☆ Nations angry with the Lord, refusing to repent!

☆ The resurrection of the righteous dead (and rapture).

☆ The rewarding of the saints, all ranks.

☆ The pouring out of God's wrath.

We've spent a lot of time discussing the happenings in the sky, but that's because we've been waiting for the beast to gather his armies to Armageddon. I've listed the sequence of happenings as I understand them, but as I've already stated, I can be wrong. There's no way to be 100% certain, (especially with the seals, trumpets and bowls), until the events take place.

● With the sounding of the seventh trumpet, a frightful moment has arrived.

The happy sounds we've been enjoying are suddenly hushed. **There's a silence** (7th seal, Rev. 8:1). Our socializing is over for a time. The situation on earth is **nearly ripe.** Something awesome is about to occur. From heaven a loud voice calls to the seven angels charged with dealing out God's wrath.

 "Go and pour out the seven bowls of God's wrath on the earth!" (Rev. 16:1 NEB).

Ah, so that's what the silence in heaven was all about. The dreadful moment of God's wrath has come at last. Heaven holds its breath, the silence before the storm. Seldom is God seen in anger. I leave it to you to read the devastation of earth that follows the emptying of those bowls (Rev. 16:1-21).

THIRD WRATH — GOD'S WRATH

The earth now shudders under the THIRD WRATH coming against it.

I hope you're keeping track of these wraths; the **first wrath** came when **antichrist** tried to force the world into his Jewish mold, killing one fourth of mankind in the process (the first 4 seals). The **second wrath** came when the **beast** vented his fury against all mankind, forcing them to worship his image. One third of mankind perished that time, with the seas and vegetation suffering similarly (the first four trumpets).

But now, when **God's wrath** (the 7 bowls) is poured out, TOTAL RUIN is unleashed against man and nature. The seas die completely (fulfilling Jacques Cousteau's prophecy). The rivers turn to blood. The sun's heat intensifies, scorching men. Their bodies are afflicted with malignant sores. They writhe in agony, in the dimness of a darkened sun (dust clouds likely). Do these afflictions lead any to repent? Not a one. Instead they gnaw their tongues and blaspheme the God of heaven (Rev. 16:8-11). Apart from the sealed Jews, those on earth will curse God. **All of them.** For the saved have been removed.

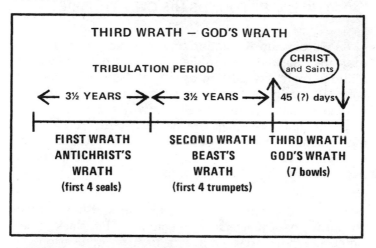

What part will you and I have in ministering the wrath of God? We'll probably sit this one out . . . and watch. Actually, God doesn't want us avenging ourselves on anyone. As for His enemies, He insists . . . "Vengeance is Mine, I will repay!" (Heb. 10:30). At this point, I'm ready to believe God will handle the wrath Himself. We can help Him with other things.

VENGEANCE. God has held His peace for over 4,000 years. He has refrained from venting His wrath as He once did in the days of Noah. Truly He is patient. But now the time has come for His patience to end. Without hesitation,

He gives the command to the angels. Men and the planet reel under plagues pouring from the sky. In one place God's wrath is described as being "mixed in full strength in the cup of His anger" (Rev. 14:10). What is so amazing, is that no matter how awful the anguish, men refuse to repent. They'd rather endure bitter pain than admit they were wrong about Jesus. Bear in mind, it is no longer a matter of faith. They now see Him. So even by sight, they don't want Him. But some of these people will survive to enter the millennium.

THE BEAST SOUNDS HIS OWN TRUMPET

As we pick up the action on earth, we find the valley of Jezreel packed with soldiers from all over the world. Millions more are putting ashore at Haifa. In the dim light, it's tough to assemble such a mass of men, but it's being done. (With the 6th bowl), the Euphrates is dried up and the kings of the east, with 200 million more men, swell the beast's army to an incredible mass of men (Rev. 16:12). The whole surrounding area is packed solid. Everything is in readiness.

The unholy trinity leaves Jerusalem and heads north to army headquarters at Megiddo. The sleek black limousine pulls to a stop at a high point overlooking the plain of Esdraelon. The beast (empowered by the dragon), and the false prophet exit the car and stand on the crest of the hill.

In plain sight of all the people, the beast surveys his sprawling army. The proud generalisimo prepares to give the signal that will put this mass in motion. As he beholds all the sophisticated weapons of war, his soul swells with pride. This is his big moment. To his mind he is invincible. Behind him, his generals await his orders.

The beast nods his head.

The false prophet gives the word, "**Let the trumpets sound!**"

At the blast of the trumpets, the army comes to attention. A hushed silence hangs over the valley.

The false prophet moves forward to speak. "**Hear o ye peoples of the earth. Remember this day when the strong hand of the beast leads you into battle against Jesus and His army!**"

The beast raises his arm above his head, his fist clenched.

At the sight of that raised arm, the people shout, "**LONG LIVE THE BEAST! LONG LIVE THE BEAST! LONG LIVE THE BEAST!**"

The earth trembles. The canyons echo the sound of more than a half billion voices.

The beast drops his arm. He shouts the command:

"**ON TO JERUSALEM! ON TO JERUSALEM!**

The awaiting generals hurry to their commands. The beast and false prophet seat themselves in the command car. Satan, indwelling the beast, heads the movement of men and machines toward Jerusalem for the greatest battle in the history of the world!

HERE COMES THE JUDGE

The waiting is over.

The Lord makes His move.

> "**Then I saw heaven wide open, and there before me was a white horse; and its rider's**

name was Faithful and True, for He is just in JUDGMENT and just in WAR. His eyes flamed like fire, and on His head were many diadems . . . He was called the Word of God, and the ARMIES of heaven followed Him . . . From His mouth there went a sharp sword with which to SMITE the nations; for He it is Who shall rule over them with an iron rod, and tread the winepress of the WRATH and RETRIBUTION of God the Sovereign Lord . . ." (Rev. 19:11-16 NEB).

The battle of Armageddon is at hand. The Lord momentarily turns from His bride to fix His gaze on the beast and his armies. You and I are part of the entourage (armies of heaven) ready to descend to engage the beast. Actually, the Lord doesn't need an army, but from here on, **we're** included in everything He does (I Thess. 4:17b).

 "Then I saw the beast and the kings of the earth and their armies mustered to do BATTLE with the Rider and His army" (Rev. 19: 19 NEB).

The earth below is still darkened as a result of the 5th bowl. Suddenly Jesus' eyes FLAME LIKE FIRE! The effect is staggering. Have you ever emerged from a darkened auditorium into broad daylight? Then you know how painful the light can be. That's the effect the brightness of Jesus' eyes will have on the beast . . .

 " . . . whom the Lord Jesus will destroy with the breath of his mouth (with the effect of a mighty sword), and annihilate by the radiance of His Coming" (2 Thess. 2:8 NEB).

Two thousand years ago on the Damascus road, the apostle Paul was struck blind by a flash of light from

206

heaven, causing him to fall to the ground (Acts 9:3-9). Now the beast and his army fall back, blinded by the Lord's radiance.

The beast is blinded and clothes are ripped from his body, as he is consumed by the radiance of the Lord's coming!

● The 7th bowl is poured out (Rev. 16:17-21). The earth heaves, convulsing under the force of incredible earthquakes. The continental plates move back together. Mountain ranges gyrate like disco dancers. The oceans disappear. Men run for cover as the ground ripples and rolls under their feet. The landscape is sprayed with 100-pound hailstones. Cities crumble under meteoric showers.

Frail humans, caught in earth's convulsions, die like flies. The carnage in the valley of Megiddo is indescribable, but John tries to relate it anyway:

" . . . an angel standing in the sun . . . cried out with a loud voice, saying to all the birds which fly in midheaven, 'Come, assemble for the great supper of God; in order that you may eat the flesh of kings and the flesh of commanders and the flesh of mighty men . . . ' " (Rev. 19:17,18 NAS).

What a banquet for the birds! Blood flows out of the winepress of God's wrath "up to the horses bridles, for a distance of 200 miles!" (Rev. 14:20). How graphic! John translates God's anger into human blood. It all happens so fast. The battle of Armageddon is over almost before it starts. The Lord SPOKE . . . and it was done!

THE UNHOLY TRINITY UNDONE

"The beast was taken prisoner, and so was the false prophet who had worked miracles in its presence and deluded those that had received the MARK OF THE BEAST and worshipped its image. The two of them were thrown alive into the lake of fire with its sulphurous flames" (Rev. 19:20 NEB).

Observe how the beast and the false prophet are caught in God's wrath. The dragon's turn is reserved for later. God has other plans for him:

"Then I saw an angel coming down from heaven with the key of the abyss and a great chain in his hands. He seized the dragon, that serpent of old, the devil or Satan, and chained him up for a thousand years; he threw him into the abyss, shutting and sealing it over him, so that he might seduce the nations no more till the thousand years were over . . . " (Rev. 20:1-3 NEB).

So, for the next thousand years the devil is going to be out of action. But the Lord isn't through with him. He still has a vital role to play in vindicating God's judgment of men.

The wrath of God continues.

JERUSALEM IS DESTROYED
BEFORE JESUS DESCENDS

Cities are reduced to rubble as God continues to shake and reshape this planet into a paradise for His Son. **Jerusalem, the capitol of the beast, is split into three parts as God pays her back "double according to her works . . . "** (Rev. 16:19;18:6). She has been found guilty of the blood of the prophets and saints slain throughout the world (Rev. 18:24). The 18th chapter of Revelation is a dirge, a eulogy over the demise of this great city, the beast's capitol.

When the earthquakes cease and the planet makes its last quiver, **the Lord, accompanied by ALL HIS SAINTS, descends to Mt. Olivet.** That sacred spot has itself undergone **DRAMATIC CHANGE.** The mountain is split right through the middle, creating a valley which runs east and west, through which water flows in both directions (Zech. 14:4,8).

WATER. With contamination of the seas and rivers resulting from the plagues, the Lord will have opened new sources of water. Even as I write, the World Health Organization estimates as much as 80% of the world's cases of disease is traceable to unclean water. Man's greed and shortsightedness has made a mess of the world. He has created problems he can't undo. When the Lord touches down, we can expect to find an entirely new system for watering the earth.

WHO WILL WELCOME THE LORD?

When Jesus and His "bride" touch down, who will be on hand to greet them? Will crowds of survivors swarm to welcome them? Say, did I mention there would be survivors? Indeed there will. It is not God's intention to wipe out all of mankind with the plagues. Besides the 144,000 sealed Jews, there will be survivors from the nations.

Ah, but will the crowds be excited about His return? Will they give Him a ticker tape parade, wildly cele-brating His victory? Will there be dancing and shouting in the streets, making THIS PAROUSIA similar to the ones made by World War II heroes in New York? Hardly. Don't forget, those on earth have beheld the Lord in the sky for some days. Even when they could see Him, they didn't want Him. Though it was absolutely clear WHO HE WAS, they refused to repent (Rev. 16:11). So when Jesus assumes control of the world, to most of the sur-vivors it will be little more than a change of dictators.

JUDGMENT OF THE NATIONS

Once He is on earth, the Lord will immediately set up His headquarters in Jerusalem. Then He will summon the rulers of the surviving nations. They too, will be coming for judgment, but not for themselves as individuals. The Lord is going to judge the nations. Why? They have to be assigned places in the kingdom too.

Did you know there will be RANKS among the nations operating in the Millennium? Indeed. Some will be favored and some will be penalized. And what will be the basis on which the Lord will judge them? Ah — on the basis of their ATTITUDE and TREATMENT of the Jew. Even though God punishes His nation, He isn't happy to have other nations take it upon themselves to abuse them. So countries like Spain, Germany and Italy, where Jews have been mercilessly persecuted, can expect to pay for it in the kingdom.

On the basis of their attitude toward the Jew, various nations will be assigned their places in the kingdom (Matt. 25:31-46). Those that have been kind to the Jew will enjoy favored status. Those who have abused him and despised him, will be held accountable.

NOT ALL FUN AND GAMES

The kingdoms of this world become "the kingdoms of our Lord, and of His Christ" **only because they are SUBDUED,** not because the people welcome Him with joy (Rev. 11:15). Consequently it is going to be necessary for Jesus to "rule all the nations with a rod of iron" (Rev. 12:5). That casts a strange pall over the millennium. There appears to be more to the millennium story than most have been led to expect. It also gives us a clue as to what many of us will be doing. Yes, we're going to reign with Jesus, serving probably AS HIS "ROD OF IRON" (Rev. 2:26,27).

Shortly after touchdown, you and I will assume our offices in the Lord's government. We will have received our PERMANENT RANKS. Every administration needs a chain of command to function properly, and Jesus' administration will be no exception. According to our rank, we will take up jobs that will make the world run on a "ROD OF IRON" basis.

211

● What will life be like in the millennium? What will the planet look like? Will the kingdom age really be "heaven on earth?" The guessing ends with the next chapter.

Chapter Ten

The Millennium— "Thy Kingdom Come"

"I SHALL RETURN!"

Remember those famous words of General Douglas MacArthur, when he was forced to retreat from the Philippines, May 6, 1942 during World War II? By that did he mean he was going to conduct commando raids to rescue those left behind? No way. He saw himself returning with power and military might to put down all resistance and dramatically retake the islands.

And that's exactly what he did. It took some time (over 2 years), but the day came when he waded ashore from a landing craft with plenty of power and might behind him and retook all the islands lost to the Japanese. The whole world knew about it, too.

ANOTHER GENERAL — ANOTHER DAY

Nearly 2,000 years ago, our general, the Lord Jesus, bade farewell to His followers on Mt. Olivet. He solemnly promised . . . **"I WILL COME AGAIN, AND RECEIVE YOU UNTO MYSELF!"** (John 14:3). That promise has to be more trustworthy than one made by General MacArthur, as remarkable a soldier as he was.

When the Lord ascended, two angels advised His disciples to stop staring into the sky, and return to Jerusalem. **"This (same) Jesus,"** they affirmed, **"will come in just the same way as you have watched Him go into heaven"** (Acts 1:11).

In our last chapter we saw this is exactly what the Lord will do. He will return in power and glory to reclaim the world, seizing it from Satan and his forces. Without doubt, His return will be a military campaign in which He will retake the world by the **power of His might.** The entire world will know about it, for "every eye shall see Him!" (Rev. 1:7).

TOUCHDOWN OLIVET — CIR. 2000 A.D.

 "Thy kingdom come. Thy will be done on earth, as it is in heaven" (Matt. 6:10 KJV).

How many times have you repeated that prayer? Quite a few, right? The day the Lord Jesus and His army (made up of believers) descend to Mt. Olivet, that prayer will be answered. You may not have realized what you were asking, but through your prayers the world will receive its greatest blessing since the garden of Eden. The coming of the Lord brings the kingdom of heaven to earth.

THE MILLENNIUM IS THE KINGDOM

Today we don't speak much of the KINGDOM. We're more likely to use the term, "millennium." Somehow we've substituted two latin words, *mille* (1000) and *annum* (year) for the biblical word, "kingdom." But that shouldn't keep us from recognizing the millennium for what it really is — the KINGDOM OF CHRIST. He will arrive as the King of the world, a position which makes Him the "King of Kings."

Consider also that the kingdom is Jesus' INHERI- TANCE. The Lord is returning as the SON OF DAVID, **not as the eternal God** (Luke 1:32). Yes, Jesus is God, but He is **not** coming to earth **as God**. He is coming AS A MAN. Even now, He is "the man Christ Jesus" (1 Tim. 2:5). That is the way He plans to return. Why? It is the only way He can INHERIT the kingdom. It is also the only way we can be "JOINT-heirs with Christ" (Rom. 8:17). He has to be an heir to inherit . . . and so do we.

> MAN. We evangelicals are so defensive about the deity of Christ, we scarcely think of Him as a MAN. **We know He is GOD,** but somehow we think it tarnishes His greatness to refer to Him as a MAN. So we skip over that exciting truth. This is why His exaltation is so fabulous — HE EARNED IT— AS A MAN! If He earned it as God, honestly, who'd be impressed? He came into this world as a Man. He died as a Man. It was a Man Who was raised in the **power** of the Father (Rom. 1:4). And it is a Man Who is returning in the **glory** of His Father (Matt. 16:27). It is a Man Who is getting "married" on that day. And it is a Man Who is going to sit **on the throne of His father David** (Luke 1:32). All the glory, honor and joy the Lord receives in that day **will be AS A MAN.**

Further, the Lord Jesus is returning as the SECOND ADAM. The first Adam was placed in the garden of Eden to RULE OVER IT, but he **failed** and surrendered the world to Satan. The SECOND (last) ADAM, the Lord Jesus, obeyed God completely, EARNING the right AS A MAN to rule over a world redeemed from Satan — a

215

garden paradise **with the curse of sin removed. That is what the** KINGDOM **(millennium) is all about — the personal reign of the Lord Jesus over a redeemed world** (Rom. 5:17, 1 Cor. 15:45,47).

Therefore with the arrival of the Lord at Olivet, the KINGDOM OF HEAVEN comes to earth.

SOME BIG CHANGES AHEAD

We noted previously that one of God's purposes for the tribulation was to get things POLITICALLY READY for Jesus. The destruction of the beast and his armies will end Satan's control of the world. The earthly systems will be dissolved. Then — with cataclysmic upheavals (resulting from the seven bowls of God's wrath) the physical earth is reshaped. A dust cloud may linger. It's hard to flatten mountains and shove continents together without stirring up a little dust.

Cities will have to be rebuilt, including Jerusalem. As the seat of the beast (political Babylon), the city of David was the special target of God's fury. With most of the land levelled, we can be sure a new temple will be constructed from which Jesus will reign. A new city of Jerusalem will rise from the ruins of the old one. How it will all be accomplished, I don't know. In any event, there will be a massive rebuilding program with things quite different from before.

DIFFERENT THAN BEFORE

When Jesus returns, little will be as it was:

" . . . the creation itself will be liberated from its bondage to decay and brought into the glorious freedom of the children of God" (Rom. 8:21 NIV).

216

The world will be transformed into a GIANT GARDEN. It will be EDEN all over again, but on a WORLD-WIDE BASIS. Those surviving the tribulation to enter the paradise of Christ's kingdom will scarcely believe what they see, the contrast will be so great. Those born into it, of course, will know nothing else. Right now, our minds can't possibly conceive how glorious it will be. Many philosophers and psychologists have argued that man, given a perfect environment, would himself blossom into perfection. Well, we'll see. That theory will be tested during the millennium.

The weather will be different.

No more storms, no floods. If some expositors are correct, there'll be no more rains, snow or wind. The atmosphere will be restored and the earth will be watered BY A MIST as it was until the time of Noah (Gen. 2:5,6; 7:11,12). While there could be a lovely network of seas and gently flowing rivers, the oceans will be gone. The bulk of their water being shifted from earth back into the atmosphere to form a canopy filtering out the dangerous cosmic rays and insuring uniform heat for the entire world. The earth will become a giant greenhouse with constant temperature all year round.

The soil will produce differently too.

Weeds will be a thing of the past. The earth will yield crops in such abundance, the population will have more than enough to eat. There'll be no poverty of any kind, no welfare programs. With the curse removed, man will no longer have to survive by the sweat of his face (Gen. 3:17-19). The abundance of food will generate such prosperity, it will be as the prophet Micah said, "and each man shall dwell under his own vine, and under his own fig-tree, undisturbed . . . " (Mic. 4:4 NEB).

217

The animal kingdom will be changed also.

"Then the wolf shall live with the sheep,
and the leopard lie down with the kid;
the calf and the young lion shall grow up together,
and a little child shall lead them;
the cow and the bear shall be friends,
and their young shall lie down together.
The lion shall eat straw like cattle;
the infant shall play over the hole of the cobra,
and the young child dance over the viper's nest.
They shall not hurt or destroy in all my holy
    mountain . . ."
(Isa. 11:6-9) NEB).

That famous passage from Isaiah indicates the animal kingdom will be as it was before the fall. There was no "bug-eat-bug" program in the garden of Eden. That came with the fall. There was no predatory instinct, for they were all vegetarian, dwelling peacefully with each other and the first couple. When artists seek to picture the millennium, they generally reproduce the scene described by Isaiah.

Can you picture the tranquility of the forest and creatures living in harmony with each other, with no fear of being abused or hurt by man? Adam (the original "Dr. Doolittle"), enjoyed some kind of COMMUNICATION with the animals. Whether this will be so for everyone in the kingdom isn't clear. Likely you and I will be able to "talk with the animals," since we'll be functioning at a different level. In any event, it is going to be remarkable living in an era when neither men nor animals prey on one another. With the PREDATORY INSTINCT (due to the curse) removed, can you imagine what it will be like in those households where the people really love pets?

Socially it will be ideal.

Throughout the ages men have dreamed of an era of peace. Even Hitler had such a dream. With the return of Jesus, that longing will be realized. There'll be no wars of any kind, no crime, for as Micah also said . . .

"They shall beat their swords into mattocks
   and their spears into pruning-knives;
nation shall not lift sword against nation
   nor ever again be trained for war"
(Mic. 4:3 NEB).

With Satan bound, those surviving the wrath of God will notice something different about themselves. Much of the evil that formerly lurked in their minds and led them to exploit others will be gone. **They'll still have the SAME HUMAN NATURES, fully equipped with original sin.** But those natures will be more manageable with Satan out of the picture.

The kingdom will see a big difference in human behavior. A great many businesses that exist today (because of satanic pressure), will no longer be around. Gone will be the liquor stores, asylums, munition plants, distilleries, psychiatrist's offices — why there won't even be any auto repair shops. When there are no RIP-OFFS, it will be obvious to all of us the big part SATAN PLAYED in triggering sin in people's lives.

The medical profession will be in deep trouble.

So will the pharmaceutical laboratories. With no more sickness or disease, they won't be needed any longer. If accidents are possible (which I'm inclined to doubt) the body will heal itself in a hurry. Doctors won't have to assist in the birth of babies, for childbirth will be easy and natural. With the **curse removed,** there'll be no pain whatever (Gen. 3:16). Wow! Can you imagine how the population will explode when people can have as many babies as they want — and be able to afford them!

NO DOCTORS. Are you aware the greatest killer today is STRESS? Those practicing holistic medicine (treating the whole man), cite stress as the number one killer. With Satan bound, the STRESS THAT KILLS will no longer plague men. This means there'll no longer be worry, fear and anxiety, stresses which utterly devastate mankind today. Heart attacks will be unknown. No one will catch cold, let alone suffer cancer. There'll be no arthritis, no cripples. Senility and insanity will disappear . . . and I doubt if there'll be any funerals. This will be a deathless kingdom, in which healing will be automatic. It will flow from the atonement, even as salvation now flows from Calvary for those who put their trust in Jesus.

Right now doctors and researchers are earnestly looking for ways to prolong human life. They might as well forget it. Once the kingdom arrives, **longevity will be the automatic by-product of removing the curse.** There was NO DEATH, you see, before the fall of man. Nothing died. Consequently man's life span will again be as it was in Eden.

Politically the world will be different.

With the Lord Jesus in charge, the second part of "The Lord's Prayer" . . . "THY WILL BE DONE ON EARTH, AS IT IS IN HEAVEN" . . . will also be fulfilled. As a **righteous king,** He will insist on righteousness throughout His kingdom. As long as the devil is allowed to reign as the "god of this world," EVIL remains the character of life on earth (2 Cor. 4:4). But with Jesus in command, God will INSIST that righteousness be the character of the kingdom. All operations throughout the world will be strictly righteous in conduct (Heb. 1:8,9).

The kings of the earth, reigning by permission of the Lord, will be obliged to EXECUTE His command for righteousness and peace. Nothing else will be tolerated. No one will be exploited by government or big corporations. There'll be no armies, no weapons, no abuses of any kind. It's hard for us to picture a sinless society, with every man and woman and child safe from all harm, while the earth explodes with its bounty. The old world, with its evil struggle for survival, will seem like a bad dream.

BAD DREAM. Bear in mind there WILL BE SURVIVORS of the great tribulation. The awesome earthquakes will not destroy all human life. We've already noted how Jesus is going to judge the nations (Matt. 25:31,32). And then we have the 144,000 Jews who are sealed to survive (Rev. 7:4). In all, there could be as many as one million survivors (not counting the saints, of course) who could bring into the kingdom the MEMORY of life on earth BEFORE SATAN WAS BOUND. Even though the earth is repopulated with MANY BILLIONS, stories of the "bad old days" will be passed on to succeeding generations. The tales of how people once did evil and the exploits of the wicked will be kept alive and handed down from father to son. Satan won't be on hand to perpetuate the narrative, but sinful human nature will see that it lives on.

THE PEOPLE OF THE KINGDOM

Three groups of people will be in the millennium, participating in Christ's kingdom:

1. The unsaved Gentiles who will multiply and rebuild the nations.

2. Unsaved Jews, who will rebuild Israel and enjoy favored nation status as they inherit the promises made to Abraham.

3. The believers of ALL AGES who return with Jesus as His "bride."

THREE GROUPS OF PEOPLE IN THE MILLENNIUM

❶	**❷**	**❸**
SURVIVING GENTILES (UNSAVED NATIONS)	144,000 JEWS (UNSAVED NATIONAL ISRAEL)	CHRISTIANS "BRIDE" OF CHRIST (SAVED FROM ALL AGES)
Those who DID NOT partake in First Resurrection	Those who DID NOT partake in First Resurrection	Those who DID partake in First Resurrection
RESTORED bodies	RESTORED bodies	GLORIFIED bodies
servants of "bride" of Christ and Israel	Enjoy favored nation status, inherit promises made to Abraham	Reign with Christ over Jews and Gentiles (Rev. 5:10, 20:6)

Now for a closer look at these three different groups.

 THE UNSAVED GENTILES

Though the forces arrayed against the Lord at Armageddon are obliterated, it is not a global slaughter. It is NOT God's intention to exterminate the Gentiles. Remnants of the nations must survive to enter the kingdom. True, the world's population will be decimated by the seven last plagues (God's wrath), but survivors will be needed to fulfill God's plan for the kingdom.

223

Will the unsaved Gentiles have glorified bodies too?

That's a fascinating question. The answer is NO. However, the bodies of the surviving Gentiles will suddenly STOP DYING! There'll no longer be ANY DEATH in them. Any damage they might have suffered in the past will be corrected by the creation of new cells, according to the instructions in the DNA molecule (genetic structure). God originally designed man to be perfect, and those same instructions reside within the DNA. **With the curse gone,** these bodies will restore themselves quickly.

Babies conceived and born into the kingdom will enter the world in perfect condition. The program for human bodies (unsaved) in the kingdom will be as it was BEFORE THE FALL. There will be no miscarriages, no imperfections, no retardation.

> **STOP DYING.** Try to picture, if you can, the perfection of the bodies of the unsaved Gentiles. The earth will yield only nutritious foods. With Satan bound, the deadly emotions of worry, fear, hate and jealousy will be a thing of the past. With the WATER MANTLE replaced in the atmosphere, as it was before the flood, mankind will be protected from the cosmic radiation that has definitely shortened human life since the deluge. They are simply human bodies as they existed before the fall and once again capable of living indefinitely. They are NOT a special creation, **they are NOT glorified bodies.** They are simply human bodies with the curse removed. Our bodies, on the other hand, are "like unto His glorious body" (Phil. 3:21).

Are the NATURES of the unsaved changed in any way?

Again, the answer is NO. There is no change in them whatsoever. Since these people are UNSAVED, their natures remain unchanged. This is not only true of those who survive to enter the millennium, but also those

224

BORN into it. The kingdom will be populated with people possessing the SAME NATURE man has had since ADAM. Theologians refer to it as "the adamic nature." The reason is: **these people have no way to acquire a new nature.**

So while the **human** body will be different, in that it doesn't die; and man's surroundings will be glorious with all satanic pressure removed; **nothing about his NATURE will be different in any way.** Those who survive the tribulation will BRING their fallen natures into the kingdom and they will PASS THEM ON to their offspring.

• With the physical creation so changed, one might expect man's nature to be changed as well. But that's not the case. I can almost hear someone protesting . . .

"Hey, that's not fair! If God really means to place the millennium people in the SAME SITUATION as Adam, He ought to give them the same sinless nature Adam had before he fell!"

If the Lord gave a sinless nature to the millennium people, it wouldn't be fair, all right. Not fair TO US!

NOT FAIR. When you and I are saved, we have to choose Jesus by **faith.** That's what gives us our righteousness and the divine nature. When we come to Christ, we have nothing to go on but God's Word and the witness of His Spirit. We have to put our **faith** in Jesus even though we have a fallen nature. And that same opportunity was open to all men BEFORE THE RAPTURE. For Him to alter the natures of the tribulation survivors AUTOMATICALLY, would definitely be unfair TO US! To give such a nature to unsaved survivors would give them an advantage over us and make God guilty of partiality. No, He does NOT CHANGE their natures. He merely changes the **setting,** the outward circumstances.

225

Faith will not be necessary in the millennium, for God's program shifts from FAITH TO SIGHT. Even so, millennium man will still be given a choice. At the end of the 1,000 year period, the devil will be loosed, providing the citizens of the world an opportunity to choose between God and Satan. We'll see what they do with that choice a bit later.

What will the nations do?

Business as usual? Hardly. There won't be any more crooked dealings. Nations will develop their resources for the **good** of mankind. Selfishness will be outlawed. Commerce will be furious. Technology will mushroom. Discoveries will abound. Energy will be limitless. The various countries, under the leadership of Israel and her Messiah, will work together to create a **superworld.**

> **SUPERWORLD.** Can you imagine what this world would be like if all the scientific research presently going into weapons of war were to be directed to the **blessing** of mankind! We'd have astonishing breakthroughs in every field. That's the way it will be in the kingdom. All human effort will be harnessed to produce giant leaps in communication, transportation, energy and agriculture. Researchers in behavorial science tell us man presently uses less than 7% of the design capacity of his brain. That has to be due to the fall. Can you imagine the **thinking power** of the MILLENNIUM MIND once that curse is lifted? It will be dozens of times greater! The breakthroughs will defy anything we can conceive. Millennium engineers will be able to harness the powers of the universe, providing inexhaustible energy for running the superworld issuing from their minds.

Sounds heavenly, doesn't it? Imagine how glorious this planet will be with the Lord Jesus directing boundless vitality into all kinds of human endeavor? After all, man IS the image of **The Creator** and should be able to create quite a world for himself. But it really isn't going to be all "sweetness and light." Why not? Even though the citizens of the kingdom have restored bodies, their **unsaved souls** will soon resent the righteous reign of Jesus, which resentment He will control with a "ROD OF IRON" (Rev. 2:27; 12:5; 19:15).

② THE UNSAVED JEWS

We're obliged to refer to ALL JEWS as unsaved, for if they were saved, they would no longer be a part of the Jewish nation. They'd be in the body of Christ. **These Jews will have the SAME NATURES AND BODIES as unsaved Gentiles.** The **nation of Israel** will be made up of those Jews who survive the tribulation (at least 144,000) and acknowledge Jesus as their crucified Messiah.

> **JEWS.** When Scripture speaks of the Jewish nation as being "born in a day," it is referring to the moment when the Jewish people behold Jesus when He appears and recognize Him as their rejected Messiah (Isa. 66:8). The Word says, "They shall look on Him Whom they pierced" (John 19:37). Observe how this OCCURS BY SIGHT, not by faith. The Jews will perceive this is the SAME JESUS they spurned centuries before and their hearts will be broken. This will bring NATIONAL REPENTANCE. The ENTIRE nation will acknowledge its terrible sin and God will forgive **that sin.** Israel will immediately be RESTORED TO FAVOR as God's personal nation on earth. **Please note this is NATIONAL SALVATION, not personal or individual salvation.** The citizens of this nation are not "sons of God," in the sense we are, for the privilege of exercising faith in Christ ends with His appearance. Salvation is never by sight, but always by faith. Therefore this is NOT **spiritual** salvation the Jews enjoy.

Can you see that when an entire nation is saved, it cannot mean salvation in the personal and individual sense? Jesus' invitation, "whosoever will may come," makes salvation a PERSONAL matter. The apostle Paul also insists spiritual salvation is personal (Rom. 1:16). So when he speaks of Israel's salvation . . . "And so shall all Israel be saved," that has to be NATIONAL salvation (Rom. 11:26). Therefore we are to understand that while Israel does become the favored nation of the kingdom, that nation is made up of UNSAVED JEWS (Rom. 9-11; Isaiah 51:11, 60-62, 66:7-14a; Ezekiel 20:39-44, 37:21-28, 39:22-29).

NATIONAL SALVATION

Most people are of the opinion that a day is coming when every single Jew who looks on Jesus will receive spiritual salvation. It's true they will be "saved" — **but not spiritually.** They are RESTORED PHYSICALLY according to God's promise to Abraham. National salvation is NOT spiritual salvation. Israel's redemption as a nation is **physical** only.

Jesus will reign on the earth as KING OF THE JEWS. He will occupy the throne as the Son of David (Luke 1:32). The Jewish nation will be catapulted to wealth and power as Jesus rules from Jerusalem. Why? God has to keep the promises He made Abraham. He pledged Himself to preserve Abraham's earthly descendants and make them the rulers of the world under their Messiah-king. **Therefore the favored nation status of the Jews is not due to their worthiness as a people, but God's faithfulness to keep His Word.** In this He demonstrates His honesty and the greatness of His mercy (Gal. 3:16; Gen. 22:16-18; Psa. 2:8).

❸ THE BELIEVERS (THE "BRIDE" OF CHRIST)

Naturally this category interests us the most. We're all curious as to what believers will be like and what we'll be doing in the kingdom. I'm going to discuss our bodies first. It's so fascinating. Granted, some of what I say will be speculative. I admit that. But all of it will be based on the Word. The Holy Spirit will help us, so be ready to evaluate what you read on the basis of His witness.

We'll be like Jesus in our physical appearance.

Surely no one will fault that statement, inasmuch as John says " . . . but we know that, when He shall appear, we shall be like Him; for we shall SEE HIM AS HE IS" (1 John 3:2). Jesus will be the SAME PERSON Who ascended from Olivet, though His body will be different. **It will be a GLORIFIED BODY. Apart from His body, though, He will be AS HE WAS WHEN HE WALKED WITH HIS DISCIPLES.** You and I will be the SAME PEOPLE, too, but with our **new natures,** for we are "partakers of the divine nature" (2 Pet. 1:4). **Going into the kingdom will NOT CHANGE anyone with respect to his person.** Beyond that, though, everything changes.

• To get an idea what our millennial bodies will be like, we need to know what Jesus' body will be like when He returns. Our best clue is found in the TRANS-FIGURATION. You recall the story, don't you? How Jesus invited James, Peter and John to accompany Him to the top of Mt. Hermon (?). There He was transfigured before their eyes (Matt. 17:1-5). His countenance became dazzling, seemingly as bright as the sun. Even His clothing was affected by it, so that it too was "white as light."

John, who was with Jesus on that mountain, describes the GLORIFIED CHRIST in the first chapter of The Revelation. There again, Jesus' face is AS THE SUN, shining in its strength. That is very different from the way Jesus looked when He appeared to the two men on the road to Emmaus or to His disciples that cloudy morning on the beach (Luke 24:13-21; John 21:4). Had He appeared in glorified form, He would have lit up the shoreline.

TRANSFIGURED. Some have thought that after Jesus was crucified, He arose in His glorified body, merely because He appeared in the midst of His disciples when they were gathered behind locked doors. It was as though He had walked through the walls (John 20:19). But those holding this notion forget He also WALKED ON WATER before He was resurrected. Is one feat more remarkable than the other? The truth is, Jesus was NOT RAISED in a glorified body, but in the VERY SAME body in which He died. He made it clear He was going to rise in the same body, insisting this would be the ONE GREAT SIGN He would give that generation (Matt. 12:39,40; John 2:19-22). If Jesus rose in any body other than the one in which He died, that one sign would not have been fulfilled. We must therefore assume THE TRANSFIGURATION affords the best indication of the body Jesus will be wearing upon His return to earth.

". . . and in their presence He was transfigured; His face shone like the sun, and His clothes became white as the light" (Matt. 17:2 NEB).

Our bodies, Paul asserts, will be changed and "fashioned like unto His glorious body" (Phil. 3:21). Concerning our glorified bodies, he has much to say in the RESURRECTION CHAPTER (1 Cor. 15:42-44):

> "It is sown a NATURAL body;
>   it is raised a SPIRITUAL body.
> It is sown in corruption;
>   it is raised in incorruption.
> It is sown in dishonor,
>   it is raised in glory.
> It is sown in weakness,
>   it is raised in power."

That tells us much. The apostle says the human body we presently wear is a *PSUCHIKOS* BODY. It is an earth-suit, one that imprisons the spirit. We're stuck with it. We have to feed it and put it to bed. It can't get around very fast. If it gets sick, we're out of action. To place the IMAGE OF GOD in a two-legged vehicle such as that, is clearly a terrible compression. It is indeed a prison. Man, a spirit-being, is capable of far more than his *psuchikos* body will permit.

The glorified body, on the other hand, Paul calls a *PNEUMATIKOS* BODY (spiritual body). It is totally different from the earthly body, though the form is very similar. It has two arms and legs, and the facial expressions may resemble the former. But there the similarity ends. **This body, rather than being a PRISON for the man inside, will be the slave of his spirit.** It will permit him to do many remarkable things, such as traveling at the speed of thought.

But we should not confuse this GLORIFIED BODY with the **restored bodies** of the unsaved millennium man. The bodies of the unsaved citizens of the kingdom will be subject to the laws of space and time. Ours, since they are of another class, will not. Functioning at an altogether different level, we will not be limited to time and space. Thus we're in a position to note the basic difference between the two:

IN A SPIRITUAL BODY, THE FLESH IS
SUBJECT TO THE PERSON'S SPIRIT,

IN A NATURAL BODY, THE PERSON'S
SPIRIT IS SUBJECT TO THE FLESH.

SUBJECT. You and I are LIMITED to the capacities of these bodies we now wear as "earth-suits." Even though we are God's image, our thinking is limited to the capacity of the brain. We don't know anything unless the knowledge is placed in the brain. We're restricted to time and space, totally isolated from the spirit-realm (our natural habitat). We're slaves to the demands of the body with regard to sleep, food and the instincts. But once we're in our GLORIFIED BODIES, the situation will be REVERSED. **In that day, our bodies will be subject to US.** Our travel, for example, will be different. We'll need only to say . . . "I AM IN BRAZIL" . . . and we're there that instant. While the glorified body can eat and drink, it will not need food for fuel or sustenance. It will live off the limitless energy of the spirit. It is my opinion, we'll be able to function at the MIND-LEVEL, far beyond anything a brain can perform. Our new bodies will perfectly obey the desires of our spirit.

I feel comfortable with what I've just said. If anything, I've probably **understated** what we'll be like. The point to remember is:

LIKE GOD, WE ARE SPIRIT-BEINGS AND IN THAT DAY WE'LL BE WEARING SPIRITUAL BODIES. YOU KNOW WHAT YOUR SPIRIT CAN CONCEIVE. IMAGINE A BODY ABLE TO CARRY OUT THOSE CONCEPTIONS!

Can you see why the Lord would CHANGE our bodies at the rapture? Only a SPIRITUAL BODY would be able to join Him in the sky (1 Cor. 15:42; Col. 3:4). To operate beyond earthly laws (gravitation, oxygen, etc.) and be able to perform anything we command requires a spiritual body. Although able to function in the earthly environment, I'm sure we'll be able to put on these bodies . . . and put them off . . . on command. Even as a light bulb can put on and put off light.

Wow! Will we be different!

Ever walk through a Christian rest home, trying to imagine what those aged, worn out saints must have been like in their youth? It's tough to see them slumped in wheel chairs. And then to let your mind go to the moment when Jesus shouts from the sky! In a split-second those same people will be throbbing with ageless beauty, transformed into a state of perpetual youthfulness and vitality! How different we'll all be from what we were!

Ah, but we'll also be different from those who are NOT in Christ — the millennium people. In their HUMAN BODIES, they'll walk about on earth locked into space and time. Their appearance as citizens of the kingdom will be quite unlike ours, for the SONS OF GOD will display a glory too obvious to miss. We'll be set apart from the earth-bound citizens of the kingdom and easily recognizable. The glory of our appearance will undoubtedly be our kingdom uniform, our badge of authority. We're going to need those badges as we reign with Christ.

We'll be like Jesus in our natures.

When we make the transition from NATURAL BODIES TO SPIRITUAL BODIES, an amazing thing happens. (I'm thinking of those who die in the Lord). The OLD NATURE is discarded with the old body. You've read the apostle Paul's frequent references to the circumcision of the heart. He calls it the "circumcision made without hands," which means it is done by God (Rom. 2:29; Col. 2:11).

When we come to Christ, that old nature is circumcised off the soul, but continues to reside in the flesh. Then when physical death occurs (or we're changed), **it is discarded with the flesh.** Once we're with Jesus, **ALL THAT REMAINS IS THE NEW NATURE (Christ's own nature), and thus we are clothed in His righteousness** (Eph. 4:22,24; Col. 3:9,10). Having nothing but the new nature will make us very different from the other citizens of the millennial kingdom.

234

The glory that will radiate from us in those days will be due to the righteousness of the Lord in us (2 Cor. 5:21). True, we have that righteousness at this moment, but it is veiled in the flesh and mingled with the old nature. But once the flesh is gone — and the old nature with it — our SPIRITUAL MAKEUP will be just like the Lord's! That's what will make our bodies appear different. They'll be bodies that will reflect the glory of Christ's righteousness in us (Heb. 2:10).

What we'll be doing.

Here is further fascination.

Once in the kingdom, we will have already received our job assignments — in the air. That is, we'll know our tasks BEFORE we touch down with Him at Olivet, able to start work immediately. Some saints will be stationed at headquarters in Jerusalem. There will be a variety of positions from cabinet rank on down. Certainly there will be ambassadors to the Jews and other nations. The closer we are to Jesus, the higher the rank. Those who have been less faithful to Him in this life will have the routine jobs, those of lesser rank.

RANK. When it comes to the particular jobs you and I will have in the kingdom, our RANK will be the key factor. (Our rank, you recall, is determined at the judgment seat of Christ). All who reign with Jesus will be perfect, but we need to understand something about perfection — IT DOES NOT MEAN EQUALITY. To see the difference, consider light bulbs. We have 10 watt . . . 25 watt . . . 60 watt . . . 100 watt . . . and so on. Each is as perfect as the other, for all are manufactured with the same precision. But not all SHINE with the same intensity. Not all give off the same amount of light, therefore not all can do the same job. So it is with God's sons, all perfect, yet not all equal. While all believers will be perfect, they will vary in MATURITY. When we die (change) we carry into glory the accumulation of character development gained during our earthly probation, when we walked by faith. To the degree we MATURE in the likeness of Jesus, to that SAME DEGREE we determine what our rank will be.

To maintain a smooth running government, the Lord will need LEADERS in many agencies. Some, for example, will be in charge of accident prevention. If there is to be "NO HURT" anywhere in the kingdom, a lot of saints will be involved in that ministry. They have to be on the spot BEFORE an accident can occur. That's why they have to be able to move at the speed of thought. Think of the people who'll be involved in INVENTIONS . . . ANIMAL POPULATION . . . SPACE FLIGHTS . . . GLOBAL HEALTH AND PROSPERITY . . . as well as MAINTAINING ORDER. **By far, the most critical task of Christians will be working with the Lord to see that righteousness becomes the law of the land.** Frankly, I doubt if we CAN OVERSPECULATE concerning our assignments. Bear in mind though, we are qualifying for those jobs RIGHT NOW. I hope that truth seizes you as it does me!

● Did you know the millennium IS NOT our final destination? We're headed for the **eternity of heaven.** But we need schooling for that, schooling as future kings. Our life on earth with TWO NATURES was but **grade school.** There we were schooled in righteousness. But in the millennium we're in **high school.** There we learn to REIGN with Christ, working in a body that is SUBJECT TO THE SPIRIT (Rev. 5:10). This is one of the more exciting reasons for our being in the millennium. Yet even that is ONLY PART of our training in the SCHOOL OF KINGS.

When the millennium is over, we will go on to the **college of life that is lived in the spirit ONLY.** We'll be ready to reign over whatever God has for us in

236

eternity. What that will be, we can only guess. But since Jesus is there, it will be great (1 Cor. 2:9).

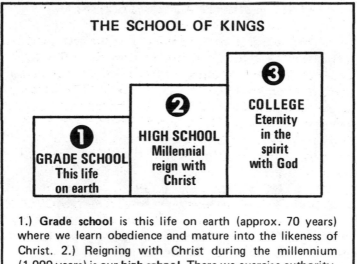

THE SCHOOL OF KINGS

❶ GRADE SCHOOL This life on earth

❷ HIGH SCHOOL Millennial reign with Christ

❸ COLLEGE Eternity in the spirit with God

1.) **Grade school** is this life on earth (approx. 70 years) where we learn obedience and mature into the likeness of Christ. 2.) Reigning with Christ during the millennium (1,000 years) is our **high school.** There we exercise authority, dealing with people at the mind level. 3.) Finally we graduate into eternity, **college level,** ready to rule angels (1 Cor. 6:3). There we'll handle omnipotence, omniscience and omnipresence — the tools of eternity. You'll want to do your best in God's SCHOOL OF KINGS.

● I haven't told you the whole story of what we'll be doing in the kingdom. Something very unusual develops in the millennium, something that will require a "ROD OF IRON" to handle it.

Don't you find it strange the Lord must USE FORCE to keep things orderly in a righteous kingdom? What does that tell us? Ah — those old natures are going to BE ACTIVE in the citizens of the kingdom. Even with Satan bound, we're going to find the "millennium man" doesn't like righteousness for a steady diet. More on this—next.

Chapter Eleven

Trouble In Paradise!

"Have you been to the Holy Land yet?"

That question is put to me so often, I almost feel guilty when I reply, "No, not yet." Trips to the Mideast are so commonplace, it's getting to be that any pastor who hasn't walked where Jesus walked feels shy on credentials. But it really doesn't matter all that much, for you and I will be there before long, anyway. We'll be seeing plenty of Jerusalem after we touch down there with Jesus.

JERUSALEM — CITY OF THE GREAT KING

When the kingdom is in full operation, Jerusalem will be **the** place to go. It will be the most glorious action center of the world. People will come from all over the globe to catch a glimpse of the King. The tour business will mushroom, for the world capitol will be filled with exciting things to see.

Let's fantasize for a moment. Imagine a WORLD MUSEUM at Jerusalem, filled with exciting relics and scenes of the past. On certain days the crowds will see ABRAHAM, ISAAC, JACOB, and MOSES, and hear their stories of what it was like when people had to live BY FAITH. The faith-life is going to sound adventurous, even romantic to those who know nothing but the tranquility of the kingdom. They'll drool over the daring escapades of the heroes of faith.

Imagine those visiting the great MENTAL MUSEUM (pictures projected from the patriarchs' minds), and having NOAH HIMSELF recall visually (using huge full color 3-dimensional holographic images) what it was like in the ark. I'm sure technology will be so advanced, they'll think they're in the animal stalls, even hearing and smelling what it was like. Ah — think then, how scary it will be to join DANIEL for a return trip to the lion's den! It won't be real, of course, just an EXPOSURE of Daniel's memory. One treat the children will love is walking with MOSES between those walls of water as they cross the RED SEA. Wow!

LEARNING THE WAYS OF THE LORD

In the kingdom, everyone from the lowest to the highest will be schooled in the ways of the Lord — whether he likes it or not. Children may also be graded on what they learn in the EDUCATION CENTERS.

"And it shall come to pass in the last days, that the mountain of the Lord's house shall be established in the top of the mountains, . . . and people shall flow unto it. And many nations shall come, and say, Come, and let us go up to the mountain of the Lord, and to the house of the God of Jacob; and He will teach us of His ways, and we will walk in His paths: for the Law shall go forth of Zion, and the

Word of the Lord from Jerusalem" (Isa. 2:2, 3; Mic. 4:1,2 KJV).

Life in the kingdom will be SATURATED with the teachings of the Lord, and people will be **compelled** to walk in His ways. So central will Christ be to the lives of the people that "there shall be upon the bells of the horses, HOLINESS UNTO THE LORD . . . yea, every pot in Jerusalem shall be holiness unto the LORD of hosts . . ." (Zech. 14:20,21). Of course that's but another way of saying that every area and aspect of a person's life will be harnessed to the WAYS of the Lord.

THE GREAT MILLENNIAL TEMPLE

If you visit Washington, DC, you can tour the WHITE HOUSE. Similarly, people will be able to pass through the **TEMPLE OF THE LORD** at Jerusalem. It will be the most glorious structure in the world. School children will likely be required to give written reports on the temple in connection with their assignments. The stream of visitors will be endless, for universal prosperity means everyone will be able to afford the trip. They'll come from every city and village throughout the world.

In fact the Lord will **expect** them to come at least once a year:

"And it shall come to pass, that every one that is left of all the nations which came against Jerusalem shall even go up FROM YEAR TO YEAR (whether they like it or not) to worship the King (outward and ceremonial), the Lord of hosts, and to keep the feast of tabernacles" (Zech. 14:16 KJV).

Inasmuch as the kingdom program is BY SIGHT and not by faith, the Lord will insist the citizens of His kingdom observe His memorials year after year. **This**

will be the principal means by which the WAYS OF THE LORD will be kept before them. As a communion service keeps the Lord's death before us, so will the ANNUAL FESTIVAL serve to remind the kingdom people "the earth is the Lord's" (Psa. 24:1).

FEAST OF TABERNACLES. In Old Testament times, the Jewish year was marked by three major festivals — Passover, Pentecost and the Feast of the Harvest (Tabernacles), held in the fall. The latter marked the completion of the fruit, wine and oil harvests. Beyond that, it pictured the day when the earth would yield its bounty under the personal reign of the Lord Jesus. During the millennium, this feast will continue to be observed as a memorial, akin to the way we celebrate the 4th of July. On that day we remember our independence from England — our freedom. But in the millennial Feast of Tabernacles, the whole world will celebrate the fact that the earth has been set free from the curse of sin. It is the removal of that curse that allows the ground to bear in abundance. Hence the feast to memorialize the great release.

WHY A TEMPLE?

Have you ever wondered WHY there will be a temple in the Kingdom? As you recall from Old Testament history, the purpose of a temple was to provide a means whereby the UNSEEN GOD could dwell in the midst of His people. The presence of God was certified by the Shekinah glory in the wilderness tabernacle (Ex. 40:34-38). The tabernacle was later replaced with a more permanent meeting place between man and his God, when David's son, Solomon, erected a temple at Jerusalem. Man, of course, could not meet God face to face. Inasmuch as he was a sinner, the glory of God would consume him. **So the temple was a "bridge," so to speak, between man and God.**

But here in the kingdom WE STILL FIND A TEMPLE. Glorious, to be sure, but nonetheless a temple.

Why? Ah, because of the sinful nature of the residents of the kingdom. These people have no righteousness. There is no way the GLORY OF GOD can dwell FULLY in their midst. **The only way God can be among them, is in the form of THE SON OF MAN.**

Now it's true that Jesus is returning "in the glory of His Father," but we've already noted how He is the SAME JESUS Who walked on earth before — AS A MAN. **Jesus continues to minister for men AS THEIR HIGH PRIEST, thereby bridging the gap between sinful men and a Holy God.** People coming to the temple are NOT COMING TO GOD ALMIGHTY, but to Jesus their HIGH PRIEST. **The sin-barrier still remains between the unsaved of the millennium and the God of heaven** (Heb. 5:1-10).

> **TEMPLE SACRIFICES.** Certain Scripture passages speak of animal sacrifices being offered in the future temple (Ezek. 40-46). And because of this, some have felt the sacrificial system would be reactivated in the millennium. To have animal sacrifices would require the DEATH OF THE ANIMALS. But in a sinless kingdom there is NO DEATH, not even of animals. Besides, since there is NO SIN, there is NO NEED FOR SIN OFFERINGS. The sacrifices were eaten by the priests. But in the kingdom, meat is not eaten. It would seem then, that those passages implying animal sacrifices in the millennium, actually refer to the FALSE MILLENNIUM which antichrist will seek to establish. To give authenticity to his plan, he will reinstitute the sacrificial rituals of the O.T. Undoubtedly there will be FEASTS in Jesus' kingdom, but it is difficult to conceive of animals being slain in a kingdom where there is "no hurt."

So what's the reason for the temple? It will stand as a testimony to the SIN-BARRIER between God and sinful man. True, sinful acts will be impossible under the "Rod of Iron," but the DESIRE to sin will still be there. That desire is going to create a problem, one that will last the entire 1,000 years.

THE CITIZENS OF THE KINGDOM

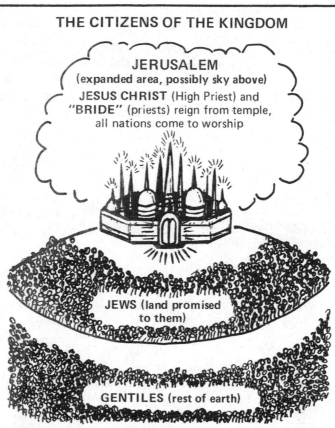

JERUSALEM
(expanded area, possibly sky above)
JESUS CHRIST (High Priest) and
"BRIDE" (priests) reign from temple,
all nations come to worship

JEWS (land promised
to them)

GENTILES (rest of earth)

The citizens of the kingdom, because of their sinful natures, will have no way to approach God. Therefore they need a HIGH PRIEST. **Jesus** is their High Priest. However, this High Priest RULES the world as a RIGHTEOUS KING. He loves righteousness and hates evil. He WILL NOT TOLER- ATE EVIL anywhere in His kingdom. Therefore He will IMPOSE righteousness on the populace. Christians, serving as priests under King Jesus, will assist Him in executing His righteous reign over the HEARTS and MINDS of men (Rev. 5:10). The Jews will serve as ministers to the Gen- tiles, instructing them as to how to get along in a godly kingdom, by explaining the ways of the Lord (Zech. 8:23; Isa. 11:10).

TROUBLE IN PARADISE?

Indeed. But what kind, you ask? Ah — unsaved man is not going to like a steady diet of righteousness. In the kingdom, you see, people will be FORCED to deal fairly and squarely — whether they like it or not. They will be required to walk in the ways of the Lord. At first it may seem like fun. After coming out of the great tribulation and being relieved of the struggle to survive, everyone will think . . . "Hey, this is great! Man, what a country club!"

That's what the kingdom will be like — until the novelty wears off. It won't be long before unsaved man grows weary of righteousness.

WEARY OF RIGHTEOUSNESS? Certainly. This is how sin got started in the first place. It began in heaven, you know. One fellow (Satan) got tired of all that holiness and having to do things God's way. So in the midst of a perfect environment, he elected to rebel against God and "do his own thing" (Ezek. 28:14,15; Isa. 14:12-15). That same spirit flared in the children of Israel. When they were in the wilderness, God provided for them supernaturally. There was plenty to eat and their clothes didn't wear out. But what happened? In time the novelty wore off. They became bored and began to dream of the good old days of "fish . . . cucumbers, and the melons, and the leeks, and the onions, and the garlic" of Egypt (Num. 11:5). They rebelled against God's wondrous provision. Why? Because it was in their hearts to do so. It will be the same in Christ's kingdom.

THE NATIVES ARE RESTLESS

Human nature is the same in any age — even in Christ's kingdom. Unsaved citizens will come to HATE His righteous ways. Even with Satan bound, it won't be long before men will yearn to do evil. The tribulation

244

survivors will be there. They're going to live the entire 1,000 year period. They'll constantly refer to the "bad old days" when a man could sin freely, when people weren't **forced** to walk in the ways of the Lord. And they're going to instill in their offspring the "glory" of those former days when a man could "do his own thing." They'll actually glamorize evil.

> **GLAMORIZE.** In spite of our technological advancements and devices for easier living, do we not tend to glamorize the past? Do we not immortalize the outlaws of frontier days. We look with nostalgia on steam locomotives and pot-bellied stoves. We try to recapture the past with dress, design and Disneyland. No parade is complete without its old cars, suspenders and handlebar moustaches. Well, that's the way the JEWS and the GENTILES will feel about sin in the millennium. They'll dream about it . . . long for it . . . but **they'll be prevented from doing it by the "ROD OF IRON."**

RULING WITH A "ROD OF IRON"

As promised earlier, I will explain what I think the "ROD OF IRON" is all about (Rev. 2:27;12:5;19:15).

Have you ever wondered WHY Jesus must rule in this fashion? You wouldn't think force would be necessary in a kingdom of righteousness and peace, where there is actually no need to exploit one's neighbor. We must keep before us the fact that ALL OF THE TRIBULATION SURVIVORS entered the kingdom with their **old human natures.** It's the only nature they have. Without the NEW BIRTH there is no way to acquire the new nature. The same will be true of all those born into the kingdom.

Consequently, the tendency to DO EVIL is still with them. Even with Satan bound, that tendency can lead to trouble. So by now, you can guess where I'm headed.

245

It seems the kingdom will have to be POLICED! Policed? Yes!

Kingdom Cops

The only use for a "rod of iron" is to ENFORCE the will of the Lord, to execute His righteous rule. We've already seen how everyone will be required to LEARN the ways of the Lord and WALK in those ways. Plenty of Scripture insists on that. Ah, but WHO will do the enforcing? Now we come to the fascination — no one can do this but Christians (kingdom cops) operating in the REALM OF THOUGHT and with the SPEED OF THOUGHT. It will take a lot of saints to make up the "rod of iron."

So — here's another reason why a SPIRITUAL BODY is necessary. To keep out evil, it will be necessary to check it WHERE IT STARTS — in the minds of the unsaved citizens. Consider this: at the first hint of evil anywhere in the kingdom . . . pphhhhhttttt . . . there's a cop! The moment an unsaved man BEGINS to entertain an evil thought, a Christian will suddenly appear alongside him to steer him away from the notion. Sin won't even be allowed to get started. O, will men hate that!

When you choke off evil before it develops in a person's mind, you are definitely controlling the situation with a ROD OF IRON. I'm sure the word "IRON" is used to represent UNBENDING ENFORCEMENT. James tells us that LUST is actually CONCEIVED IN THE MIND and then "it gives birth to sin" (James 1:15). Thus, sin will not even be allowed to get started.

As the 1,000 year reign rolls on, people are going to get **fed up with holiness.** They'll come to hate it, particularly when they find themselves checked at every turn. This will set them up as easy victims for Satan when he is finally released.

246

THE FINAL REBELLION AGAINST GOD

At the end of the Lord's 1,000 year reign on earth, Satan is "loosed (for) a little season" (Rev. 20:3). That rascal never gives up.

 "And when the thousand years are expired, Satan shall be loosed out of his prison, and shall go out to deceive the nations which are in the four quarters of the earth . . . to gather them together to battle: the number of whom is as the sand of the sea" (Rev. 20:7,8 KJV).

Immediately upon release, Satan goes out to deceive the millions (perhaps billions) born during the millennium. And it won't be difficult for him. **After people, equipped with sinful natures, have lived in a "NO SIN" kingdom for 1,000 years, Satan's words will seem like honey.** They will be drawn to him "like a moth to a flame." They will seize this last opportunity to escape the "rod of iron" and be free of its rule. The devil will deceive them into thinking **his rule** will be better than Jesus' righteous reign. The world will follow Satan *en masse,* so that their numbers will be as the "sand of the sea."

What will the devil do with all these people?

What are his plans for them?

SATAN'S LAST FLING

He will USE THEM in yet another revolt against the Lord. Leading them, as a general before his army, Satan and this horde will swoop down on the Lord and His saints headquartered at Jerusalem. See how relentless this fellow is? He still dreams of overpowering the Lord and seizing the throne:

"And they went up on the breadth of the earth, and compassed the camp of the saints about, and the beloved city: and fire came down from God out of heaven, and devoured them. And the devil that deceived them was cast into the lake of fire and brimstone, where the beast and the false prophet are, and shall be tormented day and night for ever and ever" (Rev. 20:9,10 KJV).

It's a futile move, of course. FIRE FROM HEAVEN consumes the entire population. That takes care of the devil. His fate is settled — forever.

Consequently, every tribulation survivor who entered the millennium as well as those born into it perish outside of Christ. It is clear there could not possibly be a FINAL JUDGMENT until all these people have made their choice between Jesus and Satan . . . **and died in their sins.** Even when they CAN SEE JESUS, they still prefer Satan.

THEY CLEARLY HAD A CHOICE

Do you catch what this is about? The Lord used the devil for one final test. He used him to show that **He was totally FAIR in using the FAITH-METHOD to select or screen out those who would be in the eternal family.**

After men have lived under the personal reign of Christ for 1,000 years, they are given a choice. Do they want God or Satan? God, you see, has ALREADY GLEANED from the world those of mankind who really love Him. And He insists it was fair. He further insists that those WHO REMAIN, DON'T WANT HIM! **The only way He can demonstrate that claim is to turn the devil loose again and give the ENTIRE WORLD a chance to follow him.** Then it would be absolutely clear whom they preferred.

248

A WORLD OF ADAMS

God insists all men are like Adam. He declares EVERY MAN a sinner, with each preferring to "do his own thing," rather than obey God (Isa. 53:6). To prove the correctness of His affirmation, God places a MULTITUDE OF MEN in another garden, one similar to Adam's. There these men are confronted with a choice much like Adam's. Besides providing an inheritance for Jesus and keeping God's Word to Abraham, the kingdom also proves the accuracy of God's claim that **all men are just like Adam.**

GOD HAS PROVED HIS POINT

What do you know . . . God was right!

As He announced earlier, the human heart is "desparately wicked" and hostile towards Him. Thus ends the earthly story. Out of all those souls, not a one, "no, not one" preferred righteousness over evil. All would rather be in Satan's kingdom than the Lord's (Rom. 3: 10-12; Jer. 17:9).

> **BILLIONS.** Does it bother you that God would bring billions of souls into the millennial kingdom and not have one of them saved? This is not unusual for God. During all the ages from Adam onward, He has had ENTIRE CIVILIZATIONS come and go without one word of the gospel reaching them. Multitudes have perished without the Word of God. Unfair, you say? No. God, who knows the human heart, determines WHO is born into WHAT FAMILY and into WHAT COUNTRY and in WHAT MOMENT OF TIME. He knows **in advance** those who will reject Him. Their names are recorded from BEFORE the foundation of the world (Rev. 17:8). By His omniscience, He can collect entire nations of unbelievers . . . and He has! That He would use more billions in the millennium to prove Himself fair and just, is consistent with His track record. Should you

find this idea baffling, the author's book, **DOES GOD CONDEMN THOSE WHO NEVER HEAR THE GOSPEL?**, will put you at ease about it.

WAIT A MINUTE DR. LOVETT . . .

"Dr. Lovett, are you saying NO ONE IS SAVED during the millennium?"

I know that's a startling idea, perhaps staggering — particularly since we can look back and see how people have been saved out of the **various dispensations of the past.** Ah, but they were all saved BY FAITH. Please remember this is only my opinion. In spite of the universal knowledge of the Lord during the millennium, **I am convinced NOT ONE SOUL will be salvaged and brought into the eternal family.** Why would I hold such a daring opinion? The following specifics convince me:

1.) First, I am persuaded the Lord will NOT RETURN until the last person to be included in the "body of Christ" is saved. Once that body is complete (and I'm sure it is a specific number), the church age will end and there'll be no further additions to the family of God. The door is "shut" (Matt. 25:10).

2.) The Holy Spirit's work of SEALING THE SAVED ends with the appearance of the Lord. Why? Saints are sealed "UNTIL THE DAY OF REDEMPTION" (Eph. 1:13,14). Once that day passes, the sealing work is over. Inasmuch as salvation requires that a person RECEIVE CHRIST VIA THE SPIRIT, that will be impossible once He appears in Person (John 16:7). It is Jesus' work as the SPIRIT-BAPTIZER that places us in the divine family (John 14:20; 1 Cor. 12:13). That work ends when the age of the Holy Spirit ends. Once Jesus returns in the flesh, His ministry per the SPIRIT OF CHRIST will be finished. No one can be baptized into the body after that.

3.) Inasmuch as salvation is BY FAITH and the millennium is BY SIGHT, I see no way for the millennium people to exercise faith in an UNSEEN LORD. Certainly we agree that "without faith it is impossible to please Him" (Heb. 11:6).

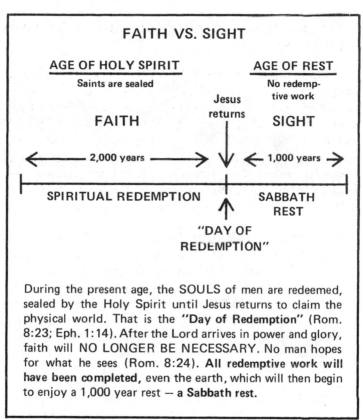

FAITH VS. SIGHT

AGE OF HOLY SPIRIT		AGE OF REST
Saints are sealed		No redemptive work
	Jesus returns	
FAITH		SIGHT
←——— 2,000 years ———→	↓	← 1,000 years →
SPIRITUAL REDEMPTION	↑	SABBATH REST
	"DAY OF REDEMPTION"	

During the present age, the SOULS of men are redeemed, sealed by the Holy Spirit until Jesus returns to claim the physical world. That is the "Day of Redemption" (Rom. 8:23; Eph. 1:14). After the Lord arrives in power and glory, faith will NO LONGER BE NECESSARY. No man hopes for what he sees (Rom. 8:24). All redemptive work will have been completed, even the earth, which will then begin to enjoy a 1,000 year rest — a Sabbath rest.

4.) The REDEMPTIVE WORK of Christ is clearly over when He comes to enjoy His inheritance. Everything that is going to be redeemed WILL HAVE BEEN REDEEMED as He begins His earthly reign. Right now, in the present stage of God's program, the SOULS of men are being redeemed. But when the Lord appears (and we appear) the PHYSICAL CRE-

ATION will also be redeemed (Rom. 8:21-23). That will be the END of the redemption business. As far as I can see, there is NOTHING REDEMPTIVE in the millennial kingdom. Instead, it is a JUSTIFICATION of God's insistence on salvation by faith.

5.) The judgment of God's own people occurs BE-FORE the millennial kingdom begins. The saints (all those in Christ) are judged and receive their assignments PRIOR to the kingdom. If people are to be saved DURING the millennium, it would require another judgment for the new saints. Scripture gives no hint of such a thing, neither has any commentator I know of suggested it.

6.) The millennium is clearly not a place of choice WITH RESPECT TO SIN, but rather one of COM-PELLED OBEDIENCE ("rod of iron"). However, MILLENNIUM MAN is offered a SINGLE CHOICE when Satan is released at the end of the 1,000 years. It's not a FAITH-CHOICE, but a SIGHT-CHOICE. The results indicate it was not a choice for salvation. Rather it serves to prove what God has stated all along — men don't want Him (John 3:19). The SIGHT-METHOD failed in the first Eden, and it will also fail in the last Eden. There will be no way for anyone to say, "Had I been in Adam's shoes I would have done differently." They are cut off forever from the "tree of life" (Rev. 2:7; Gen: 3:22).

THINK I'M WRONG?

You may feel I've really missed the target, too far out. That my reasons don't hold water. You could be right. But this is the way I understand the Word as well as the counsel I am receiving from the Spirit. I'm not defensive about it. Rather, I'm happy to have you check with the Holy Spirit on every point. But as I review God's program, **I see no way for anyone to be saved apart from faith.**

252

WHY GOD CHOSE THE FAITH-METHOD

The super rich have a serious problem — knowing who their real friends are. When you are wealthy and powerful, it's obvious people are going to flock to you and cater to your whims. They want what you **have**. They'd like to get their hands on some of it. So if you want to determine who are your REAL FRIENDS, you must employ some kind of a **screening device** to separate the genuine from the false. God's problem is just that. When men see Him in His glory, they want WHAT HE **HAS**, but they may not WANT **HIM**.

So God has come up with a **screening device** — THE FAITH-METHOD. By means of it, He can separate those who truly WANT HIM from those who merely want WHAT HE CAN GIVE THEM. Thus it has ever been God's way to provide men with enough evidence for FAITH TO OPERATE, but not enough to CONVINCE the unbelieving doubter. God could easily convince men of His reality and power, but that won't bring Him what He wants — genuine friends and family. Those who truly love Jesus by faith, love God FOR HIMSELF! **Those who don't like Jesus (as we know Him), don't like God. It's that simple** (John 14:7-10; 10:30-38).

WHEN IT'S ALL OVER

Once the nations following Satan are consumed, (Israel undoubtedly joins the rebellion), God is finished with the earth. It has served its purpose. PROGRAM EARTH IS ALL OVER. God has extracted (screened out by faith) a nice family for Himself, even though it took billions of souls to accomplish it.

When the Lord established the FAITH-METHOD of bringing "sons to glory," He knew only a few would make it. This hurts, because it is God's desire "that none should perish." However, if men do not want Him,

253

He will not impose Himself on them (John 3:16). Jesus Himself announced that most of the people on this earth would travel the BROAD WAY TO DESTRUCTION. Very few, He said, would find the straight and narrow way to life (Matt. 7:13,14). From the beginning, God was prepared to separate the MANY FROM THE FEW.

Now that we have the earthly program ending, where do we go from here? The answer is truly "out of this world" . . . as we'll see next.

Chapter Twelve

From Here To Eternity

"Do you have the correct time, please?"

I turned in my place before the bank teller's window to answer the person behind me. My hand automatically shoved back my sleeve for a glance at my watch. Oh, Oh! In my hurry to get to the bank before closing, I'd left it on the dresser. Man, that's upsetting. I mumbled an apology, but the frustration drew my mind to the whole business of time.

I couldn't help but think how people are forever wanting to know the **correct time.** It seems we live in a timed world. Everything within our universe is measured in terms of time. Not just physical things, but our lives as well. Everybody is trying to do things "on time." Well, those musings gave the Holy Spirit something to work with. He struck me with a question . . .

"Is there such a thing as the correct time?"

THE CORRECT TIME

My first reaction was, "Of course there's such a thing." But you don't give the Holy Spirit a glib answer. He's always after something deeper than appears on the surface. So I began to think a little further. For starters, it was clear there is NO TIME IN HEAVEN. Why? Heaven is ETERNAL. As most Bible students realize, **time and eternity are two separate realms — one having to do with flesh, the other with spirit.** The two don't mix.

And yet you and I are spirit-beings, and we live in a universe timed to the fraction of a second. Somehow God has taken men designed for eternity and blended them into time. We're eternal beings with wrist watches — a real mix of flesh and spirit. Seems incongruous, somehow.

It remains mysterious until we understand **time belongs exclusively to the physical world and God is using it to get us ready for eternity.** As for the Spirit's question concerning the correct time, we can't answer that until we know **how God is using time.** So let's begin here.

HOW GOD USES TIME

See that line with the infinity symbols at either end? I'm going to let it represent eternity. I haven't any idea what eternity is like, but we know it has **neither beginning nor ending.** For what I seek to share with you, a never ending line is adequate.

Now let's place a DOT (•) squarely in the middle of the line, so that now our line looks like this:

256

We'll let that dot represent the point in eternity where God said . . . "Let us make man in our image, after our likeness . . . " (Gen. 1:26). Don't ask me WHEN this happened, for it occurred outside of space and time. There is NO "WHEN" in eternity. We have no tools for examining eternity. Logic and reason are limited to the dimensions we know.

But here is what happened, apparently: **God has COMPRESSED into that single dot the entire human story from Genesis to Revelation.** All we know of human existence is but a solitary event in eternity, so that we may display the contrast like this:

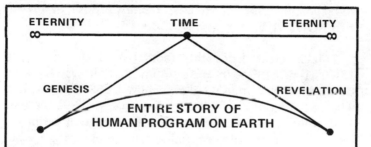

The drawings have but one purpose — to show the relationship between **time and eternity.** It is one thing for me to say they are totally different and separate, another to illustrate that difference graphically. When you grasp the difference between the **LINE and the DOT,** you've got it. When you understand **all of time is COMPRESSED INTO THAT DOT,** you lay hold of the ingenious thing God has developed with His invention of time. In no way is eternity (whatever it is) disturbed, and yet God is able to run out a complete program for man, using TIME as a separate medium. I know that sounds wild. Don't try to master the concept. Just let yourself understand that **time and eternity are two different ARENAS, where two different types of existence are experienced.** Arm yourself with that much, and you'll behold God's program in a new way.

Does it seem God has gone to a lot of trouble in setting up a time-space program? Sure He has. But it's worth it, considering what He's getting out of it. When we examine God's purpose in making man, we'll see why it's worth it.

GOD'S PURPOSE IN MAN

God wasn't out of work when He made man. It wasn't because He didn't have anything else to do. Fact is, He was LONESOME. How do we know? He tells us . . . "God is love" (1 John 4:8). Can you imagine anything worse than being a God of love WITH NO ONE TO LOVE! Writing under the inspiration of the Spirit, **the apostle John insists God's one purpose in man is FELLOWSHIP.**

This is clear from the fact that God made man LIKE HIMSELF — in His own image. Fellowship would be impossible if man were somehow LESS THAN GOD. That would put us in the PET category. Thus we read that when TIME CEASES TO BE, God will be in the midst of His people, rejoicing with them as a Father with His children (Rev. 21:3-7).

For the fellowship between God and man to be genuine, the love between them has to be voluntary. There is no way God can create people with a passion for Him. Love is based on free choice. Therefore man must be totally free to LOVE GOD OR REJECT HIM. The love God wants must be freely given. You know that. It's not really love unless it is freely bestowed from the heart. So at best, all God could do was make men like Himself, capable of loving Him . . . but with NO GUARANTEE THAT WE WOULD LOVE HIM. Man can't be free and controlled at the same time.

What's more, the LIKENESS between God and man must also be exact. If a fellowship is to exist, each must be able to contribute to the other. That's what a fellow-ship really is — a mutual sharing, acting and reacting to another. For this fellowship to make sense, it must OCCUR AT THE SAME LEVEL — the spirit level. Since GOD IS SPIRIT, it follows that man (His image) is essentially SPIRIT, too.

> **SPIRIT.** God is spirit (John 4:24). That is easily settled, for there is no way for man IN THE FLESH to see God (1 John 4:12). It is also certain, that if man is truly the IMAGE OF GOD, he must also be spirit. The image must be like the object. This means that man, like God, is invisible. True, we see the body housing a man, just as men beheld the body Jesus was wearing. But the MAN HIMSELF remains unseen. We meet this truth every time we see a corpse at a funeral. The body is there, brain and all. Yet the man is obviously GONE! **The body, therefore, is nothing more than a two-legged vehicle which allows a SPIRIT-BEING to participate in space and time.** All we know about anyone, is the personality he projects through the physical body. The man himself will never be truly known until he is displayed in eternity (1 Cor. 13:12b). That even applies to the Lord Jesus.

GOD'S PURPOSE IN TIME

For man to be truly like God, there is one feature he must have — A FREE WILL. God is free to make His decisions. Man must be free to make his decisions as well. If he can't, he's not like God at all. But that creates a problem. In allowing man to DECIDE FOR HIMSELF whether or not he will love God, God takes the "divine risk" in creating such men. It IS possible, you see, for man to REJECT GOD and love someone or something else. But what is God to do, since fellowship is only possible with those who love Him? The answer: **man's free will has to be TESTED to see what he will do with it.** It needs to be seen WHO OR WHAT man will love.

THE BIBLICAL ACCOUNT OF MAN'S TESTING

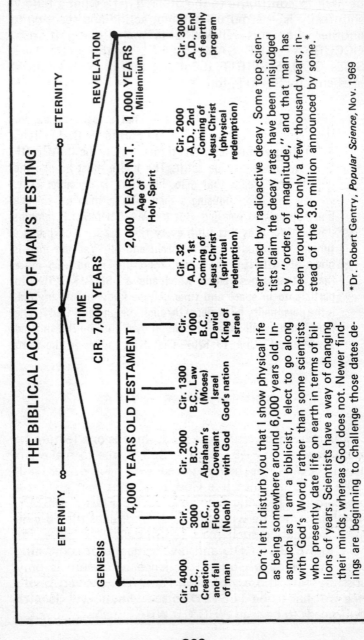

ETERNITY ∞

ETERNITY ∞

GENESIS   REVELATION

TIME
CIR. 7,000 YEARS

4,000 YEARS OLD TESTAMENT				2,000 YEARS N.T. Age of Holy Spirit	1,000 YEARS Millennium
Cir. 4000 B.C., Creation and fall of man	Cir. 3000 B.C., Flood (Noah)	Cir. 2000 B.C., Abraham's Covenant with God	Cir. 1300 B.C., Law (Moses) Israel God's nation	Cir. 32 A.D., 1st Coming of Jesus Christ (spiritual redemption)	Cir. 2000 A.D., 2nd Coming of Jesus Christ (physical redemption)	Cir. 3000 A.D., End of earthly program

(additional column: Cir. 1000 B.C., David King of Israel)

Don't let it disturb you that I show physical life as being somewhere around 6,000 years old. Inasmuch as I am a biblicist, I elect to go along with God's Word, rather than some scientists who presently date life on earth in terms of billions of years. Scientists have a way of changing their minds, whereas God does not. Newer findings are beginning to challenge those dates determined by radioactive decay. Some top scientists claim the decay rates have been misjudged by "orders of magnitude," and that man has been around for only a few thousand years, instead of the 3.6 million announced by some.*

———————————
*Dr. Robert Gentry, *Popular Science*, Nov. 1969

Therefore God came up with a remarkable device — TIME. **Since time has a beginning and ending (duration), it can be used to test man's free will.** A test, you see, has a beginning and an ending. Obviously it can't be done in eternity WHICH HAS NEITHER. So God created the earth, placed man on it — and put the whole program INSIDE TIME.

> **DEVICE.** Indeed, for that is precisely what TIME AND SPACE are all about. **God created this world merely to give man an opportunity to exercise his freedom of choice in a TEST SITUATION.** It is a TEMPORARY DEVICE for testing ETERNAL BEINGS. You cannot test in eternity, but you can test in time. That is why TIME is but another word for the story of man on the earth and God's dealing with him to determine his fitness for eternal fellowship. On earth, a man can do as he pleases with his love and devotion. In the process, God reveals Himself to that man. The individual is free to love or reject the ONE revealed to him. If he chooses to love God, he is suitable for the eternal fellowship. If he rejects God, he must spend eternity separated from God. That's what hell is all about (Matt. 25:41b).

NO WATCHES IN ETERNITY

Once the testing of God's image is finished, there will be no further need for time and space. **The universe as we know it, will be discarded.**

 "And I saw a great white throne and Him Who sat upon it, from whose presence earth and heaven fled away, and no place was found for them" (Rev. 20:11 NAS).

Jesus Himself verified this, **"Heaven and earth will pass away,** but My words shall not pass away" (Matt. 24:35).

Some scientists accept the "BIG BANG" theory as explaining the earth's creation. That is, earth was formed by a mighty explosion in space. Should this really be the case, the scientists holding to this theory will get a thrill out of Peter's explanation as to how the world will **disappear**. The "day of the Lord," says the apostle, will end like this:

 " . . . in the which the heavens shall pass away with a GREAT NOISE, and the elements shall melt with fervent heat, the earth also and the works that are therein shall be burned up" (2 Peter 3:10 KJV).

Talk about BIG BANGS! If the world began with a bang, it is going to end with one, too. And this time it won't be any theory. That verse pictures the earth as a super firecracker. When it speaks of elements being consumed, that has to be an ATOMIC EXPLOSION! Observe that it is not merely our planet that disappears, but all the heavenly bodies. **The entire universe will release the energy holding it together.** Of course, it was nothing more than an EXPRESSION of the mighty power of God in the first place (Heb. 11:3; 1:3, 10-12).

BIG BANG. The modern school boy knows all matter is composed of atoms. And atoms are merely particles of electricity, with huge amounts of space (vacuum, actually) between the particles. Some scientists have noted that all the really solid stuff in the entire universe would not make up more than a cup. To be sure, no one could lift it, it'd be so dense. The atoms are held in their spaces by energy. When you break the atom, you release the energy holding it together. This energy comes directly from Christ, Who holds this world together with the "Word of His power" (Heb. 1:3; Col. 1:17). All God has to do is release the power holding ALL the atoms and the physical universe would disappear as Peter states . . . "with a loud noise!" The detonation of a billion megaton bomb would be a peep compared to the explosion of the physical universe.

END OF PHYSICAL PROGRAM?

"Just a minute, Dr. Lovett. You've dropped another bombshell. Are you saying God is all through with the physical universe? That the 'new heaven and a new earth' are not physical?" (Rev. 21:1).

In fairness, I should mention that some Bible students do not believe Peter's BIG BANG, which comes at the end of the millennium, puts an end to the physical program. They see ANOTHER PHYSICAL WORLD emerging from the fireball, one purged and purified, ready for further human occupation. It is their conviction that the future fellowship is NOT SPIRITUAL, but physical. That God Himself, Who is SPIRIT, will somehow dwell on earth in a physical form and that we'll be with Him.

I won't raise a big fuss over that. It's a lot like the rapture question — if these brethren are correct in their theory, all of us will still make out fabulously. As long as we're with the Lord, we can't lose. However, the idea of our ETERNAL FELLOWSHIP being confined to a physical world creates a number of problems for me, one in particular: **anything physical is FINITE and therefore temporary.** How can ETERNAL fellowship be fulfilled in a TEMPORARY situation? The apostle Paul insists everything physical is temporary:

 "Meanwhile our eyes are fixed, not on the things that are seen, but on the things that are unseen: for what is seen passes away (is temporary); what is unseen is eternal" (2 Cor. 4:18 NEB).

To me, it doesn't make sense trying to compress eternity into time. I don't see how it would accomplish anything for God, since He's interested in an ETERNAL FELLOWSHIP. Surely He anticipates the day when "time shall be no more," and **our fellowship is fulfilled in the spirit.**

NEW JERUSALEM NOT PHYSICAL EITHER

Even so, some dear brethren insist they see it in the Word . . .

"And I John saw the holy city, new Jerusalem, coming down from God out of heaven . . . And I heard a great voice out of heaven saying, 'Behold the tabernacle of God is with men, and He will dwell with them, and they shall be His people, and God Himself shall be with them, and be their God' " (Rev. 21:2,3 KJV).

We've all heard those verses. Fact is, the last two chapters of the Revelation are devoted to describing a city that DESCENDS out of heaven; one with golden streets, jasper walls and foundations of all kinds of precious stones. But isn't it obvious that all these materials belong to this PRESENT CREATION — the very one scheduled to pass away? When we refer to them as precious, are they not precious to THIS LIFE only? What reason do we have to suppose God cares about gold and silver or anything made up of atoms? The whole ball of wax is destined to perish (Heb. 1:10-12).

CITY. Readers studying the last two chapters of the Revelation could conclude John is speaking of an actual city on earth. They are not stupid for reaching that conclusion. But they ought also to consider that John is trying to describe something OUT OF THIS WORLD . . . and at the same time, using terms with which we are familiar. Very likely the apostle Paul saw the same things, but made no attempt to explain them. He chose, instead, to say that his vision brought words that are impossible to explain (2 Cor. 12:4). Don't you get the feeling old John is struggling to picture for us a glory we can't possibly fathom now, but will when we're with the Lord? I do.

As I see it, we'll BE THROUGH with such things once the millennium has passed. They belong to the physical creation, the TESTING GROUND. **Once the testing is over, the IMAGE OF GOD should take up residence in God's environment, heaven itself.** We're destined to live with God in eternity, not in some city that floats down out of the sky. (A little later we'll discuss what I think the new Jerusalem really is.)

MAN NOT DESIGNED FOR A FINITE WORLD

Another difficulty: man, the image of God, is in his essence a SPIRIT-BEING. In his makeup, he is LIKE GOD. While he can be placed in a physical body and LIMITED TO THE BRAIN that comes with the body (as was Jesus), **it is not his natural habitat. Man was NOT DESIGNED for a finite world, but for the INFINITE REALM of the spirit.** We even sing that truth . . . "This world is not my home, I'm just passing through."

Just because it is possible to put a spirit-being in a human body, doesn't mean that's where he belongs. There isn't a body of any kind that can be completely satisfying to a spirit. And if you put him there with a command to STAY, it would be an awful imprisonment. Man is clearly designed for GOD'S REALM, a spiritual environment.

GOD IN FLESH AGAIN?

It's difficult for me to picture God perpetuating the TEST ENVIRONMENT and living in it Himself. If the future fellowship is to be limited to a physical realm, it would require God to limit Himself to some kind of a physical body also. We've already seen that a physical body, locked into space and time, cannot participate in the spirit realm. It is isolated from eternity.

SO, NO BODIES IN ETERNITY

If our fellowship with God is to be genuine, we'll have to be with Him AS EQUALS. There must be uninhibited communication — SPIRIT TO SPIRIT. Since **flesh** and **spirit** are different in kind, it is impossible for physical bodies, no matter how glorious, to be a part of that fellowship. But that, naturally, raises a question:

"If we don't have bodies in eternity, what do we have?

A FORM NOT MADE WITH HUMAN HANDS

The exciting answer to our question is found in a familiar passage, one that has to do with Jesus . . .

"Who, being in the FORM OF GOD, thought it not robbery to be EQUAL with God: but made Himself of no reputation, and took upon Him the FORM of a servant, and was made in the likeness of men" (Phil. 2:6,7 KJV).

The answer is right there.

Before Jesus left heaven to be born as a MAN, He was **equal with God.** And He was in the **form of God.** Obviously, there is a **FORM of some kind as perfectly suited to heaven as the human body is to the physical world.** Paul said as much to the Corinthians:

"Now we know that if the EARTHLY TENT we live in is destroyed, we have A BUILDING from God, an ETERNAL HOUSE IN HEAVEN, not built with human hands" (2 Cor. 5:1).

See the two realms in that verse — heaven and earth? Note the TWO FORMS, spiritual and physical. We're told that if anything happens to our earthly body, we

already have a SPIRITUAL FORM (of some kind) that majestically clothes us in heaven. Now that form is the SAME FORM Jesus had (even now has) before and after His incarnation.

> **FORM.** What form did Jesus have in heaven? It definitely was **NOT a physical body.** Can we be sure? Yes, He had to PUT ON a physical body to enter this world. Hence the manger scene in Bethlehem. What happened to the FORM He had in heaven? **Nothing.** He still had it. After all, it is SPIRIT. He didn't have to lay aside His spirit-form to take on a PHYSICAL form. The two easily coexist. You and I are in that situation. We're spirit-beings in earthly bodies. The fact is, Jesus COULDN'T lay aside His spiritual form — it is part of His spiritual being. Jesus, to "empty Himself," as Paul says, simply took on the FORM OF A SERVANT and was "found in fashion as a man" (Phil. 2:8). He was the eternal God, but confined to a human body and limited to a human brain the same as we. The EMPTYING of Christ consisted of His being LIMITED TO A PHYSICAL BODY. In that same sense, you and I are EMPTIED of what we really are as the image of God.

TIME AND ETERNITY EXIST SIDE BY SIDE

Ask me where heaven is and I'll hold my hand 5 inches from my chest and say . . . "Right here." We tend to think of heaven as being miles and miles straight up. **In reality we're in heaven now.** It's all around us. You want me to explain?

Heaven and earth can coexist because spirit and flesh are utterly different realms. We find a helpful illustration in the world of radio and TV. The very room in which you are reading this book is filled with radio waves. You can't see them, nor can you feel them. But they're there, aren't they? Turn on a TV set and you will transform those waves into something you can see and hear. Turn the set off and where do the waves go? They're still there. They don't go anywhere.

Your room can be filled with radio waves and your physical existence unaffected by them. You have no contact with them. You're unaware of them. They don't bother you. Give that some thought. The radio world and your personal existence function side by side, yet totally independent of each other. They occupy the same space, yet there's no contact.

It's like that with the spirit-world.

The spiritual realm, like radio waves, occupies the SAME SPACE we do. We're not conscious of it because our brains are designed to limit our awareness to the FIVE SENSES. However, once we're released from these bodies, able to function at the MIND-LEVEL, the spirit-world will be as real to us as the physical world is now.

When we understand that TIME AND ETERNITY COEXIST, certain Scriptures make sense. Take Jesus' baffling words . . . "Before Abraham was, I AM" (John 8:58). He could say that because He knew He existed in both realms, time and eternity. This is why Paul can say of us that we "SIT TOGETHER IN HEAVENLY PLACES IN CHRIST JESUS" (Eph. 2:6,7). **You and I can be here and in the heavenlies AT THE SAME TIME!** How come? Because we're eternal-beings who have an existence in the flesh . . . **and in the spirit.**

On the surface we appear to be limited to one spot. But only the body is limited to that spot, not us. Since WE ARE SPIRIT, we are also in eternity, in heaven, in Christ. I know that sounds wild, but you'll just have to wait until we're out of the flesh and operating at the MIND-LEVEL, for confirmation. Then we'll see how we were indeed citizens of two realms simultaneously (Phil. 3:20; Eph. 2:19,22).

BLAST OFF TO THE ULTIMATE DIMENSION

Once everything physical is destroyed, all else that takes place must occur in the SPIRIT-REALM. That BIG BANG is going to take everyone out of the flesh. Everybody will be in the spirit once that happens. Don't worry, there'll be no pain connected with the transition. It'll all be done in the twinkling of an eye. Then God will get on to an all important matter — holding court for the **unsaved of all ages.** We know it is IN THE SPIRIT, for even death and hell deliver up their dead to this judgment (Rev. 20:13).

There is **no way** the unsaved could be judged before the millennium. Why? There were multitudes who had yet to be born into the earthly kingdom. But once the earthly program ends, their judgment is the first thing on the agenda. **The eternal fellowship can't get under way until God makes disposition of those who don't want Him.**

THE GREAT WHITE THRONE JUDGMENT

Everybody will be summoned to this event:

> "And I saw a great white throne, and Him that sat on it, . . . and I saw the dead, small and great, stand before God; and the books were opened; and another book was opened, which is the book of life: and the dead were judged out of those things which were written in the books, according to their WORKS . . . and death and hell were cast into the lake of fire. This is the SECOND DEATH. And whosoever was not found written in the book of life was cast into the lake of fire" (Rev. 20: 11-15 KJV).

This judgment must be distinguished from the "judgment seat of Christ," where the works of the saints are evaluated. Even though you and I are present at this "great white throne" judgment, **we are merely spectators.** Our judgment took place BEFORE THE MILLENNIUM so that we could receive our RANKS and be assigned our kingdom tasks. The only reason we appear at this judgment is because the Lord is here. Once believers are gathered unto the Lord, they are NEVER to be separated from Him again (1 Thess. 4:17). Wherever the Lord is, that's where we'll be (Matt. 24:28).

Jesus is the Judge.

The Person sitting on the great white throne is the Lord Jesus. The Lord Himself explained the reason for that:

 "For the Father judgeth no man, but hath committed all judgment unto the Son: . . . and hath given Him authority to execute judgment also, BECAUSE HE IS THE SON OF MAN" (John 5:22,27 KJV).

Only A MAN can judge men, a man Who has been in their shoes. Therefore the one seated on that throne is the MAN, CHRIST JESUS!

Our Lord is uniquely qualified to judge the unsaved, since He knows BY EXPERIENCE that Satan can be resisted. He also knows a man CAN LIVE to please God, if he really wants to. He did it Himself — **as a man.** Having been there, He will be well qualified to pass judgment and assign the unsaved to their fate.

As the unbelieving dead are brought before the great white throne, the "BOOKS ARE OPENED" (Rev. 20:12). (The "book of life" is kept at hand to show that God KNEW HIS OWN from the beginning of the world.) The "book of works" is undoubtedly the recording from the computers OF THEIR OWN MINDS, providing

270

incontestable evidence for their judgment. The human mind keeps a running account of every thought, feeling and decision a person makes, revealing his motives as well.

According to works.

What an education it will be to watch the Lord Jesus evaluate the **DEEDS of the unsaved** and decree their eternal fate! Remember, we're going to be judging angels ourselves. So this will be valuable schooling for us. ALL THE UNSAVED who have lived and died on the earth will be here, yet it will **not be a trial.** These people have already rejected Jesus' sacrifice, hence **they are already GUILTY.** They're not here to be tried, but to receive their respective **sentences.** It's like a sentence hearing in our modern court system.

The Lord's assignments will be ETERNAL, even as His assignments of the saints are eternal. Both judgments, for unsaved and saint alike, **are for WORKS done during the time spent on earth.** The only difference is: the saints live out their judgment IN HEAVEN, whereas the unsaved live out theirs in THE LAKE OF FIRE (Rev. 20:15). The saints are with their God, **Jesus** . . . the unsaved are with their god, **Satan** (Matt. 25:41).

ASSIGNMENTS. The very fact of a judgment of the unsaved, BASED ON WORKS, indicates degrees of hell. Not all will be assigned the same rank or status. There will be a "lowerarchy" of hell, even as there is a hierarchy of heaven. There are many "good people" who wouldn't hurt a fly, yet who have rejected Jesus and cannot be a part of the eternal family. They must be eternally separated from God. But even in assigning them to hell, God's justice is manifested, for their places in hell are determined BY THEIR DEEDS (Rev. 20:13). Those who have done good works will fare better than those whose works are evil only. It would not be just to lump a dear grandmother, who did much good, with a dictator who lived only to destroy. If there are no degrees of hell, then why judge the unsaved at all? A judgment always supposes a sentence of some kind.*

THE GREAT WHITE THRONE JUDGMENT

FOR ALL <u>UNSAVED</u> DEAD
(those who did NOT partake in First Resurrection)

great white throne and One who sat upon it (Rev. 20:11a)

SALVATION

book of life

ALL UNSAVED DEAD JUDGED ACCORDING TO THEIR WORKS
(Rev. 20:12,13)

WORKS

book of works

whose names were not found in the "book of life" were flung into the lake of fire (second death) (Rev. 20:14,15)

death and hell flung into lake of fire (Rev. 20:14)

LAKE OF FIRE
(SECOND DEATH — Rev. 20:6,14; 21:8)

---

*For a fuller discussion of the judgment of saved and unsaved, refer to the author's book, **JESUS IS COMING—GET READY CHRISTIAN.**

THE LAKE OF FIRE

Wondering about the "lake of fire," into which even death and hell are cast (Rev. 20:14)? What is it? Where is it? For one thing, it won't be a literal flame, for John carefully employs the word TORMENT, not the word TORTURE. There's a difference. Torture is PHYSICAL and requires a body. Torment is SPIRITUAL and afflicts the soul.

Remember how Jesus spoke of the "everlasting fire, prepared for the devil and his angels," and how sinners would share Satan's fate? (Matt. 25:41). And how John also spoke of the doom of the beast and those who follow him, saying, "the smoke of their TORMENT" would ascend up forever and ever? (Rev. 14:11; 19:20). These bespeak SPIRITUAL AGONY . . . no rest . . . a burning of the soul. That is why it is called the "second death."

As for WHERE this lake of fire might be, it won't be in heaven. Likely SOME KIND OF A GAP will be fixed between the saved and unsaved, so that those who rejected God's love will see what they missed. That may be part of the agony. When John pictures the unsaved as being OUTSIDE the gates of the new Jerusalem, I feel he is attempting to describe that GAP (Rev. 22:14, 15). It's a SPIRITUAL GAP, something our minds can't comprehend at the moment. Jesus called it the "outer darkness" (Matt. 22:13; 25:30).

NEW HEAVENS — NEW EARTH — NEW JERUSALEM

"Dr. Lovett, you spent some time telling us what the new heavens, new earth and new Jerusalem are not. As promised earlier, how about explaining what you think they are?"

"And I saw a new heaven and a new earth: for the first heaven and the first earth were passed away; . . . And I heard a great voice out of heaven saying; Behold the tabernacle of God is with men, and He shall dwell with them, and they shall be His people, and God Himself shall be with them, and be their God" (Rev. 21:1,3 KJV).

In my opinion, the "new heavens and a new earth" represent the new home of the believer after the earthly program is concluded. It is the "place" Jesus said He was going to "prepare" for us (John 14:2). Remember how He spoke of the "many mansions" in His Father's house? Well, I believe those words refer to a BRAND NEW SPIRITUAL ENVIRONMENT, all prepared through the sacrifice of Jesus for the family of God.

For John to illustrate God's dwelling in our midst, he employs the imagery of a city:

"And I saw the holy city, new Jerusalem, coming down out of heaven from God, MADE READY AS A BRIDE ADORNED FOR HER HUSBAND" (Rev. 21:2 NAS).

As I read that verse, I can almost hear the familiar refrain . . . "HERE COMES THE BRIDE . . . ♩♫ ." Don't you detect an air of pageantry in those words . . . "Made ready as a bride adorned for her husband?" To me, the setting is akin to a formal wedding. One can almost see the Bridegroom (Jesus) gazing fondly on His adoring bride (Miss Church) as she makes her way toward Him.

The NEW JERUSALEM, which he describes as a city, is (in my judgment) **the church** — the "bride of Christ." To me, John's vision is poetic imagery. **He employs a**

PHYSICAL CITY to picture the COMPLETENESS the Lord will enjoy with His bride. It's a metaphor.

COMPLETENESS. Note how the WALLS and GATES of John's city contain the names of the 12 tribes and the 12 apostles of the Lamb (Rev. 21:12-14). He is blending the saints of both old and new testaments into one, unified holy city. And when you observe how the measurements of the city form a perfect cube, you realize the "precious stones and pearls," along with the "gates and walls," signify completeness. The entire city is a HOLY OF HOLIES and the Lord God and the Lamb are its temple (Rev. 21:15-17,22). That's spiritual talk. Everything for life and fellowship is included, right down to the "tree of life" itself (Rev. 22:2). List all the elements John puts into his city and you quickly conclude our dear brother is using a city to picture a SPIRITUAL REALITY.

AND WHAT IS THE REALITY?

Well, the reality is NOT A WEDDING. John can hardly be describing the "marriage of the Lamb," for that has already occurred. The marriage ceremony took place when Jesus appeared in the sky and gathered the church to Himself! Then followed the "wedding feast" (reception), the 1,000 year reign on earth, which His bride shared with Him. It was a time of SCHOOLING for the bride, during which she learned the ropes of the reigning business.

The REAL HONEYMOON won't start until the PHYSICAL PROGRAM is finished and the Lord is with His bride in eternity. The moment TIME ENDS, eternity will begin for all of us — IN THE SPIRIT REALM. Christ and His bride will consummate their marriage with SPIRIT TO SPIRIT fellowship. This is what God purposed before the world began (Eph. 1:3-12). Thus, living with God in a face-to-face, spirit-with-spirit union is the TRUE REALITY.

" . . . the throne of God and the Lamb will be there, and His servants shall worship Him; they shall SEE HIM FACE TO FACE . . . " (Rev. 22:3,4 NEB).

As you read those words, doesn't the Spirit Himself witness they are true?

THE ETERNAL HONEYMOON

What John is trying to reveal in the last chapters of the Revelation is the COMPLETENESS AND SATISFAC-ION the Lord will enjoy with His church. Once the earthly program is out of the way, **the Lord will have His bride to Himself.** She'll be ready to ENJOY HIM and work with Him in a way that never would have been possible, had they not gone through the earthly experience together. With all fleshliness set aside, Jesus and His bride will be FACE TO FACE . . . in the SPIRIT. That's what John is trying to describe, but there are no words. The closest the apostle Paul could come was this . . .

 "But as it is written, 'Eye hath not seen, nor ear heard, neither have entered into the heart of man, the things God hath prepared for them that love Him' " (1 Cor. 2:9 KJV).

WHAT WILL WE DO IN ETERNITY?

Now you've asked a question that goes beyond my competence to answer. If John and Paul can't describe it, how can I? However, some things seem obvious. Inasmuch as God likes harmony, it would seem there would be MUSIC in heaven — if so, what music it must be! Also, it seems obvious, that since we're made in the image of A CREATOR, we'll be in the creating business ourselves. But what we might build, I couldn't guess.

276

But I feel confident about this: **whatever God will be doing, we'll be doing.** I'm certain He's had this in mind from the beginning. Surely it will take some doing for us to learn how to handle OMNIPOTENCE (all power), but God must have that in mind. Surely He wants His sons to fill His shoes. And the same could be said for OMNISCIENCE (all knowledge). For the fellowship to be on the same level, that seems very necessary.

As for OMNIPRESENCE (being in all places at the same time), I've got a hunch we're already omnipresent, but not aware of it. And no way to **be aware** of it as long as we're in these bodies. (However, in the earthly kingdom, in our glorified bodies, we'll probably get some experience in **all three of these areas:** omnipotence, omniscience, and omnipresence. It will be on a limited basis, but enough to get us ready for eternity.) **In ETERNITY when we'll be operating in the spirit, we will be fully aware of our powers.** I've said enough. Beyond this, I dare not speculate.

I COULD BE WRONG. Are you keeping in mind that I'm sharing "opinions" with you? **I do not insist I am right in** saying the **ETERNAL FELLOWSHIP will be spiritual** rather than physical. I could be wrong. If it turns out a **PHYSICAL CITY** actually descends from heaven, somehow dressed like a bride, onto a physical new earth, I won't be disappointed. Surprised, yes. But not disappointed. **What really matters for us is that we'll be with Jesus and that will be HEAVEN FOR US.**

ARE YOU READY FOR THAT REALITY?

I hope you are. So does the apostle John. He closes the Bible with this note of caution:

 "And, behold I come quickly; and my reward is with me, to give every man according as his work shall be!" (Rev. 22:12 KJV).

Do you understand the reason for his caution? The Lord is coming quickly — in a flash. I didn't say He was coming soon, but SUDDENLY. There'll be no warning, no last minute to make up one's mind whether he wants to be with Jesus or not. That has to be decided BEFORE HAND. If you've read this far and that question remains unanswered in your mind, you should settle it quickly.

Let's take a moment to talk about **meeting the Lord and making that all important decision.** Here's how to go about it. Right where you are, seated in your chair, bow your head. Get ready to pray. The Lord is eager to reveal Himself to you. Here's His invitation:

 "Behold, I stand at the door, and knock: if any man hear My voice, and open the door, I will come into him . . . " (Rev. 3:20).

© Linda Lovett 1978

That door of which Jesus speaks, is your heart. If you'll **open that door to Him**, He says . . . "I WILL COME IN." Here's what's nice; the moment He comes in, He lets you know He's arrived. **He makes Himself real to you.** You experience a fabulous peace.

Since He's made the offer, you have to take the FIRST STEP. That shows you want Him. So answer His invitation by speaking directly to Him like this:

"Lord Jesus, I want You for my eternal Friend. I want to be a part of the eternal fellowship. I'm ready to accept Your death on the cross as my sacrifice for my sins. I here and now open my heart to You, and invite You to come into my life. I now put my trust in You as my personal Savior. Amen."

Can you do that? Actually the words you say are not as critical as the attitude of your heart. **You must WANT Jesus. And you must ACT on His invitation and tell Him you really want Him.** The words you use are immaterial. The important matter is WANTING HIM. The transaction can be completed in less than a minute. So won't you pause . . . and get it settled? Then you'll be ready to join the rest of us in that great fellowship in the sky and share the fabulous inheritance awaiting the children of God!

WRITE TO ME. If you elect to ask Jesus to be your personal Savior as a result of reading this book, would you write and let me know? I'll send you something that will explain the marvelous thing that has happened to you, and show you how to proceed in the new life you've just received.

★ ★

All men are created for eternity. Not a single person was created simply for a lifetime on earth. God's purpose in creating man was for ETERNAL COMPANIONS. Everyone is designed for eternity. So while it may appear that life ends when the body dies, in reality that person is going to SPEND ETERNITY SOMEPLACE. **Where** he will spend eternity is up to him. During his single life span on earth he makes a decision about the Lord. **That decision is his own.** If he elects to receive Jesus, he has PASSED THE TEST, so to speak. If he rejects the Lord, he fails the test and dooms himself to an eternity separated from God. BUT HE WILL SPEND ETERNITY SOMEPLACE.

> **I SUGGEST YOU LAY DOWN THE BOOK AND DO NOT PLAN ON READING FURTHER UNTIL YOU MAKE THAT DECISION. WHAT YOU'RE GOING TO MEET IN THE NEXT SECTION WILL BE FAR MORE EXCITING IF YOU KNOW IT APPLIES TO YOU.**

★ ★

We have now covered the entire span of prophecy as I understand it. And that brings us to the end of PART ONE. As I said at the beginning, I do not have all the truth. I'm bound to be off on some things. But I will be close enough for every reader to recognize one thing—**the events which I have described are so close, you ought to devote the rest of your life to . . .**

GETTING READY FOR THE APPEARING OF THE LORD!

© Linda Lovett 1979

PART TWO

PREPARING FOR HIS APPEARRING

Chapter Thirteen

It Will Be
Worth It All!

What would you say is the most dramatic point in a
formal church wedding? There is a point where the ex-

citement peaks, but a lot goes on before that point is reached. The action starts with the seating of the bride's mother. After special music, a door opens and out comes the minister, accompanied by the bridegroom. The groom takes his place at the head of the aisle, and stands there waiting for his bride. Usually he has to wait awhile.

The bridesmaids and ushers must all come down the aisle to take their places. Their costumes are striking. Then come the scene stealers. The flower girl, hardly more than a toddler, brings approving smiles and whispers as the audience adores her cuteness. The little ring bearer gets no less attention.

Then the music stops. A chord is struck on the organ. The big moment has arrived. The bride's mother rises to her feet and turns toward the rear of the auditorium. That's the signal. Everyone in the place rises and does the same. And there she is — the bride herself — dressed in gleaming white, topped with a veil.

As the wedding march begins, the bride steps forward, leaning on her father's arm. Her snowy gown rustles as she walks, drawing admiring glances with every step. This is her big moment, her big day — and she knows it. She is nervous, of course, but not too nervous to soak up the attention and approving looks coming her way. Yes, this is her day, her wedding day. And her trip down the aisle is the most dramatic moment.

But all of a sudden there is a shout! Everyone is stunned!

HEY! LOOK AT ME!

Heads turn in the direction of the shout. It's the bridegroom! Oh, does he look upset. With all that attention focused on the bride, he feels left out. In his frustration he shouts, **I'm here too, you know! Look at me!"** With all that attention going to his bride, he feels the audience has turned its back on him. At the most dramatic point in the ceremony, he felt unimportant. After all, it's his wedding too!

WOULD THAT EVER HAPPEN?

No bridegroom would do such a thing. Not in a million years. Everyone wants this to be the bride's biggest moment, especially the bridegroom. Why then, would I introduce such melodrama? Why would I want to picture a frustrated bridegroom. To make a point . . . one that comes across powerfully if you can imagine an upset bridegroom.

I want you to consider a groom who felt left out because of all the attention directed to his bride. If you can do that, here's the point I seek to make.

THE HEAVENLY WEDDING — THE GROOM'S BIG DAY!

By heavenly wedding, I'm referring to the "MARRIAGE OF THE LAMB." We've spoken of it before. but here's the Word on it:

 "Let us rejoice and be glad and give the glory to Him, for the marriage of the Lamb has come and His bride has made herself ready" (Rev. 19:7 NAS).

We've already noted how **this event takes place when the saints are gathered unto the Lord at the rapture.** It is a wedding in the sky. A glorious spectacle. The pageantry, set against brightly colored clouds, will be breathtaking. If earthly weddings are exciting, the wedding of the Lord Jesus should be a heart-stopper. It will dazzle every eye in heaven and on earth.

Now to my point. Will you observe that this is HIS WEDDING? To be sure the church is the BRIDE, but here the emphasis is different. **This is the greatest day in the life of the Lord Jesus!** This is HIS wedding day. Indeed it is a great day for the BRIDE, **but the center of this wedding is JESUS,** not the church. It is my intention to focus our attention on Him rather than the church.

"Of course the attention belongs to Jesus!" That's what you'll say to me. "He's the center of everything!" Ah — but I submit few people have this on their minds when we think of the Lord's return and our meeting Him in the sky. I think I can safely say the average Christian is more concerned with **what happens to himself** in that day than with what happens to the Lord.

We're all quite selfish at this point. We're inclined to forget it is HIS big day, viewing it instead, as OUR big day. Am I being unfair? I have tested a number of Christian audiences at this point and my claim holds up. A unique story reveals how I stumbled on to this.

A CAR CAUGHT MY ATTENTION

One day I was riding with a Christian brother as our car drew alongside another with a big sign painted on the side, announcing, "JESUS IS COMING, ARE YOU READY?" As we paused for a traffic light, my friend stared at those letters, then nudged me . . .

"Now there's a real fanatic!"

"Yeah," I responded, secretly wishing I had the same boldness for Christ.

"I wonder," mused my friend, "if people really pay any attention to that stuff?"

"I do," I replied. "In fact, I'm asking myself right now if I'm ready to meet the Lord. And I'm getting some disturbing answers. You know, I'm going to put that same question to my congregation next Sunday and see what answers I get."

I QUIZZED MY CONGREGATION

The following Sunday I told my people about the car we had encountered and its challenge painted in huge letters . . . "JESUS IS COMING, ARE YOU READY?" I wanted to know if they were challenged as I had been. So I asked for a reaction . . .

"As you think about Jesus' return and our meeting Him in the sky, what's the first thing that comes to your mind? Anyone?"

Hands went up. Different ones voiced their first impressions:

"It'll be great not to have to get up and go to work in the morning. I'm tired of the struggle to survive."

"Boy will I be glad to get out of this body. I've suffered aches and pains for so long, it'll be a relief to feel good again."

"I've got loved ones waiting for me I can't wait to see again!"

"Praise God, think of all the bills I won't have to pay!"

"For me the greatest blessing will be getting away from the temptations and trials that dog my steps."

"I can't wait to get into the new body and be able to move about in the sky. I hope we can look down and shout . . . 'I told you so!' "

"People have been pushing me around all my life. I think it will be super to reign with Jesus and be able to tell somebody else what to do for a change."

"I hope He doesn't come right away. I'm not ready yet!"

That's a cross section of the responses I got. When I put the same question to different audiences later on, the answers were much the same. Scan the list and observe how they all have one thing in common:

EACH REPLY HAS TO DO WITH US . . . WHAT IT'S GOING TO BE LIKE FOR US IN THAT DAY . . . HOW WE'RE GOING TO BENEFIT. WHAT A GREAT TIME WE'LL HAVE. BUT IT IS ALL SELF-CENTERED. NOT A ONE REVEALS ANY CONCERN FOR WHAT THIS DAY IS GO-ING TO MEAN TO THE LORD JESUS. IT'S AS IF IT DOESN'T MATTER THIS IS THE GREAT-EST DAY IN HIS LIFE.

Wouldn't you know, we have even put our self-centeredness to song. I'm sure you know the chorus:

"O that will be glory for ME,
   glory for ME, glory for ME.
When by His grace
   I shall look on His face,
that will be GLORY FOR ME!"

It's obvious whose glory we're interested in — OUR OWN. Very clearly, the BRIDE holds more attraction for us than the GROOM. See now why I told the story of a frustrated bridegroom? I can almost hear the Lord Jesus saying . . .

"Hey, look at Me! This is MY DAY too! I'm sup-posed to be the happiest, most celebrated Person

287

here! And you're focusing all your attention on the bride!"

The Lord would never say that, He's too unselfish. But He'd be justified in taking us to task for our attitude. We ARE more concerned with what that day brings to us, than what it brings to Him. Shame on us for being so self-centered. It's my intention to SHIFT OUR FOCUS from ourselves to Jesus and get us thinking in terms of what that day means to Him.

WHAT IS JESUS' JOY NOW?

Once our focus is shifted from ourselves to Christ, certain Scriptures expand with new meaning. Here's one that speaks of Jesus' great day:

 " . . . Who for the JOY THAT WAS SET BEFORE HIM endured the cross, despising the shame, and is set down at the right hand of the throne of God" (Heb. 12:2 KJV).

Tell me, what do you think is the JOY that was set before Jesus? Someone will say . . . "It's right there in the verse, being seated at God's right hand." But surely that can't be it. He's in that position NOW . . . and He's still suffering. A day doesn't go by but what you and I give Him all kinds of grief.

GRIEF. Though the apostle Paul cautions . . . "And grieve not the Holy Spirit of God, whereby ye are sealed unto the day of redemption," we nonetheless grieve Him plenty (Eph. 4:30). As long as the Lord continues to build His church, He's going to suffer a lot. As we Christians persist in our cold-heartedness, selfish living, backbiting, gossiping and looking to the world for our pleasures and security, we rend His heart continually. Each of us brings pain to the Lord by our neglect of His Word and of Him personally. Our thought-life and the way we treat other Christians must tear Him apart day by day. It's a good thing He is long-suffering. He's been suffering a long time (2 Pet. 3:15).

So, in spite of His exaltation to God's right hand, the Lord is far from enjoying it. Do not most believers insist on doing their own thing — you know, raising families, pursuing careers and achieving financial security? Very few are interested in what the Lord is doing. Fewer still even care. Even though He has invested **everything** in us, few are willing to forego success and security to get involved with Him and make Him Number One in their lives.

Thus while Jesus' exaltation is an honor, there is little joy in it for Him now. We must look to the future. There is but **one event** that will make it all worthwhile for Jesus. That will be the day He takes His "bride" to Himself, His wedding day. Only then will His labors and sorrows end. **Only then will He know the JOY of being with those who love Him,** who are purchased with His blood (Acts 20:28).

THE HAPPIEST MAN ON EARTH

A lot is going to happen that day. Not only will Jesus GET MARRIED, but He will also RECEIVE HIS KINGDOM (Matt. 25:31). That's a lot for anyone — even Jesus. To my mind, this has to be the biggest moment in His life — the happiest! That brings to mind a verse we gloss over, perhaps because it has little to do with us:

 " **. . . therefore God, Thy God, hath anointed Thee with the oil of gladness above Thy companions"** (Heb. 1:9 NAS).

Catch what that verse is saying? A day is prophesied when the Lord will be the HAPPIEST MAN ON EARTH! Observe the words . . . "THY GOD, hath anointed Thee . . ." For Jesus to HAVE A GOD, He

289

must be in the role of a MAN. For God to anoint Him, He has to be in the role of the SON. (Anointed with the "oil of gladness" is a Hebrew expression for happiness of soul).

Will you observe that His joy EXCEEDS that of His companions? And WHO ARE HIS COMPANIONS? You and I — plus the saints of all ages. When we're all with Him that day, He will be the happiest MAN in our midst. Most of us think of Jesus only as the God of glory, not needing anything from us. But, because He is returning as a MAN, we can ADD TO HIS COMPLETENESS. In fact . . .

THIS MAN LOVES YOU DESPERATELY!

I am convinced the Spirit is backing me when I say the Lord Jesus loves you DESPERATELY, that He is OBSESSED with you. Recall Gethsemane where He poured out His heart for you, and consider how that same passion took Him to Pilate's judgment hall and the cross. **That cross is proof of His obsession.** You are the center of His life — you're all He has to live for.

© Linda Lovett 1971

If no one ever talked to you like this before, it's time you heard it. The fact is (if I may be blunt), the Lord is "head-over-heels" in love with you — yes, even "hooked" on you. He is the One Who should sing . . . "O, love that wilt not let Me go!" Next time you hear that song, think of it as expressing **Jesus' obsession with you. He can't let go.**

WANT TO LOVE HIM THAT WAY?

Of course. I know you do. Deep in your spirit you ache to love Him with the same passion with which He loves you. You want to be as OBSESSED with Him as He is with you. And it thrills you to think a day is coming when He will be FILLED with all the joy and satisfaction He can hold. Just as He has filled you with "joy unspeakable and full of glory," so do you want the same for Him (1 Pet. 1:8).

Don't you think we should **make it our business to see that HE IS the happiest Man on earth,** revelling in the "joy that was set before Him!" How much would it mean to Jesus to receive a kingdom if He couldn't share it with His bride? Very little. While the kingdom is a precious reward for His obedience, it is NOT HIS PASSION. His yearning is for His bride. The Lord is not obsessed with a kingdom, **He's obsessed with you and with me.**

What do you think will fill and thrill the Lord most on the day of His return? What do you think will make Him jump for joy and burst out singing . . . "It was worth it all?"

JOHN THE BAPTIST KNEW

 "Ye yourselves bear me witness, that I said, I am not the Christ, but that I am sent before Him. He that hath the bride is the Bridegroom: but the FRIEND of the Bridegroom,

which standeth and heareth Him, rejoiceth greatly because of the Bridegroom's voice: this my joy therefore is fulfilled" (John 3:28, 29 KJV).

This is another passage we gloss over. But a closer look will stir us a bit.

First a little background.

In New Testament times, Jewish marriages were usually arranged by the parents. Couples would rarely see each other until it was time for the marriage to be consummated. When that moment arrived, the FRIEND OF THE BRIDEGROOM would set out for the bride's house, accompanied by the groom. There the lad would behold his intended for the first time. The FRIEND presided over the meeting and was the chief agency of communication between the parties.

As a reward for his effort in making all the arrangements and handling the preparations, the FRIEND was allowed to be present when the bridegroom got his first glimpse of his bride. He would hear his exclamations of delight as he discovered how beautiful she was. The **joy of the friend** was made complete through witnessing the groom's delight. Thus John the Baptist said . . . "This my joy therefore is fulfilled."

Now it's true that you and I are the church, the "bride." But there's a sense in which we are JESUS' FRIEND as well. For you see, **there is a lot we can do to get things ready for His return. A lot we can do to make His bride more radiantly beautiful.** How would you like to be next to Jesus on that day when He looks on His beloved and hear Him exclaim . . . "SHE'S ABSOLUTELY BEAUTIFUL. JUST GORGEOUS!" And then as her loveliness fills His eyes, to hear Him further say...

"O, IT WAS WORTH IT ALL! I'D GLADLY GO
THROUGH THE PAIN AND SUFFERING AGAIN
FOR THE JOY OF THIS MOMENT. MY HEART
IS LITERALLY BURSTING WITH PLEASURE.
THANK YOU, FRIEND, FOR YOUR PART IN
MAKING THIS THE GREATEST DAY OF MY
LIFE!"

That's what this chapter is all about.

WE CAN ADD TO JESUS' JOY IN THAT DAY

"Come, Lord Jesus — and I pray that when
You come, You'll be so thrilled with Your
bride, it'll bring tears of joy to Your eyes. I
pray that Your delight will be boundless . . .
ecstatic . . . overwhelming. O Lord, I long for
You to be filled with joy unspeakable. May
Your soul be totally satisfied as You behold
Your bride."

Dear reader, I pray something like that every day. And
have done so for a number of years, ever since God
called me to be His "MARANATHA MAN." Familiar
with the word, "maranatha?" Paul uses it to close his
first letter to the Corinthians. It means . . . "O, Lord,
come!" As Jesus' return draws closer, we're beginning to
see this word showing up everywhere. You run into it
more and more. Well, I've taken that word . . . and by
the leading of the Lord, developed the idea of the
MARANATHA MAN and MARANATHA WOMAN.

I use these terms, MARANATHA MAN and MARA-
NATHA WOMAN, to describe those believers who
LOVE THE APPEARING OF THE LORD. This too,
comes from a statement by the apostle Paul. You've
heard this verse . . .

"Henceforth there is laid up for me a crown

of righteousness, which the Lord, the righteous judge, shall give me at that day: and not to me only, but unto ALL THEM ALSO THAT LOVE HIS APPEARING" (2 Tim. 4:8 KJV).

Some reading that verse take it to refer to those who merely BELIEVE in the Lord's return. Others have felt it refers to those who LONG for His coming, or are filled with ANTICIPATION and EXCITEMENT over it. But that is not what the apostle had in mind. From the context of his letters, it is clear that **to love the Lord's appearing means to be more concerned for CHRIST'S JOY in that day than your own.**

MARANATHA MEN/WOMEN

So what do I mean by a MARANATHA MAN or MARANATHA WOMAN? Someone who loves Jesus so much it hurts. He is so grateful for what Jesus has done for him, he is ready to PUT HIM FIRST. By first, I mean ahead of FAMILY, PLEASURES and COMFORTS — yes, even careers and financial security. That sounds like a lot, **but when you consider what Jesus sacrificed for us, does He deserve less?** Does He not have a perfect right to expect us to "... Seek ye FIRST the kingdom of God . . ." (Matt. 6:33)?

● Do you know why we're left on earth AFTER we're saved? Why God doesn't take us to heaven the moment we're born-again? Life in this God-hating world is a PRESSURE COOKER. We're tough, you and I . . . hard nuts to crack. We hate to change. But that's what God wants. **The whole point of leaving us on earth is that we might "be conformed to the image of His Son"** (Rom. 8:29). Did you know that the more we become like Jesus, the more beautiful we are in God's eyes? Jesus is the perfect example of what God wants us to be like, what He NEEDS in the way of friends.

CHANGE. In the Christian life, "change" is the "name of the game." Someone once said, "You don't have to teach a child how to be bad." How true. To teach him to BE GOOD is a stupendous task. It's uphill all the way, like working against gravity. Who has to show a man how to lose his temper, let his tongue rattle unchecked, or be impatient? How natural are unforgiveness and selfishness. Ah, but to be forgiving and kindhearted take real effort. And so if God hopes to make us like Jesus, **it's going to take a lot of time in the pressure cooker** — years for most of us. During that time He sees to it we have lots of opportunities to work on our tongues and tempers and develop a patient and charitable spirit. The more we MATURE in Christ's likeness, the prettier we are to God. To become lovely in His sight, we must work on these things continually. If we truly care about the Lord's joy in that day, we'll give this matter TOP PRIORITY.

But someone might ask, "How far are we supposed to go in putting Christ first?"

I'll let the Lord answer that.

 "He who loves father or mother more than Me is not worthy of Me; and he who loves son or daughter more than Me is not worthy of Me" (Matt. 10:37 NAS).

Children are about the dearest things to our hearts. How we sacrifice for them. We scrimp and save and go without many things for their sakes. If they get hurt, we wish it could have been ourselves instead. If you are a grandparent (and I am), you know how powerfully those darlings seize the priority in our affections. Why we even put baby-sitting ahead of serving the Lord. In nearly every area of our lives, whether Bible study, prayer, fellowship or service, it is clear that Jesus is NOT FIRST.

CONSEQUENTLY THE BRIDE
IS FAR FROM READY

In view of what we've seen, how do you think the CHURCH would look to Jesus, should He return right now? Not very inviting I'm afraid. It would seem that many in the body of Christ would "be ashamed before Him," were He to appear this moment (1st John 2:28). If we were totally honest about this, I suppose many of us would want Him to hold off for a time, so we could clean up our act and be more prepared for His return.

Alas, the church is ugly right now. Her selfish and cold-hearted indifference toward Jesus can hardly make her an attractive bride. Evangelical Christianity is shot through with self-seeking, back-biting, gossiping spirits, ready to exploit God's people for money. It's enough to "turn-off" the Bridegroom. Of course, there are some who put the Lord first, and with those the Lord is delighted. **But with most, the hard fact is, they're simply not ready.** And our Lord, praise His name, delays His return so that we might work with Him to get His bride ready.

Think what would happen if all of us who truly love Jesus BANDED TOGETHER for the purpose of making sure the day of His return WAS the greatest day of His life! Suppose we SET OUR HEARTS on making sure He was thrilled to His "shoe tops!"

And how might we do that? First of all, by doing all we could to make sure He is not disappointed with US, and then, by getting OTHERS to commit themselves in similar fashion. Think what it would be like if you and I shifted our focus from this world and set our affections on Jesus, and devoted our TIME, TALENT and TITHE to **preparing for His appearing!** That has to be **the noblest call of all!**

THE NOBLEST CALL

For nearly two centuries, world-evangelism has been the major thrust of the Holy Spirit. Yes — there will undoubtedly be a healthy ingathering before this age ends. But with the time of the Lord's return approaching so swiftly, some scholars and theologians expect the work of the Spirit TO SHIFT to preparing the BRIDE for the "Marriage of the Lamb." I am one who feels this way. That is, I feel the Spirit urging me to challenge His people to become MARANATHA MEN and WOMEN.

THE SPIRIT'S CALL

Several years ago, an event took place that burned into my spirit — **the vision of the Lord rejoicing over His bride.** He led me to the top of a mountain overlooking the city of Los Angeles. As I sat there viewing the millions of homes sprawling in every direction, I felt a whisper in my soul . . . "YOU ARE MY MARANATHA MAN!" I knew what "maranatha" meant, hence it was easy to sense what He was saying . . .

"Let Me work through you to help get My bride ready for My return. If you will challenge My people, I will back you, and raise them up by My Spirit!"

I trembled at the thought. Who was I to receive such a call? All I could think of was my own sinfulness and unworthiness. Had not that call been accompanied by an outpouring of grace and assurance, I would have asked Him to give the job to someone else. You see, I'm not really a public person. I like to do my work quietly, privately. But here was God asking me to RALLY those who "love His appearing!" His grace brought a verse to mind . . .

 "Faithful is He that calleth you, who also will do it!" (1 Thess. 5:24 KJV).

As I sat there awed, overwhelmed, it hit me what He was asking me to do. **He wanted me to summon the "FRIENDS OF THE BRIDEGROOM," people who would work to get things ready for His return!** People who would want to BEHOLD HIS JOY when He received His bride. People with the humble spirit of John the Baptist, **who cared more for Jesus' happiness than their own.** Obviously, this is the MARANATHA VISION.

In the pages ahead, that vision will unfold. Also, you'll see how you can get in on it yourself.

GETTING IN ON THE VISION

Are you one in whom the Spirit has cultivated such a love? Do you want to see Him so happy He can hardly stand it? Would you be willing to SACRIFICE time, talent and tithe to get others ready for His return? If so, then you qualify as a MARANATHA MAN OR MARANATHA WOMAN. I'm persuaded the Spirit of God is calling out dedicated Christians for this glorious task. **Getting the "bride" ready has to be the BIG WORK of the Spirit now — and you can get in on it.**

● Do you recall what I said about the POPULATION EXPLOSION, and how it is going to put the **BULK of Jesus' church on earth during the tribulation period?** There will be more saints on earth DURING THIS TIME than the sum of all who have lived and died throughout the ages past. For all practical purposes we can assume **the church is on earth right now.** Consequently we are approaching the golden hour of the maranatha vision.

By now you've faced the proposition that the church will go through the tribulation. You can also see WHY — **she's not ready.** It's going to take tribulation to refine her, to strip away the things that hold her attention and keep her from occupying with Jesus. Once believers are DETACHED from the THINGS of this world, it'll be easy to shift their focus to Jesus.

WITH THAT DAY ALL BUT UPON US, THE TIME TO PREPARE YOURSELF AS A MARANATHA MAN OR MARA-NATHA WOMAN IS RIGHT NOW!

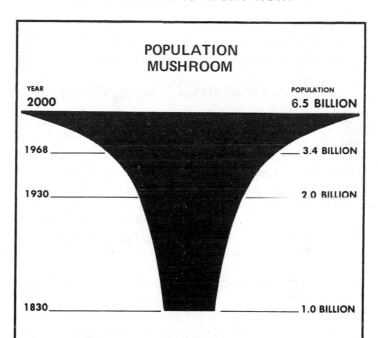

POPULATION MUSHROOM

YEAR	POPULATION
2000	**6.5 BILLION**
1968	3.4 BILLION
1930	2.0 BILLION
1830	1.0 BILLION

Out of the huge mass of people on earth during the tribulation (6.5 billion?), a smaller mass (numbering in the millions) will be born-again believers. Can you visualize the "FUN" we're going to have helping God's people? Not only will the great mass of God's people be on earth because of the population explosion, but the refining heat of the tribulation fire is going to make believers WANT help. That's when it will be exciting to help the "bride" make herself ready. (Rev. 19:7). What an adventure, moving among believers — sealed by the Spirit!

IT WILL BE WORTH IT ALL!

I know some shudder at the thought of going through the tribulation. But I assure you (having also been assured by God), that if you set your heart on helping God's people, you're going to have a GREAT TIME when the pressure is on. It is going to be a fabulous adventure — one you won't want to miss.

The more committed you are to the Lord Jesus, the more exciting the coming days will be for you. So purpose now to get yourself ready to stand fearless in the face of antichrist . . . with singing in your heart . . . "It will be worth it all, when we see Christ!" Why? Because you've spent yourself making it "worth it all" for Jesus. As this chapter closes, may I expose you to this important fact:

> NO MATTER HOW ROUGH THE TRIBU-
> LATION, HOW FEARFUL THE DAYS MAY
> SEEM UNDER ANTICHRIST, YOU'LL BE
> BETTER PREPARED FOR THEM . . . AS
> A MARANATHA MAN OR MARANATHA
> WOMAN!

The next three chapters will give you a feeling for what you could personally encounter in the coming tribulation. Anything is much easier to handle when you're PREPARED FOR IT . . . as you'll see.

Chapter Fourteen

Prepare To Operate Underground

"Honey, would you look at that!"

My wife turned to see the object of my consternation.

Right there, in the next parking space, was a car adorned with the numerals **666**. We had just arrived at the shopping center, but the strange sight greeting us made us momentarily forget our errand.

"Why would anyone deliberately put that on his car?" asked Margie.

"Oh, probably to get a rise out of Christians, I suppose." But then I added my own feelings, **"I know I wouldn't want to be identified with that number!"**

WHAT'S SO BAD ABOUT 666?

 "Here is wisdom. Let him that hath understanding count the number of the beast: for it is the number of a man; and his number is six hundred threescore and six" (Rev. 13:18 KJV).

You've heard this number before. It would be a rare (or new) Christian who didn't know that 666 is the number ascribed to the "beast" of the Revelation. Don't ask what it means. I don't know — yet. At the proper time, we'll all know.

666. For 19 centuries people have speculated as to the meaning of these numbers. All sorts of devices for getting the names and titles of people to add up to 666 have been attempted. Some feel they can positively identify a particular caesar or pope. The theories are almost endless. But one approach deserves merit. It is based on the idea that SIX is the **number of man** in Scripture. Thus 666 would refer to a TRINITY OF MAN. As 777 could be taken to indicate the Holy Trinity of Father, Son and Holy Spirit, so might 666 refer to the UNHOLY TRINITY of Satan, antichrist and the false prophet. While it is clear the unholy trinity will be operating on the earth at a certain point, we will probably have to wait until the beast is revealed before we understand how John means for these numerals to provide positive identification.

With this number specifically assigned to Satan's man (the beast), believers feel uncomfortable when that number is used to identify them or their possessions. **666 represents the epitome of evil and rebellion against God.** It's not that God cares how we use numbers. He doesn't. It's the TAINT of the world's most evil man we abhor.

Now as to WHEN this man will appear and just WHO HE IS, will have to wait on the sequence of events. The way things are shaping up, that might not be too far away — a few years, perhaps.

ANTICHRIST INTRODUCED

The FALSE PROPHET, sounding much like a "John the Baptist," will do a masterful job selling antichrist to Israel. Coming to the nation with his "signs and miracles" he will say, **"I have come to introduce the PRINCE OF ISRAEL!"** The word will spread quickly, inflaming Jewish minds with the possibility that antichrist is the promised Messiah!

Will the Jews go for it? Do kittens like cream? The result will be explosive! As far as Israel is concerned, the kingdom of heaven WILL be at hand. The people will seize this man, as they once laid hold of Jesus, insisting He accept the throne (John 6:15).

ANTICHRIST MAKES 7 YEAR
COVENANT WITH ISRAEL

Very slyly, antichrist will agree to accept the leadership of Israel for seven years. **In pretended humility,** he will say the seven years are to make sure he is God's choice. It's as though he wants to give God a chance to put His seal of approval on his administration. Such FEIGNED HUMILITY will fan Jewish fever even hotter. The Jews will hurriedly enter into such a covenant with him. The moment they do, it marks the official beginning of the tribulation period.

TRIBULATION. We can assume that once antichrist is acclaimed ruler of Israel, he will ACT OUT the role of Messiah and seek to fulfill Israel's destiny. Prophecy clearly states that Israel is to be the SUPREME nation of the world with the Gentile nations subservient to her. This means antichrist will exalt Israel's interests above those of other nations. The Gentiles won't mind going along with the RULER when it comes to putting down Christianity, but living in a JEWISH WORLD is something else. They can hardly be expected to get excited about it. Rather, they will give antichrist some opposition. The ruthlessness with which he will deal with the Gentile nations and the force employed to impose his will, will bring on the tribulation. For 3½ years, the world will reel under the wrath of antichrist, while Israel will bask in his blessing.

HE RENOUNCES CHRISTIANITY

I expect antichrist to RENOUNCE Christianity, and at the same time ANNOUNCE HIS PREFERENCE FOR JUDAISM. Claiming to be of Jewish descent, he will declare to the world that **Judaism is the ONLY religion revealed by God.** That Moses was the only person authorized by God to show men how to worship Him.

Armed with great power, he'll be able to denounce Christianity and get away with it. But that is only his **first move.**

Eager to please the Jews, he will then set about to **IMPOSE JUDAISM on the rest of mankind,** claiming it is the only religion sanctioned by God, and must fulfill its destiny as a "light to the Gentiles" (Isa. 42:6; 49:6).

"Let's make this a Jewish world," he'll shout, "and enjoy the good life as we all live together under the God of Abraham!"

JUDAISM. Since Judaism IS BIBLICAL, the deception will be powerful. Anyone can read in the Old Testament how God established a way for the Jewish people to worship Him. There is no arguing that God gave Moses a system of worship. Everything antichrist will say about it will be solidly biblical. But what he will NOT REVEAL is that Judaism has fulfilled its purpose and been set aside by God (Heb. 8:13; 10:9). Judaism was all finished when Jesus accomplished His sacrifice for our sin (Heb. 10:4,10). But as I say this, I ask you to keep in mind the difference between the RELIGION and the NATION. Judaism and Israel are two different matters. God has future plans for the nation, but He has NONE for Judaism. Resurrecting this obsolete religion will be antichrist's idea, not God's.

THE GREAT FALLING AWAY

Remember our earlier reference to the STAMPEDE TO JUDAISM? This is how it starts. **As soon as Christianity is outlawed, severe penalties will be announced for those who persist in worshipping Jesus as Lord.** With Christianity saturated with "tares" (phony Christians), professing Christians will desert the ranks in droves. Literally hordes of so-called "believers" will forsake Jesus for Judaism. This will be the great "falling away" predicted by the apostle Paul (2 Thess. 2:3). Knowing this IN ADVANCE should strengthen, rather than weaken, your faith when you see it taking place.

Why will all these so-called "Christians" flock to Judaism? To escape persecution, of course. Once antichrist sets out to woo Israel, he'll go all the way in exalting Judaism (the religion of Israel) on a worldwide basis.

DANGEROUS FOR TRUE BELIEVERS

Shortly after antichrist's announcement, **it will be dangerous for Christians to identify themselves openly as believers in the Lord Jesus Christ.** Here's what we can expect:

1. For a few weeks, **Christians will cautiously make their way to church,** amazed however, to see how few show up. The "tares" will be gone, having defected to Judaism. Only a handful of faithful ones will be left. More shocking, some who used to make the loudest professions will be among the missing. A feeling that all churches are about to be BANNED, will sweep over everyone.

2. Here in the United States, **churches will immediately lose their tax-exempt status.** Our government (such as exists) would not dare incur the displeasure of the world ruler by supporting Christianity with tax advantages.

3. In another swift move, one calculated to please the Jews, **antichrist will OUTLAW Christianity completely.** The nations cooperating with him, though reluctant at first, will enforce the ban making it illegal for believers to assemble. This will further decimate the Christian ranks **driving the faithful underground.**

4. **The NEW TESTAMENT will be banned.** People will be ordered to surrender their copies for burning. Homes will be searched for illegal Scriptures. When found, the owners will be arrested.

5. In time, **all nations will join with antichrist in exterminating Christianity.** Even though they may not be excited about Judaism, they will cooperate in persecuting the Christians. They'll have to please the world ruler to survive.

In the face of such trials, you can see how only those grounded in the Word will cling to the faith. The temptation to SHIFT over to Judaism will be very great. Can't you hear so-called "Christians" saying . . .

"What's the difference? After all, Moses was God's man as surely as Jesus. If we follow the teachings of Moses, are we not obeying the Lord? Are we not keeping the faith? Surely there can't be that much difference between the Old and New Testaments — if both are from the same God!"

But as the writer to the Hebrews warns, " . . . if any man draw back (to Judaism), My soul shall have no pleasure in him" (10:38). Even so we can expect to see millions forsake Jesus and embrace Judaism. The apostasy will be great. The sight of so many turning back to the old system will put pressure on those who know better. So it is vital that you determine within yourself NOT TO BE DECEIVED; to resist this move and stand fast for Jesus no matter the cost.

● For Christians, it will be a matter of living in a world ruled by a man who hates them, and in countries obliged to persecute them. This sounds frightening. But it helps to remember the church of Jesus Christ THRIVES on persecution. What's more, individual believers will enjoy the GRACE OF GOD in a way not otherwise possible. Thus we come to the heart of this chapter . . .

LIVING UNDER ANTICHRIST

As we enter the WEEK OF TRIBULATION (the 7 year period referred to as the 70th week of Daniel), things will become progressively worse for believers. The first 3½ years will see Christianity outlawed, accompanied by increasing persecutions. Then, in the "middle of the week," Satan will ENTER ANTICHRIST TO FORM THE "BEAST." The "beast" will devote himself to

307

outright extermination of every Christian he can find (Rev. 12:17). In view of this **progression of persecution,** believers should prepare themselves to meet the coming days in three stages:

1. PREPARE TO GO UNDERGROUND

The Christian church **as an organized institution** will disappear. Once Christianity is outlawed, its social influence will end. From then on, it will be a matter of **gathering in secret to strengthen each other and be refreshed in the Word of God.** Witnessing will be risky, with severe penalties imposed on those caught doing it. Believers will dare not be found with Bibles for fear of arrest and punishment. Consequently, all Christian activity will be forced underground.

2. PREPARE TO BE ARRESTED

The persecutions will increase steadily, reaching a point where Christians will be arrested whenever they can be identified. It will be a time of betrayal (Luke 21:16). As we reach the "middle of the week" (the first 3½ years having passed), the world ruler will decree that no one may "buy or sell," except those who bear the MARK OF THE BEAST, or the NAME of the beast, or the NUMBER of his name. Beyond that, the IMAGE of the beast will be displayed world-wide, with people everywhere required to worship it. It will be almost impossible to escape detection. Those in isolated spots may well escape, but **most of us should be ready to have our property seized and ourselves placed under arrest.** If we're prepared for this, we're more apt to honor the Lord and rely on His grace when it happens.

3. PREPARE FOR EXECUTION

Those refusing to worship the IMAGE of the beast will

be sought out and executed. **Task forces will be assigned to ferreting out Christians and exterminating them.** Some, as we noted earlier, will escape to be raptured, but that number is likely to be tiny. Most of us should plan on being in the "great multitude, which no man could number" (Rev. 7:9-15). **The Word definitely teaches the bulk of God's people will be slain.** The choice will lie between accepting "the mark of the beast" to stay alive, or willingly dying for Jesus. (True believers WILL NOT accept the mark of the beast). John says this is the "patience of the saints" (Rev. 14:12). **When you are prepared for death, there's nothing to it.** It can even be glorious.

TO HELP YOU GET READY

What you are about to read is calculated to help you prepare for the difficult days ahead. It's one thing to write a book that alerts you to what is coming, another to help you get ready for it. I would fail you, if I didn't do what I could to prepare you for the oncoming tribulation. How long I'll be able to continue doing so is questionable. Once the evil hour strikes, you and I will be out of touch with each other. It will be too late for me to get help into your hands. Therefore I must do what I can — NOW.

● **With the 3 stages of persecutions in mind, let's give thought to preparing ourselves as MARANATHA MEN and WOMEN.**

A fruitful way to go about this is to project ourselves, VIA OUR IMAGINATIONS, into the tribulation days and see if we can discern the kind of preparation needed to stand up for Jesus. I'm going to create some scenes . . . and as I do, check for the Spirit's witness. While the scenes are speculative, they'll give you an idea of what it takes to get ready.

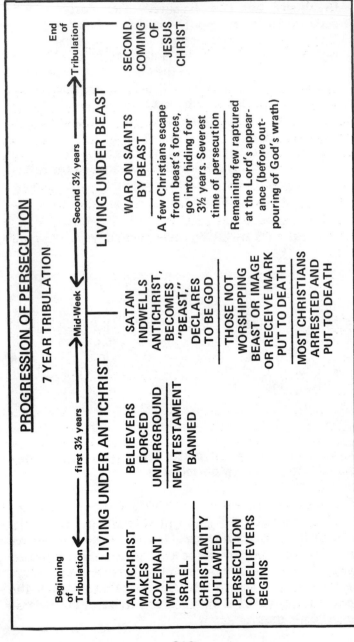

PROGRESSION OF PERSECUTION

7 YEAR TRIBULATION

Beginning of Tribulation ← first 3½ years → Mid-Week ← Second 3½ years → End of Tribulation

LIVING UNDER ANTICHRIST

ANTICHRIST MAKES COVENANT WITH ISRAEL

CHRISTIANITY OUTLAWED

PERSECUTION OF BELIEVERS BEGINS

BELIEVERS FORCED UNDERGROUND

NEW TESTAMENT BANNED

SATAN INDWELLS ANTICHRIST, BECOMES "BEAST," DECLARES TO BE GOD

THOSE NOT WORSHIPPING BEAST OR IMAGE OR RECEIVE MARK PUT TO DEATH

MOST CHRISTIANS ARRESTED AND PUT TO DEATH

LIVING UNDER BEAST

WAR ON SAINTS BY BEAST

A few Christians escape from beast's forces, go into hiding for 3½ years. Severest time of persecution

Remaining few raptured at the Lord's appearance (before outpouring of God's wrath)

SECOND COMING OF JESUS CHRIST

We'll begin with the first stage:

PREPARE TO OPERATE UNDERGROUND

It's sometime nearing the end of the twentieth century. Antichrist has banned Christianity. Churches are closed and believers gather underground for fellowship. There's no gasoline available — at least not for you — so you're using a bicycle. You're in the process of chaining it to a phone booth, when you glance across the parking lot. A man lingers suspiciously near the entrance of an alleyway. Normally you wouldn't pay any attention, but his actions catch your eye. He nervously looks in either direction before disappearing between the buildings.

Oh-oh, you hope no secret police caught sight of that. You've got an idea what it's all about. You've seen it before. The man is probably a Christian headed for a secret gathering. You shake your head wondering how the poor brother has managed to survive, his actions are so obvious. But since you belong to Jesus too, you wish you were going to that meeting with him. It's been some time since you heard someone say . . . "Praise the Lord!" Christians don't do that anymore, not since the government outlawed the faith, banning all gatherings. Fact is, you don't even keep a New Testament in your house any more. Were it accidentally discovered, it would mean real trouble for you.

It tugs at your heart to think a group of believers could be meeting close by. You'd love to be with them. The desire is so overpowering, you forget your errand and find yourself moving in the direction of that alleyway. Maybe you can see where the brother goes . . . that is, if he is a brother. It bothers you that his trail is so easy to follow. If you catch up to him, maybe you could warn him about it.

You round the corner in time to see a leg disappear into the back of a restaurant. You rush to the spot, glancing back carefully over your shoulder to make sure you're not being observed yourself. Looks okay. You put your ear to the grimey door. Nothing. You try the knob. It opens. You pass a washroom. Ahead is the kitchen. Beyond, you can see the customers in the dining room. But there's no group anyplace. Ah, then you see it. A door marked "storeroom." That has to be it.

A few steps and your ear is against the panel, eavesdropping. Sure enough, whispered voices. You barely make out some words . . . "Lord Jesus . . . almost got caught . . . got to hold out!" You're satisfied. The knob turns silently in your hand. The door yields. You find yourself staring into half a dozen startled faces.

"Who are you?" is the frightened challenge.

"Relax, I'm a Christian." That identification brings sighs of relief. One of the group, apparently the leader, is curious. "How did you find us? We didn't think anybody knew about this place?"

"Easy. I just followed the brother who came in. He gave himself away before he turned into the alley. I wasn't sure he was a Christian, but the way he was acting made me think he was. So I took a chance and followed him. He lead me right to you."

All eyes turn on the poor brother. His face drops into his hands as he moans, "I'm sorry fellas. I'll make sure it doesn't happen again."

"Wow!" explodes the leader, "If you found us that easily, the police could too. If they get a line on any one of us, we're all dead!"

But as Christians are inclined to do, the blunder is forgiven and you find yourself worshipping with them, sharing vital truths of Scripture and reveling in prayer. **How blessed to be with those who love the Lord!** It'd be fun to sing together, but the sound of your voices would reach the customers. That could bring government men in a hurry.

"Tap-tap-tap . . . tap-tap." That's the code. Another brother is outside the door. He enters, almost breathless. He has news:

"Quick, turn on the radio. They're announcing another Bible-burning for tonight! The city council is ordering Christians to surrender every book that has to do with Christianity in any way. They even want commentaries, novels . . . everything! I tell you, they're determined to destroy anything that has to do with the Lord!"

You attended the last BURN. For the sake of family security, you elected to turn in all of your New Testaments. It was hard to stand in the fair grounds and watch that mountain of truth go up in smoke. But these are hard days. To your mind, it was safer to do that than be caught with biblical contraband. Now it looks as if you'll have to watch the rest of your Christian library destroyed. **All that you'll have left will be your personal knowledge of basic Bible truths!**

CAN YOU FEEL THE THREAT?

I hope you sense a bit of it, because that's my purpose in telling such a story. I want you to sample the feelings we'll experience when our faith is banned. The pressure will be on believers in every village and settlement, as well as the policed cities. Officials will be under strict orders from the state. Little groups of Christians will band together in secret, risking the constant danger of being discovered . . . OR BETRAYED.

TO KEEP A NEW TESTAMENT IN YOUR HOUSE WILL BE DANGEROUS. SEARCH AND SEIZE ORDERS COULD FIND EVERYTHING YOU OWN CONFISCATED BY THE STATE. YOU COULD BE ARRESTED, EVEN EXECUTED.

Since you know this is coming, how do you think a believer should prepare himself? **There's only one way — stockpiling biblical gems in his HEART. Then, when the written page is denied him, he can survive out of the treasure in his heart.** When the WORD is taken from us, you can be sure it will come about swiftly. There'll be no time to prepare then. **Therefore the wise Christian will busily stock up on biblical treasures — NOW!**

> **NOW.** Once the New Testament is banned, there'll be little Bible study. Some believers will stash Scripture portions here and there, hoping to use them in underground cells. There will be some of that, but it is foolish to wait until then to lay hold of the Bible's treasures. The time to do it is NOW. The moment the tribulation gets under way, it will be too late to master the critical truths of the New Testament. There are truths believers MUST HAVE as **working knowledge** in order to stand fast under trial. A good way to acquire them is through home Bible study groups. Consider opening your home right now, and get a group digging into the principles that will fortify them in the coming crisis. Every week is precious. The evil hour is approaching with lightning speed.

HOW TO PREPARE YOURSELF
WITH THE WORD

The time is so short, I doubt if anyone could master the whole New Testament now. But there are three New

Testament books in which every Christian should feel at home:

a. **The Gospel of John:** The matter of **Christ's deity** is more powerfully settled in this gospel than in any other book. It was written for this purpose. To stand in the face of mockery, persecution and the big Jewish shift, you'll need this truth engraved in your understanding.

b. **Romans:** Paul was getting ready to leave for Jerusalem when he wrote this letter to the Christians at Rome. It was something like an insurance policy. Fearing he might be killed in the Jewish capitol, he wanted to leave on deposit in the political center of the world a statement concerning Christian basics . . . particularly **salvation by faith** plus nothing. This letter contains the foundation for the Christian life and how it is to be lived.

c. **Hebrews:** This book was written to **discourage the early Christians from defecting to Judaism.** Before Jerusalem was destroyed (A.D. 70), Christians suffered for their faith. Some hoped to escape persecution by shifting from Christ to Judaism. This amazing book WAS NOT included in the New Testament until some 300 years later. From that, it is obvious **God anticipated a future time** of testing when believers would again be tempted to forsake Christianity for Judaism. The first 3½ years of the tribulation will see this powerful book come into its own. Master it and you'll not only shield yourself from "the hour of temptation," but you'll be able to keep your friends and family from a dreadful mistake.

MASTERING THE BASICS

When I speak of mastering a New Testament book, I DO NOT MEAN memorizing it. **I mean appropriating its**

CENTRAL TRUTHS, making them part of your working knowledge. To make this easy for you, the Lord has led me to produce a series on these books known as **LOVETT'S LIGHTS ON JOHN, ROMANS and HEBREWS.** They open the truths for you in such a way, you can easily lay hold of them. What's more, they can make group study exciting and fun. If you decide to open your home for group study, you'll enjoy a fabulous boost by starting off with these tools.

Here are the three BIG GUNS of the New Testament. Master them and you'll have plenty of biblical ammunition to defend yourself against the demonic assaults of antichrist.

HOME BIBLE STUDY. From 1949-1966, churches were closed in China and house-to-house searches were made for religious books. Christians were routinely arrested and detained without trial. To survive, many dropped their Christian identification and kept silent. Some relaxation occurred when President Nixon opened the door to China. From 1968 to the present time, the HOUSE-CHURCH has flourished, though believers are still afraid to be seen with Bibles. Before long, it will be that way here in America. Now is the time to see if your pastor would approve a Bible study group in your home. The purpose would be to HELP the church, not compete with it. Let him know you and others want to prepare yourselves for the coming tribulation and need to master vital parts of the Word. He may offer to teach it himself. The informal atmosphere of a home is fabulous for dealing with questions and satisfying hearts in the Word. Many scholars believe the home-meeting was the secret strength of the early church.

EVANGELISM WILL BE FORBIDDEN

 "And I, if I be lifted up from the earth, will draw all men unto Me" (John 12:32 KJV).

Without doubt, the hardest task of evangelism today is leading men to Christ via a **personal interview**. On the other hand, the easiest way is from a pulpit where the invitation is given to everyone IN GENERAL and **no one in particular**. The pulpit threat is so minimal, even children become evangelists. (The youngest I've heard of is five years old). When you present Christ via a ONE ON ONE basis, the threat of rejection is so great, not one Christian in a hundred will do it — **even when he knows how**.

That's the way it is now. Ah — but in the tribulation, the situation will be reversed. With pulpit preaching banned, **only personal evangelism will remain**. It will have to be done in a very secretive manner, for anyone attempting to lead souls to Christ will lay his life on the line. However, the task will be easy, inasmuch as **people will come begging to be saved**. Fact is, with persecution so intense, it will be hard to find someone who'll take a chance on sharing Christ. But there will

317

be those who'll put the opportunity ahead of personal safety.

IMAGINE YOURSELF IN THIS SITUATION

It is late evening. You and your family are having devotions and prayer in the basement of your home. The secluded exit off the back of an alley provides a means of escape, should the secret police barge in from the front. Snug and secure inside, you are praying for those less fortunate than you. The sound of dogs baying in the distance interrupts your prayer.

Suddenly there is banging on the alley door. You open the peek hole to behold a grubby out-of-breath man. He looks vaguely familiar.

"I don't have much time. The guards are right behind me. If they catch me, I'm a dead man. I was your neighbor up the street and know you are a follower of Jesus Christ. I don't want to go to hell. Please tell me how I can become a Christian and go to heaven!"

What a spot! If you believe him to be sincere, would you dare speak to him of Jesus? Would you know how to introduce him to Christ in a way that left no doubt in his mind that he was saved? Weigh that. Today such a thing wouldn't happen, but a time is coming when there'll be people **pleading** with you to show them how to be saved.

I can understand how timidity and shyness would keep you from doing it now. But in a day when men CRY OUT for salvation, would you be able to present Jesus to them — ALIVE! And if so, would you risk arrest to do it?

SHARING CHRIST. It takes skill and courage to present Christ alive at the door of a man's heart — and have him know for sure Jesus is there, waiting to enter. The time to learn that skill is **now,** when the only threat is what someone might think of you. Mastering the technique before you come into the tribulation will free your mind from concern over what to say and do. You'll be able to concentrate on your prospect's motives and read his spirit. In the tribulation your attention will be divided and the pressures will be greater. Also, you'll have to be able to handle the thrill of leading a soul to Jesus, and at the same time discern whether or not it is a government trap. The only way you can prepare for such an event is to learn the skill NOW, and be able to use it when people are begging to be saved. That way you'll be ready to capitalize on the days ahead and get rich in heavenly treasure. But you must know how.

The basic text **SOUL-WINNING MADE EASY** is displayed above, along with the teacher's guide and accessories for learning the plan. The technique is based on the fact that Jesus is ALIVE and ready to enter any heart that will open the door to Him. If you'll equip yourself with this plan, you'll be ready for the hour when souls will be begging to be saved.

Again we see why the Lord raised up this ministry. Many of you are familiar with **SOUL-WINNING MADE EASY.** It was the first book the Lord led me to write, the one that gave me the idea of combining spiritual principles with the power of the printed page. Over the years that book has gone into millions of lives. The approach has become a standard today. It's so simple, even children can learn to use it.

Now back to the story.

You determine the sincerity of this man, and open the door briefly to let him in. Armed with the soul-winning plan, you introduce him to Christ in a few minutes. He is grateful.

"Oh, thank you for showing me how to receive Jesus. I know my sins are forgiven and I'm on my way to heaven. Now I must get away from here. The guards must not discover me in your house."

As he leaves, you whisper, "See you in heaven, brother." Turning to your family you say, "Let's pray for that new brother and thank the Lord we could introduce him to Jesus before it was too late."

YOU WILL BE NEEDED

There'll be no more evangelistic preaching. If Billy Graham is still alive, he'll be working MAN TO MAN the same as the rest of us. Who's going to introduce these people to Jesus? YOU ARE! For many of those begging to be saved, **you'll be the best one to help them.** You'll be the one they'll trust. So you'd better be ready. God will be counting on you.

Not only will you be needed to WIN SOULS, but you also must be ready to strengthen and coach new and weaker christians, so that they do not faint in the

face of fire. These are going to be great days for those who master the New Testament basics and know how to strengthen people in Jesus. What a time of fruit-bearing it will be. Can you see now why I love my job so? How glorious to equip God's people with the tools they need for the days ahead.

Please don't let my words run off your back. You're going to feel awful should Jesus appear and you haven't done anything to rescue those crying out for salvation. You'll feel ashamed to meet Jesus if you have done nothing to prepare other members of the family for the supreme test. Shame on you if you ignore this exhortation (1 John 2:28).

> **TRIBULATION SALVATION.** You may have heard the Holy Spirit was going to be taken out of the world before the tribulation. We should deal with that idea right here. With the bulk of the church on earth (saved) during the tribulation, one has to ask . . . "How is that possible apart from the Spirit of Christ" (Rom. 8:9b)? Paul makes it clear that no one can be saved apart from the Holy Spirit. This will be particularly true during the tribulation when being a Christian means certain death. How could anyone put his faith in an UNSEEN LORD and be willing to DIE FOR HIM without the Holy Spirit? Who is going to make Christ real to sinners? We can't. Only God's Spirit can do that. It is His work to DRAW and SEAL those in Christ (John 6:44; Eph. 1:13). Only the Spirit can make Christ real to men (Matt. 16:17). As long as people are being saved on the earth, it is error to teach the removal of the Holy Spirit. It is a false assumption. If you've been led to embrace such a view, this would be a good time to abandon it.

● This is as far as we'll carry the discussion of STAGE ONE — OPERATING UNDERGROUND. Inasmuch as the days will be treacherous, the wise Christian will prepare himself to work in secret, on a man-to-man basis. It will be risky to trust others. Consequently **now is the time**

321

to draw close to the Lord and learn how to lean on the Holy Spirit for discernment. With your life in jeopardy, you'll need the "spirit of discernment" to distinguish between those who are sincere and the betrayers.

Do what you can now to equip yourself for working with the Lord. No longer will you be able to rely on others for spiritual tasks. You'll have to do them yourself. If you're smart, you'll lay hold of all the spiritual ammunition you can get. When we come to STAGE TWO — PREPARE TO BE ARRESTED, you'll see why that ammunition is necessary. That's next.

Chapter Fifteen

Prepare To
Be Arrested!

It's the middle of the night. You're sound asleep.

"BANG . . . BANG . . . BANG"

Your wife nudges you. "Honey, wake up! Did you hear that? Is it backfire, or is someone at the door?"

You heard the sound. It jarred you out of a deep sleep. "I don't know dear," you reply, trying to shake yourself back to reality. "Maybe it was shots. The secret police have been in our neighborhood lately."

"You'd better go take a look."

Oh-oh, too late. Before you can slip on a bathrobe, the sounds come again. But this time they are accompanied by the sound of splintering wood. It's your front door.

A gruff command turns your heart to ice . . .

"We know you're in there. Just stay where you are."

You sit frozen on the edge of the bed, not even reaching for the light. A glance at the clock reveals it's 3 a.m. Probing rays from flashlights pierce the darkness in the hall. Seconds later you're shielding your eyes from the glare of those lights, as two uniformed men barge into your bedroom.

"Are you Bud Jennings?"

"Yes." You strain to see the face behind the voice.

"Get your clothes on, you're coming with us."

"Why, what have I done?" You have an idea, of course. They've found out you are a Christian.

"Don't argue. Make it easy on yourself and do as you're told."

Your wife is terrified, but concern for your safety overrules her fear. "Where are you taking my husband?"

"SPLAT!" A gun butt slams into your wife's face. You hear the jaw crack. Blood spurts from her nose and mouth as her head falls limp on the pillow. If you didn't recognize the uniform, the actions tell who these people are — secret police! This is bad. These brutes show no mercy. They have orders to be merciless.

"You're going to jail. We'll send a truck for your wife later."

Half dressed, you are shoved into the back of a waiting truck. Neighbors watch sympathetically through their windows. The sergeant leading the raid sneers . . .

"Ha! You Christians are a laughingstock for believing

324

some unseen God is going to come out of the sky and save you! Well, where is He now?"

On your way to the police station you are left with your thoughts. "Oh, my poor wife! Help her Jesus." Then you ask yourself, "Who betrayed us? What 'Christian brother' would have done this to his own family?"

Your reverie is interrupted as the truck squeals to a stop. As you are pushed toward your prison cell, the sergeant proudly calls to the officer in charge, "Here's another Christian for your collection."

The steel door squeaks open. A shove sends you sprawling into a tiny cell. As your face plunges toward the icy concrete, your knee slams hard against the corner of a metal bed. Paralyzing pain shoots through your leg. Your palms tear as you skid on the rough floor. You lie there, your heart pounding. It skips a beat when the heavy door clangs shut.

The bang of the heavy bolt brings a sick feeling inside you. Less than an hour ago you were snuggled in bed beside your wife. Now anything can happen . . . and there's no way of finding out how your wife survived that blow. The way Christians are being persecuted now, you might never see her again. You could die here, or be executed.

● EXECUTED? Yes. It is now the SECOND HALF of the tribulation. By a miracle you survived the first 3½ years. But now the beast has given orders for everyone to receive HIS MARK. No one can buy or sell without it. HIS IMAGE has been displayed all over the world and all mankind has been ordered to worship it. To this point you've ignored the commands, thinking you might be overlooked. But you've been discovered, or more likely, betrayed. And just when it looked as if you might survive, too.

You had planned well, living off of stored supplies.* You didn't have to "buy or sell" a single item. You didn't need the "mark" to get by. But evidently someone informed the authorities of your **involvement in secret Christian activities.** It could have been a member of your own family, for you have unsaved relatives who resent your relationship with Christ and would cooperate with the people in power. Or a paid informer, posing as a Christian, saw you at an underground meeting. But that doesn't matter now. You're here and it's clear life will not be the same again.

IN JAIL WITH JESUS

"If only my knee didn't hurt so," you groan, rubbing the upper part of your leg to move the blood downward. It feels like the cap might be broken. You can hardly stand to touch it, let alone walk on it.

 "O, Father, that hurts! But I'm sure it's nothing compared to what Jesus suffered for me!"

You glance about the cell to divert your attention from the painful knee. "Not bad," you think to yourself. "At least there's water here and a toilet. I'm sure I can lie down. Could be worse."

"Hey brother!" A voice from the next cell interrupts your painful reverie. "Don't get too attached to that nice room. You won't be here long. None of us will. They keep us here till they get a truck load and then they'll take us to a camp outside town."

---

* There are a number of books out now showing how to survive physically during the tribulation. A good one, by Jim McKeever, is called "Christians will go through the tribulation . . . and how to prepare for. it." He deals thoroughly with the matter of physical survival. Write to Jim McKeever, P.O. Box 4130, Medford, OR. 97501.

"Wow, just what I needed." Your knee throbs so fiercely you scarcely give heed to what the fellow said. But he makes sense. The cell is too good to be true.

"Wait a minute, Lord!" You remember something. You've read and used **JESUS WANTS YOU WELL** and know of the tremendous healing power God has built into our bodies.

 "I don't have to suffer like this. I know Your healing power can be triggered by faith. You've proved it often enough. There's no way they're going to bring in a doctor to help me. So, You'll have to be my doctor, Lord. Will You work with me now, as You have in the past? Can we use the healing principles to fix this knee?"

HEALING PRINCIPLES. If you've never considered the awesome healing power God has built into our bodies, you should learn of it now. Some day soon, you may find yourself in a tribulation situation with no doctor . . . and you'll need this knowledge. Seem strange to hear a Baptist speak of healing power? I'm convinced (by experience) that the Christian's MIND is a SUBSTATION for the power of God. **Tremendous healings can be effected in the human body simply by taking advantage of the HEALING PRINCIPLES God has established for our use.** Just as there are laws of electricity and gravity, so are there laws of healing. I'm not referring to CLAIMING HEALING in Jesus' name. That's the BLIND FAITH approach. I'm referring to **specific ways** of working with the Holy Spirit to trigger healing power ALREADY BUILT INTO OUR BODIES and focus it on a particular illness or injury. In coming days, when doctors are no longer available to us, we'll have to depend on DOCTOR JESUS and His healing principles.

So you begin. First you chat with the Lord, reviewing the healing laws as you understand them. This helps your faith to rise. One law stands above the rest:

> WHATEVER THE CONSCIOUS MIND BELIEVES, THE UNCONSCIOUS (substation of the Holy Spirit) ACCEPTS AS A COMMAND.

Now you're ready to use the healing plan. As you talk with Jesus about your knee, it is necessary to see it ALREADY HEALED . . . by faith. You thank Him for healing it, even though the pain is still there. Faith, you see, can go where reason cannot follow. So although it sounds unreasonable, you praise God for healing your knee and picture it as perfectly whole. No injury whatsoever. **And you believe it.** That's the faith element.

Then you use another law, the LAW OF REPETITION . . . and the next thing you know . . . the PAIN IS GONE! As you continue to affirm God's healing power working through your own mind, you stretch out your leg. Bless the Lord, there is no pain. You try standing on it! Wow! Isn't the Lord wonderful! You can walk. Now if they come to march you off to a detention camp, you'll be able to make it. You no longer need a doctor.

YOU ARE HEALED

That healing — accomplished by you and the Lord in private — makes you want to tell the whole world how fabulous He is. It does wonders for your faith to have the Lord come through when you're in a tight spot. So— at the moment, your faith is soaring. That's great, because you're going to need that kind of faith for what lies ahead.

In the midst of this testing, your mind flashes to your wife. As you remember how you left her, fearful concern sweeps you. "Is she alive? If so, does she have the faith to meet the testing awaiting her? Did I, as her husband, equip her with the necessary biblical resources?" As you think back over your times at the family altar, you're glad you shared God's Word with her. She'll know how to draw on the grace of God, the same as you. That's a relief.

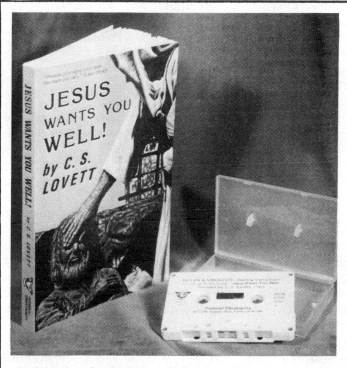

Anticipating the day when Christians will be denied medical help, the Holy Spirit has given us the healing principles. The above text, **JESUS WANTS YOU WELL!**, shows believers how to work with the Lord in using those laws. The **HEALING INSTRUCTION CASSETTE** is designed to give personal coaching in applying the laws to a particular problem. Tools offering this kind of help will not be available during the tribulation, so the time to learn the healing laws is NOW!

With your knee healed and your faith lifted to a new level, you're ready to weigh the words of the brother in the next cell. The very mention of the word "CAMP" kindles images of the days of Hitler and his horror camps. You can't shake the notion that a similar situation awaits you. One thing seems clear — you're due to be shipped off to some kind of a depot where Christians are collected . . . for what, only the Lord knows.

"I wonder how long I have before they come for me? Will it be hours . . . days? Will I be able to handle myself in a way that brings credit to Christ?"

Whatever happens, **you won't have to face it alone.** The Lord's presence is very real right now, and you have the feeling the two of you can manage whatever comes.

IN THE MEANTIME

Probably one of the hardest things for Christians to endure is WAITING . . . uncertainty . . . not knowing what's coming. Just sitting there pondering your fate can be torturous. **You must not do that.** It quenches faith. Then the Holy Spirit prods you. There is a way to transform those dread-filled hours into feasts of joy and ecstasy. How? By using the time to MINISTER TO THE LORD!

"WHAT'S THIS? HERE I AM IN A TIGHT SITUATION. I NEED THE LORD TO MINISTER TO ME . . . AND C.S. LOVETT SAYS, 'THIS IS THE TIME TO **MINISTER TO THE LORD!'** "

You already know, I'm sure, one of the best ways to take your mind from your own problems is to get concerned for someone else's needs. The Lord has genuine needs . . . and **there is no more precious experience than MINISTERING TO HIM in the spirit.**

330

MINISTER TO THE LORD. If this is a new concept for you, let me explain. Most of us think of God as living in a big white house atop a hill . . . so wealthy and powerful He has need of nothing and no one. In fact, if He needed anything, He could simply speak it into being. Right? Consequently, we gear ourselves to endless requests, always asking things of Him, never once considering He might have needs of His own. But this picture of God is faulty. **He has very definite needs with no way to fill them — apart from us.** That's why He created us — TO MEET HIS NEEDS. What are God's needs? He needs to be **loved.** He needs someone to love. How awful to be a God of love with no one to love! He needs **attention and praise.** He needs to be **comforted** at times, for He continually endures THE FEELING OF REJECTION, the most painful of all emotions. He needs to be WANTED, yes INCLUDED in all we do. He LONGS for the **companionship of His own.** Angels can't give this to Him, they're not made in His image. Above all, God needs tender **affection,** for that's the kind of a Person He is. We alone can shower this on Him.

Here you are . . . in a terrible situation . . . undoubtedly the worst of your life. Are you going to sit there on your bunk pondering your fate, and possibly allow Satan to get you stewing about it? That's no way to go, especially when those moments can be turned into one of the most ecstatic events a Christian can know. What better time to think about the Lord and His needs . . . when you have nothing to do but WAIT!

You close your eyes. You bow in prayer. **Your spirit drifts into the "secret place" of your imagination,** that delightful room in your mind where you meet Jesus in prayer. Having done this for years, you immediately feel at home in His presence.

There He is . . . **you behold Him by faith.** He is eagerly waiting for you to rush into His arms. In your imagination, you hurry to Him, throwing your arms about

His neck. You hug Him tightly. How good He feels to you and you to Him. You kiss His cheek. It's like SWEETHEARTS who've been separated all day. How glorious to hold the Lord in your arms — BY FAITH! How He loves it! His joy becomes intense when you minister to Him with words from your heart,

"Precious Savior, You're the most fantastic Friend a person could have! I love You. It's glorious to hold You in my arms and know You enjoy MY PRESENCE. You certainly are generous with Your presence. Since You made me for Your pleasure, I want to bring You all the joy I can. Whatever delight You can find in me, I want You to have it right now.

So many of Your people are suffering, Lord Jesus. A lot of them are giving their lives for You. While this is precious in Your sight, I'm sure their pain is Your pain. O, that they all knew how to put their arms about You and minister to You. It's a joy for us, Master, to be able to tell You that You mean more to us than our physical lives. It's a thrill actually, sweet Lord, to lavish our presence and hearts on You at a time when the average person would be thinking of his own situation. That's not what You did. You were thinking of US when they seized You and led You to Calvary.

For what it means to You, Lord Jesus, I wouldn't care to live without You. For me, the safest and most blessed place of all is right here in Your arms. If my life is to be taken from me soon, Master, grant that my death will bring glory to Your Name. I want You to be proud of me. Thank You for loving me and letting me know it. No matter what happens to me physically, there is no

way anyone can snatch me out of Your arms.''

When it's your turn to be seized by the secret police and dragged off to confinement, it will be a fabulous comfort to enter the **"secret place"** and minister to the Lord. In anticipation of the coming hour, the Spirit has produced a cassette showing how to do this called **HOW TO MINISTER TO THE LORD.** Via the cassette, you and I go into the "secret place" together. Once there, I will show you a new way to embrace the Lord and thrill His heart. If you do not know how to "cuddle with Christ," this cassette will teach you. Can you imagine how fabulous this will be when you face your last moments on earth!

● You've been so busy chatting with the Lord, you failed to hear the sound of heavy boots in the hall. The clang of steel brings you out of the "secret place." As the cell door swings open, your eyes focus on your captors who have come for you. The brother in the next "suite" was right, you haven't been here very long. But it was long enough. **You've enjoyed two marvelous events — the healing of your knee and ministering to the Lord in the "secret place."** You should be ready for anything now.

READY FOR ANYTHING

"Hurry up . . . get in line."

You oblige, even smiling as you rise and walk (without a limp) through the doorway to join a dozen others being escorted by armed guards. You turn around to see the smiling face of the brother from the adjoining cell.

You smile back. "You were right, I wasn't here long!"

Before he can reply, a guard barks a gruff order . . . **"No talking!"**

Well, you don't have to talk. You lift your hand, gesturing the "ONE WAY" SIGN. Your friend nods his response. An unspoken message passes between you as your eyes meet. Then you both face straight ahead.

A door swings open to the outside. Oh-oh, there's the truck. You follow the others, silently climbing inside. From your place on the hard bench, you can study your companions. They sit there passively, like sheep led to the slaughter. As you gaze into the eyes of each one, you measure his spirit. Some are ready for this, some are not. The look in the eye pretty well tells the extent to which each has prepared himself for this moment.

How glad you are you equipped yourself for these days. Some of those with you are already drawing strength from your smile of assurance. You've just come from the "secret place." No matter what lies ahead, you will undoubtedly be able to help some of these very people stand firm for Christ. You hope you'll get that chance when you arrive at your destination.

● The truck pulls out with a jerk, throwing you into the chain stretched across the back to keep the prisoners from falling out. The rear is open permitting you to observe the countryside. A chilling wind in the wake of a recent snowstorm makes you shiver. The New England countryside is blanketed in white.

After an uncomfortable hour's ride, the truck reaches the crest of a ridge. Below sprawls a massive detention camp crammed with people. A giant stand of trees has been cleared to make room for the buildings and compound surrounded by high barbed wire fences. So this is your destination. It's hard to believe this is actually taking place in America. Detention camps are so out of character with our passion for freedom.

When you pass through the heavily guarded entrance, your transportation comes to an abrupt end. You and the others are herded into an open compound, where prisoners are crammed into the enclosure like sardines.

You and your friend slowly edge your way to the fence. Some brethren are kind enough to yield the space, giving you a turn at looking across the fields of "the land of the free" . . . probably for the last time. Your friend is clearly worried,

"We're in death row, brother! I can feel it!"

At those words your fingers tighten slightly around the links in the fence. In your heart, you realize your friend is right. You understand why he feels as he does. This is a **death camp**. Yet you do what you can to ease his tension:

"**We're not dead yet. Who knows what God has for us to do before that time comes.**"

But the time **will** come, as you well know. To your knowledge Christians don't come out of these camps alive. You and your brother mingle with others in the crowded enclosure. Some huddle together for warmth. It's chilly in the open air. But that's the least of the discomfort. There's no shelter of any kind, no sanitation, no way to treat those made sick by the filth.

However you can praise the Lord. At this stage, there's nothing to lose by speaking openly of Him and singing His praises. Nearly all of these poor souls are Christians and would welcome it.

"They're not even bothering to feed us," groans your companion. "I guess they see no point, **since they're going to kill us anyway.**"

KILL. Once the beast gives orders for Christians to be liquidated, the process won't drag on. The sooner he can stamp out Christianity, the easier he'll breathe. He knows the vitality of our faith and how persecution tends to make it more virile. His approach will be out-and-out extermination. Hitler's methods will appear crude by comparison. Modern technology will give the BEAST a real boost, creating new means of high effeciency disposal; and likely the production lines of some industrial plants will be converted into execution centers.

Curiously enough, a factory of sorts adjoins your camp. A closed corridor connects the two facilities. The big sign on the roof identifies it as a FERTILIZER FAC-

TORY. That's a laugh. You shudder to think what they're using to make that fertilizer.

Satan rubs his hands gleefully when the believer's mind occupies with such thoughts. One could picture a high-speed decapitation machine that separated heads from bodies, allowing eyes and teeth to be extracted. That gruesome picture is reinforced by something John said. He predicted multitudes would experience such a fate . . .

" . . . I could see the souls of those who had been BEHEADED for the sake of God's Word and their testimony to Jesus, those who had not worshipped the beast and its image or received its mark on forehead or hand . . ." (Rev. 20:4 NEB).

You stomp your foot in anger at yourself.

"What am I doing? I know better than to let Satan maul me like this! The Lord doesn't want this depressing stuff in my mind. I've got more important things to think about. There are people in this camp who need to be encouraged. I'll be useless to God if I let the devil quench my spirit now."

SO YOU DEAL WITH THE DEVIL

"Submit yourselves therefore to God. Resist the devil, and he will flee from you" (James 4:7 KJV).

Familiar with that verse? You should be. It's one of the great promises of the Bible. Will you note, however, it **does not say** PRAY and the devil will flee. It says . . . "RESIST!" Praying and resisting are two different things. Praying is toward God. Resisting is toward the devil.

This is a military operation. We're dealing with an enemy, an adversary. It's a fight. If you don't engage Satan in face to face combat, he'll dominate your life . . . one area at a time. The only way to stop him is to meet him head on.

So it's time to act. First you submit yourself to God. Then you speak directly to Satan:

"**Satan, in the name of Jesus, depart from me right now. GO! Stop trying to fill me with fear, for it is written . . . 'Be anxious for nothing, but in everything . . . give thanks: for this is the will of God in Christ Jesus concerning you!'** " (Phil. 4:6; 1 Thess. 5:18).

THEN WHAT HAPPENS?

That action took less than 15 seconds. It is NOT God's will for His children to be victimized through fear and worry. So you exercise your right as a child of God, and take authority over the devil. **When you order him away in Jesus' Name, HE HAS TO GO!** He is a defeated enemy. You've just given the devil his marching orders and he departs at once. The thrill of it is overwhelming.

You lift your head. Your friend senses something spiritual was going on, though he couldn't possibly recognize the miracle. He couldn't know the fantastic release you're feeling! The great relief that comes when Satan flees!

DEALING WITH THE DEVIL. Did you know the Bible has as much to say about Satan and hell as it does about the Lord and heaven? Just as we must deal with Jesus for salvation, so we must deal with the devil for victory over temptation. The very word "victory" means to win in battle. The Christian life is a battle that can only be won by taking authority over Satan. There is a biblical technique

338

for squaring off against the devil. The Lord Himself used that technique when Satan sought to tempt Him after His wilderness fast (Matt. 4:1-11; Luke 4:1-13). Aware that true victory in the Christian life is obtained by using this technique, the Holy Spirit urged me to put it in print. It is called, **DEALING WITH THE DEVIL.** During the tribulation, when Satan will seek to overpower believers with FEELINGS OF FEAR, this technique will be urgently needed.

Knowing demonic assaults are certain to come when Christianity is outlawed, the wise Christian will fortify himself against that day. Terrible tales of persecution will turn the believer's heart to ice. The devil will pounce on his fears, terrorizing him to the point of numbness and surrender. That must not happen to you. Equip yourself with the skill in **DEALING WITH THE DEVIL** now. Learn how to use it and you won't cave in when Satan's attacks come.

You feel sorry for the other prisoners who cannot do what you just did. Your heart goes out to them — they're living below their privileges in Christ. You don't know how many of them you will be able to help, but at least you can show your friend how to deal with the devil.

You're an old hand at it. Long ago you learned the technique of resisting him. You can recognize a satanic thrust and deal with it IMMEDIATELY. If only your friend could do the same. It would save him so much grief, so much needless agony. Then that anxious look would disappear from his face. You'd love to help him:

"Woody, I can tell by the look in your eyes that Satan has you in the grip of fear. Every time one of the guards comes to the gate and calls out names, you turn white as a sheet.

Would you try something for me? Next time they call names, instead of freezing, start talking to Satan. I mean speak to him. Take authority over him and order him to depart from you and take his darts of fear with him. Then see what appears on your face! Everything will change for you, I guarantee it!"

Your heart is glad at his reply . . .

"Are you serious, Bud? Can we really do that? Will he actually go away?"

"Sure, I've done it for years. Nothing to it."

"Man, if you could only show me how. I thought Christians should be able to cope with their fears in a situation like this, but I don't think I can take much more!"

His hungry desperation makes it easy for you to show him the steps of the plan and how to do them in the power of the Holy Spirit. As he goes off to deal with the devil privately, you scout out others who are obviously caught in the grip of fear.

Before long, your brother comes running back.

"I did it! I did it! Satan fled just like the Word says. My fear is GONE now! Praise the Lord, and thank you so much, brother, for showing me how to resist the devil. You've saved me from awful torture!"

"I can see He's set you free. Praise His Holy Name! Now come and help me with the others until our names are called."

"How much time do you think we have?"

"I don't know, but let's make it count. If I'm called before you are, make sure you 'SET FREE' as many as you can!"

How long DO you have? You're about to find out — next.

341

Chapter Sixteen

Prepare To Graduate To Glory!

Your name is called.

"Prisoner Bud Jennings . . . front and center!"

It came sooner than expected. You don't reply immediately. Slipping into the "secret place" for a moment, you want to be refreshed by the Lord's presence before you face the guard:

 "Lord Jesus, here we go. Would You hold me in Your arms for just a bit. Strengthen me with Your presence, Lord, so I'll be a credit to You. If it's time to bring me home, help me to go out of this life with Your praise on my lips!"

The guard calls out your name again. During the short time you've been in this camp, you've heard stories. You know for certain this is a one way trip.

"Over here! I'm coming!"

You edge your way through the crowd, encouraged by comforting pats on the back. The brethren are silently saying, "Hang in there brother! Stand up for Jesus!" You smile back your assurance, letting them know God's grace is sustaining you. They watch mutely as you present yourself to the guard.

"Let me see your tag. 643821 . . . all right, walk ahead of me. Go straight to the doorway marked DEBRIEFING!"

"Debriefing," you snort inwardly, "who are they kidding?" Through the grapevine you've heard what goes on in there. They want you to deny Jesus and receive the mark of the beast. It's not a debriefing, it's a show-down! It's accept the mark or **die!**

"Stand here!" The guard is all business. Why not? It's routine for him. He points to a spot. You plant your feet on it. Momentarily he moves ahead to knock on a grey steel door. As it opens, a heavily built man with cold steely eyes looks you over. His hard looking features conjure an image — GESTAPO MAN!

"We're just about ready for him." You feel death in his voice. Now you know how Jesus felt when Isaiah said of Him . . . "like a sheep to the slaughter." Suddenly you have a greater appreciation for Jesus' suffering. Whew! **You're glad the Lord is with you.**

INTIMIDATION HEADQUARTERS

A jab from the guard's machine gun tells you to step into the room. Yes, they're ready for you now. Whoever was in the room before you has been escorted to his fate. First thing you notice are the thick carpets. What a contrast to the filthy compound. But that's the point.

They want you to notice the difference and be motivated by it.

The walls are gentle pastels. Potted plants, chandeliers and oil paintings give the place a luxurious atmosphere. A colonel sits on the other side of a massive teak desk. He smiles broadly, motioning you to take a seat on the lounge across from him.

Official looking papers are in front of him, probably your file. Above the colonel, a framed portrait of the world ruler ("the beast") looks down on the scene. The atmosphere appears to be very cordial. The colonel is most friendly:

"Well, Mr. Jennings, I apologize for the terrible conditions of our camp. We hope to make things better for you very soon. All we need is a little cooperation on your part. You look like the kind of a man who knows how to adjust and make the best of a situation. I'm sure we're going to get along fine.

Besides, Mr. Jennings, we know quite a bit about you. See how thick your file is? You didn't know it, of course, but we've been monitoring your activities for years. And not only yours, but we have a line on every Christian throughout the world. We pick up people with our computer almost from the moment they accept Jesus.

From your extensive record, Mr. Jennings, I see you're a committed Christian and so far you have refused to honor our ruler and accept his offer to become part of our one world family.

It's also clear, you've been active in underground activities. You've persuaded other Christians to reject the generosity of the government. Is this true?"

344

His saccharin-smile doesn't fool you for a minute. Still, there's no point in denying anything. Everything seems to be in the record. You might as well be open about it.

"Yes, it's true."

The colonel is almost fatherly as he continues:

"We appreciate your commitment, Mr. Jennings. I congratulate you on your loyalty to Jesus. But I want you to see how misplaced your commitment is. There's no way you believers can win against the rest of the world. I don't blame you for embracing the teachings of Jesus. He was a remarkable man. But 2,000 years is too long to wait on anyone's promises. You're too intelligent to bind yourself to promises that can't possibly be fulfilled.

We're prepared to be very lenient with you, Mr. Jennings . . . if you'll just acknowledge Jesus as a friend of the past and show respect for our ruler. Besides, you've got your wife to think about. We'd like very much to give her medical attention — before it's too late."

Wow! That's the first word your wife is still alive. But again . . . it may be a trick. You're about to speak, when the colonel silences you with a wave of his hand. He's smooth, this fellow, even friendly. He wants you to hear him out before you reply. As he continues to turn on the charm, it's obvious he considers himself a super sales-man.

"See that table over there? The little machine on top is a laser device. If you'll step over there with me, we'll painlessly tattoo a special number on your wrist and forehead. We could release you at once and get help for your wife."

TATTOO. I am employing a literal interpretation of John's reference to the "mark of the beast" and see it applied to the wrist and forehead. It could just as easily refer to finger-prints and voice prints, both accurate identification devices of our day, though wholly unknown in John's time. Others have suggested the MARK has to do with MIND-CONTROL (forehead) as well as positive control over one's actions (hands). For simplicity's sake, I have elected to go the literal route and see the mark applied as a tattoo. But this may not be the case. You will also find, I have incorporated the idea of literal beheading to round out the story. When the time comes to dispose of God's people, we can expect the "beast" to use a number of methods.

"A wonderful life awaits you in this great country of ours. And we have ways of making your fondest dreams come true. We certainly have no desire to harm you . . . we just need your cooperation. I'm sure Jesus wouldn't hold it against you for doing this. He loves you. He knows you're human and circumstances often dictate your actions. It'll only take a minute. Let's do it."

As you glance about the room, the guards on either side are all smiles. They nod their heads affirmatively, as if this were the only intelligent thing to do. The colonel assumes you're going to go along with him. He rises from his chair:

"If you'll join me here at the table, I'll show you how simple this is . . . and you'll be out of here in a flash. We don't want to keep you from your wife a minute longer than necessary."

THE SHOWDOWN

The colonel expects his action (rising from the chair) to trigger a similar response in you. He exudes confi-dence. You can almost feel unseen hands trying to lift you out of that chair to follow him. That's satanic, for sure. You shake off the spell:

"I'M SORRY, I CAN'T DO THAT!"

"What?" The colonel explodes, pretending to be shocked that anyone would turn down such an offer. He'd like you to think many of those preceding you accepted his offer and were released. But you know better.

The colonel's phony charm vanishes:

"You mean you choose death over the generosity of our benevolent ruler! I can't believe you'd do such a thing!"

"Sorry, colonel, but there's no way I can deny the Lord Jesus. It just isn't practical."

"Practical!" That gets him.

"Certainly. You see, if I reject Jesus and accept the mark of your ruler, I might enjoy his favor for a few years . . . the same as you. But then I'd be trading away a glorious eternity for those few years. That's too big a price. Besides, the Lord has made it clear that those who receive this mark, will burn IN HELL FOREVER . . . along with the world ruler. Honestly, what kind of a deal is that?

As it is, you can deny me a few years on earth, but you can't rob me of eternity. As for allegiance to a leader, I already have a leader, One Who loves me. I have found Jesus to be the most reliable and loving Friend a person could have.

You see, He was in this spot once. He had a chance to deny me, and He refused to do it. Now it's my turn.

347

I'm in the place of giving my life for Him. When you come right down to it, wouldn't I be crazy to trade eternity with someone who loves me, for a few years with someone who can only lead me into hell?"

"THAT'S ENOUGH! TAKE HIM TO THE PLANT!"

The colonel is no longer smiling. His face is purple with rage. Of course his smile wasn't genuine anyway — just part of his technique. Now that you've taken your stand, he doesn't want to hear another word. Not only has his charm failed, but he's heard (from others as well as you) that he is condemned to hell along with the beast. Your words have cut him to the quick . . . especially since you're ready to back them with your life.

AMAZING GRACE!

Did those words of testimony come out of you? Wow! You're amazed at yourself! The grace of God truly overwhelms in the moment of need. Even though you knew your life was on the line, you said those things as casually as you used to tell a gas station attendant, "fill'er up." "Amazing grace" indeed.

"C'mon." This time the hands helping you out of the chair are not unseen. They're the rough hands of the guards. No more smiles as they hustle you out the side door. Everything is done swiftly to prepare for the next victim. The colonel is set to go through his routine again.

As you are shoved into the makeshift corridor leading to the next building, you think of all those who've walked this path ahead of you. Suddenly a heart-warming sound comes to your ears. It's singing . . . and it's just ahead. One of the guards slides a huge door back on its rollers. Now you know who's doing the singing. A cluster of Christians, both men and women, stands before a moving steel conveyor system.

To the displeasure of the guards, these Christians are singing the praises of Jesus. You're not the only one enjoying "Amazing Grace." These brethren are waiting their turn on the deadly conveyor, yet their faces radiate the joy of the Lord! The very sight of these precious brethren swells your heart with courage.

NO ONE CAN DIE LIKE A CHRISTIAN!

One rumor is true. The plant is equipped with one of the new automatic guillotines. It won't be long now. A shove sends you stumbling into the group. No need to apologize. What's a bump among those who are about to die? They look at you . . . smile . . . but don't stop singing. Are they doing this to muffle the sound of the conveyor? No way — **they want the Lord's praises on their lips as they go out of this life.**

And you know what they're singing. What else but **"Amazing Grace."**

"Thru many dangers, toils and snares,
   I have already come;
'Tis grace hath bro't me safe thus far,
   And grace will lead me home.

When we've been there ten thousand years,
   Bright shining as the sun,
We've no less days to sing God's praise
   Than when we first begun."

What a blessed fraternity! What a glorious privilege! Makes you think of the gallant men and women who bravely marched into the Roman coliseum to meet the hungry lions . . . with Jesus' name on their lips. You are following in the same glorious tradition, ready to give your life for Jesus.

● The sound in the room changes. The clanking of the

349

conveyor slows down. Apparently the last batch of bodies has been processed. The casket-like cages come to a quick halt. One in front of you opens like a yawning mouth to receive its victim. As guards seize you and lift you onto the conveyor, you instinctively hum "Amazing Grace." Snap . . . snap . . . click. Your legs are clamped. Your shoulders are locked into place. Your head fits into a cradle, holding it just right for the high-speed knife.

As the other brethren are loaded, they too are filled with grace:

"Praise the Lord!" "Lord Jesus, I'm coming home!" "Bless the Name of Jesus!"

"Listen to those fools," smirks a guard.

"Yeah, they're crazy," jibes another.

It bugs them that these victims prefer death rather than deny their Ruler. One guard isn't so tough. You see a tear run down his cheek. Maybe he senses he should be on that conveyor. The testimony is getting to him.

The motors whine again. A jolt. The conveyor linkage clanks once more. You feel yourself being propelled forward . . . slowly at first . . . then faster. Now you detect a different sound ahead. It's the knife doing its job . . . fast . . . efficient . . . no outcries. You have only seconds to go . . .

 "Father have mercy on them. They can't possibly know what they're doing. Hold me in your arms Lord!"

There's barely time to slip into the "secret place." Good. You feel the Lord's presence. Your eyes close so you won't see the flash of the blade as your neck moves into place.

"ZIP" . . . that's it.

The knife does its job, but you don't feel a thing. Something else has happened in that same "twinkling of an eye." You've simply stepped from the "secret place" into the Lord's presence. His presence you **felt** before, is now HIS PERSON! There He is with arms outstretched to embrace you . . .

"Welcome to the club, son!"

Those are Jesus' first words — His welcome. He may not use those words, of course, but He'll welcome you to the fraternity of those who "die in the Lord." Your first words will probably be . . .

"Oh Lord, You're everything I thought You'd be," as you fall into your Father's arms.

You're **glad** you died for Jesus! His grace made it so easy. You shifted instantly from one reality to another . . . feeling nothing in the process (2 Cor. 5:6-8). It reminds you of the way motion picture reels were changed in movie theaters. The audience didn't realize there were two projectors up there in the booth, so SYNCHRONIZED that when one reel ended, another began without so much as a flicker. The film continued without the slightest hesitation.

DYING FOR JESUS. Only a **Christian** can consider death so casually, it can even be viewed as a glorious event. There are tremendous truths about death in the New Testament—which, when we know them — turn death into an exciting event. One of the chief truths is that **DEATH IS HARMLESS.** The devil, of course, has painted it as the ultimate agony, but he's a liar. Actually, death is one of the easiest things to endure. But Satan has used it to bind people with fear (Heb. 2:14b,15). When the New Testament concept of death becomes a part of your working knowledge, you can laugh at it (1 Cor. 15:54,55). Lavishing your death on the Lord can be thrilling. Besides, what's so great about dying in bed with a sickness? In preparation for the hour when believers will be surrounded by death, the Lord has given us an exciting tool . . . **DEATH: GRADUATION TO GLORY!** These insights provide fantastic preparation for the day when we will be living with death all around us.

ABSENT FROM THE BODY — PRESENT WITH THE LORD

"Hey fellows! Don't be afraid of death. There's nothing to it. See — it didn't hurt me . . . and it won't hurt you either. It's harmless!"

Who said that — Lazarus? He might have. But it was Jesus. That's the message that comes to us via His death and resurrection. Even now our Lord stands on the OTHER SIDE OF DEATH and shouts. . . **"I guarantee it won't hurt a bit!"**

By His sacrifice, the Lord removed the sting (stinger) from death:

> **" . . . that through death He might destroy him that had the power of death, that is, the devil; And deliver them WHO THROUGH FEAR OF DEATH were all their lifetime subject to bondage"** (Heb. 2:14b,15 KJV).

> **"And when our mortality has been clothed with immortality, then the saying of Scripture will come true:**

> **'Death is swallowed up; victory is won! O Death, where is your victory? O Death, where is your sting?'**

352

. . . God be praised, He gives us the victory through our Lord Jesus Christ" (1 Cor. 15:54b, 55,57 NEB).

THE "BLESSED" EXODUS

Do I expect to convince you that death is nothing but a "big teddy bear?" No. But I can prod you to lay hold of the New Testament concept of death to prepare you for your own exodus. It can be a "blessed event" — if you're ready for it. **To be able to die with the praise of Jesus on your lips has to be the BLESSED EXODUS!** It's so much easier when you know death is HARMLESS. Now "blessed" is not my idea. It is the apostle John's:

> **"And I heard a voice from heaven saying unto me, Write, BLESSED are the dead which die in the Lord FROM HENCEFORTH: . . .**

 . . . and I saw the souls of them that were beheaded for the witness of Jesus and for the Word of God, and which had NOT WORSHIPPED the beast, neither his image, NEITHER HAD RECEIVED his mark upon their foreheads, or in their hands . . ." (Rev. 14:13; 20:4 KJV).

Observe . . . "Blessed are the dead." To whom is that blessing directed? It's right there in the Revelation . . . THOSE REFUSING THE MARK OF THE BEAST. Look at the passages again. See how believers are faced with a choice between Jesus and the beast. This **test** is described as the "patience of the saints" (Rev. 14:12).

As I shared with you earlier, I'm satisfied the **biggest part of the "body of Christ," is going to join the Lord VIA MARTYRDOM.** If I can strengthen you to the place where you can rejoice in the face of that experience,

353

I will have served you well. I want you to be able to pass through death's door with Jesus' name on your lips. See now why I would write such a book? I want you in that BLESSED CROWD!

RATHER BE RAPTURED?

Rough days are before us, no question about that. But those days are also numbered. In fact, they'll be supernaturally CUT SHORT when Jesus appears in the sky! (Matt. 24:22). You might be thinking to yourself . . . "I HOPE I CAN STAY ALIVE AND BE AMONG THOSE RAPTURED FROM THE EARTH!" Forget It — it won't matter one bit whether you are raptured or die a martyr's death. **Both routes end up the same place — with Jesus in the sky.** The apostle Paul insists there's no advantage in being raptured (1 Thess. 4:15).

HERE'S THE IMPORTANT THING—**BEING READY TO STAND UP FOR JESUS, NO MATTER THE COST.** AND IF YOU GIVE YOUR LIFE FOR HIM, YOU ARE EVEN MORE BLESSED. UNDER NO CIRCUMSTANCES SHOULD YOU THINK OF CO-OPERATING WITH THE BEAST IN ANY WAY, HOPING TO STAY ALIVE UNTIL THE RAPTURE. THAT WOULD BE FOLLY. YOU COULD WIPE OUT A LIFETIME OF FAITHFUL SERVICE BY GIVING IN TO THE TEMPTATION TO MAKE THINGS EASIER FOR YOURSELF OR FAMILY IN THE FINAL MOMENTS OF THIS AGE. **DON'T DO IT!** YOU'LL BE SORRY IF YOU DO.

HELPING YOU GET READY
FOR JESUS' RETURN

With the passing of the years, the family of God has become very dear to me. I could reach out and hug you all. Some of the letters you beloved friends have written are so full of affection, so full of appreciation for what

I'm trying to do . . . that you've become very close to me. **I ache in my spirit to see every one of you ready for Jesus' return.**

In this second portion of the book, I have addressed the fiery trial that precedes the Lord's appearing. In the process I have mentioned certain books God has authored through me. But please don't think my motive is to sell books. Nothing could be further from the truth. The truth is . . .

I AM ABSOLUTELY CONVINCED THE MOST EFFECTIVE WAY TO HELP GOD'S PEOPLE IS WITH BOOKS . . . BOOKS BACKED BY PRAYER! GETTING LIFE-CHANGING BOOKS INTO THE HANDS OF BELIEVERS . . . AND BACKING THEM WITH PRAYER . . . IS THE WAY I DO WHAT GOD HAS CALLED ME TO DO.

BOOKS. Have you considered the **power of a book?** It is the most powerful way to touch and change a life. Abraham Lincoln testified . . . "What I am today, I owe to my angel mother and the books she taught me to read." Benjamin Franklin's testimony was similar. He said a BOOK by Cotton Mather gave direction to his life, enabling him to become the influential leader of those early days. Get a man alone with a book and he'll face truths he'd never otherwise consider. In such a moment, he can be himself, not worrying that someone else might see his reaction and judge him. A book is more powerful than TV, which bombards our minds with such a stream of ideas there is no time to absorb any of them. No sooner are you struck by one, when another hits you. But when a person READS, the SPIRIT can impress an idea on him and **he can pause and reflect.** As the idea penetrates and seizes his soul, he is compelled to ACT. **That is the power of books backed by prayer.** No wonder God chose A BOOK to transmit His revelation — THE BIBLE.

Now that you understand my conviction, you can see why I would speak of the tools God has given me. They do the job. **Note how each one I've mentioned helps to get us ready for the Lord's return.** Each one encourages the reader to be a MARANATHA MAN or MARANATHA WOMAN.

Start thinking of yourself as a MARANATHA MAN or MARANATHA WOMAN. Remember how I defined them: **people who LOVE the appearing of the Lord.** Not people who merely ANTICIPATE His return or are EXCITED ABOUT IT, but **those who want Jesus to find HIS BRIDE READY when He comes.**

A MARANATHA MAN IS ONE WHO SEEKS TO **PUT CHRIST FIRST** IN HIS LIFE AND DOES WHAT HE CAN TO **HELP OTHER CHRISTIANS** DO LIKEWISE. ONLY IN THIS WAY CAN THE BRIDE MAKE HERSELF READY.

Earlier I promised to explain why one could endure the tribulation easier as a MARANATHA MAN or WOMAN. By now you've probably figured it out for yourself:

1. Pity the man or woman who does not know how to **DEAL WITH THE DEVIL** in that hour. Demonic assaults will be the order of the day. **The believer who knows how to put Satan to flight will be IMMUNE to attacks of fear,** whereas those without this skill will have to grin and bear it.

2. If Christians can neither buy nor sell in those days, they will also be denied doctors. Surely doctors will be forbidden to tend believers. But Jesus is the Super Physician. **The man or woman who knows how to work with Him to trigger the AWESOME POWER of the body to heal itself, will be a great blessing to his friends and family.**

3. For the believer thrown into prison and left, perhaps to die, **MINISTERING TO THE LORD can bring the joy of heaven into his cell.**

4. When you face execution, knowing that DEATH IS HARMLESS allows you to laugh in its face. Instead of cringing in despair, **you'll be able to use your death as a testimony to those watching. The most powerful witness men can behold is the JOY on the face of a Christian when he gives his life for Jesus!**

So you see, being a MARANATHA MAN or WOMAN makes it possible for you to USE the tribulation as a testimony to the power of God. Armed with these insights, you can take the worst Satan can dish out and use it to bring credit to Christ. On top of that, if you can WIN SOULS as well as master the basics of **ROMANS** and **THE LETTER TO THE HEBREWS,** you'll be a powerhouse for Jesus. The tribulation will be your brightest hour. In view of this, don't you think it's time to commit yourself to the Lord as . . .

A MARANATHA MAN OR WOMAN?

Epilogue

MARANATHA

"THAT YOU
MAY WIN THE PRIZE"
(1 Cor. 9:24)

MAN

" . . . that we may present
every man perfect in Christ Jesus!"
— Col. 1:28

Paul's statement pretty well describes what we're trying to do here at Personal Christianity. What could delight the Lord more than having you and me at our best when He returns? This is what will make His "BRIDE" beautiful in His eyes.

She is far from that now, as we've seen. So far, in fact, the Lord is going to let her pass through the refining fires of the tribulation. Then — when she has been stripped of the earthly bonds holding her affection, it will be a lot easier for her to put Jesus FIRST.

When the fiery days come, **the Lord is going to need MARANATHA MEN AND WOMEN who know how to work with Him.** God's people are going to need COACH-

ES, concerned friends who can guide them in those bewildering days. Without such counsel, they won't know what's going on. They won't be able to cope. They will desperately need friends who can show them how to roll with the punches and change into the likeness of the Lord.

Thus I invite you to become a Maranatha Man or Maranatha Woman. I want you to work with me . . . I need you to help in preparing the BRIDE for Jesus' return. No, I don't expect you to commit yourself merely on the basis of what you read here. You need to know more about me; know more about my motives and how I expect to get the job done. Therefore I want to make you an interesting offer:

If you will write to me, saying . . .

"Brother Lovett, as I read your LATEST WORD ON THE LAST DAYS, I felt God's Spirit urging me to get ready for the days ahead. While I may not agree with you in every detail, I believe we should prepare ourselves. Also, I agree we should do what we can in helping the "bride" to make herself ready for the Lord's return."

If you'll drop me a note revealing your interest in this matter . . . (and please believe it isn't necessary for you to agree with all the points in this book) . . . here's what I'll do in return:

THAT YOU MAY COME TO KNOW ME AND HOW GOD RAISED ME UP TO HELP THE BRIDE MAKE HERSELF READY, I WILL SEND YOU (WITHOUT CHARGE) A COPY OF MY AUTOBIOGRAPHY . . . C.S. LOVETT: MARANATHA MAN!

Once you read this book, you'll sense God's call to be

a part of this great work the Holy Spirit is doing prior to Jesus' return. Your heart will beat with mine and you'll be saying . . . "Let's go brother!"

This 240 page book lays bare the life of C.S. Lovett. You'll laugh, you'll cry, you'll praise God when you see how He took a useless nobody and transformed him into a productive servant. You'll be saying . . . "If God can make a MARANATHA MAN out of C.S., He can make one out of me!"

Precious friend, this invitation is as personal as I can make it. True, you're reading my words in a book, but

won't you please receive them as coming from me personally? Write to me, I'll get your letter. I'll read it. Be sure to mention number **M-5485**, and I'll see that a copy of **MARANATHA MAN** gets on its way to you.

That's the first step in our working together for Jesus. After that, you and I will be doing lots of things together. And in the process of helping God's people, we'll become personal friends. I can hear you now, saying to me and other friends . . .

"Hey! I love being a part of the MARANATHA VIS-ION! I can't think of anything more wonderful than being a MARANATHA MAN and working to get the 'bride' ready for the appearing of the Lord Jesus!"

SAMPLE LETTER

To make it easier for you to send for our free book, **C.S. LOVETT: MARANATHA MAN,** I have prepared a sample letter you can use as a guide. (Please, only one free book per family.)

Dear brother Lovett,

I have read your book, LATEST WORD ON THE LAST DAYS, and I feel God's Spirit prompting me to prepare for the days ahead. I consider myself as one who LOVES THE LORD'S APPEARING, and would like to help the "bride" make herself ready for Him.

Would you please send me a free copy of M-5485 C.S. LOVETT: MARANATHA MAN. As I read it, I'll be looking for the Holy Spirit to show me any part He might have for me as we move into the final hours of this age.

Eagerly, in Christ,

Signed _____

Mail to:

Dr. C.S. Lovett
Maranatha Man
Personal Christianity
Box 549
Baldwin Park, CA 91706

TITLES MENTIONED IN THIS BOOK BY C. S. LOVETT

No. 526 ▪ **LOVETT'S LIGHTS ON JOHN with rephrased text**, 336 pages, illustrated, paperback

No. 538 ▪ **LOVETT'S LIGHTS ON ROMANS with rephrased text**, 432 pages, illustrated, paperback

No. 541 ▪ **LOVETT'S LIGHTS ON HEBREWS with rephrased text**, 352 pages, illustrated, paperback

No. 201 ▪ **SOUL-WINNING MADE EASY**, paperback

No. 202 ▪ **SOUL-WINNING CLASSES MADE EASY** (teacher's guide for no. 201, paperback)

No. 537 ▪ **JESUS WANTS YOU WELL!** paperback

No. 523 ▪ **DEALING WITH THE DEVIL**, paperback

No. 502 ▪ **DEATH: GRADUATION TO GLORY**, paperback

No. 520 ▪ **JESUS IS COMING—GET READY CHRISTIAN!**

No. 501 ▪ **DOES GOD CONDEMN THOSE WHO NEVER HEAR THE GOSPEL?**, 64 pages, paperback

---

All of Dr. Lovett's works are available from:

PERSONAL CHRISTIANITY
Box 549,
Baldwin Park, CA 91706

SINCE 1951
HELPING CHRISTIANS "PREPARE FOR HIS APPEARING"